UNDERSTANDING CLASSICS

EDITOR: RICHARD STONEMAN (UNIVERSITY OF EXETER)

When the great Roman poets of the Augustan Age – Ovid, Virgil and Horace – composed their odes, love poetry and lyrical verse, could they have imagined that their works would one day form a cornerstone of Western civilization, or serve as the basis of study for generations of schoolchildren learning Latin? Could Aeschylus or Euripides have envisaged the remarkable popularity of contemporary stagings of their tragedies? The legacy and continuing resonance of Homer's *Iliad* and *Odyssey* – Greek poetical epics written many millennia ago – again testify to the capacity of the classics to cross the divide of thousands of years and speak powerfully and relevantly to audiences quite different from those to which they were originally addressed.

Understanding Classics is a specially commissioned series which aims to introduce the outstanding authors and thinkers of antiquity to a wide audience of appreciative modern readers, whether undergraduate students of classics, literature, philosophy and ancient history or generalists interested in the classical world. Each volume – written by leading figures internationally – will examine the historical significance of the writer or writers in question; their social, political and cultural contexts; their use of language, literature and mythology; extracts from their major works; and their reception in later European literature, art, music and culture. *Understanding Classics* will build a library of readable, authoritative introductions offering fresh and elegant surveys of the greatest literatures, philosophies and poetries of the ancient world.

UNDERSTANDING CLASSICS

'I hate and I love.' The Roman poet Catullus expressed the disorienting experience of being in love in a stark contradiction that has resonated across the centuries. While his description might seem to modern readers natural and spontaneous, it is actually a response planned with great care and artistry. It is that artistry, and the way in which Roman love poetry works, that this book explores. Focusing on Catullus and on the later genre of elegy – so-called for its metre, and a form of poetry practised by Tibullus, Propertius and Ovid – Denise Eileen McCoskey and Zara Martirosova Torlone discuss the devices used by the major Roman love poets, as well as the literary and historical contexts that helped shape their work. Setting poets and their writings especially against the turbulent backdrop of the Augustan Age (31 BCE–14 CE), the book examines the origins of Latin elegy; highlights the poets' key themes; and traces their reception by later writers and readers. It shows that a highly developed sense of place and landscape informed the elegists' explorations of passion and desire. In their romantic attachment to the bucolic countryside as well as to the city of Rome, their pursuit of both men and women, and their vibrant exchange with other genres and authors, the Roman love poets are seen to have explored the act of writing as much as the experience of love itself.

DENISE EILEEN MCCOSKEY is Professor of Classics and Affiliate in Black World Studies at Miami University, Ohio, and is the author of *Race: Antiquity and its Legacy* (I.B.Tauris, 2011).

ZARA MARTIROSOVA TORLONE is Associate Professor of Classics at Miami University, Ohio. She is the author of *Russia and the Classics: Poetry's Foreign Muse* (2009) and *Vergil in Russia: National Identity and Classical Reception* (2014).

Latin Love Poetry offers a clearly written and comprehensive synthesis of the most important scholarship on Latin erotic elegy from the last thirty years. A worthy successor to Lyne's *The Latin Love Poets* (1981), it will be this generation's *vade mecum* for all those entering the field.

—Paul Allen Miller, Professor of Classics and Comparative Literature, University of South Carolina, author of *Latin Erotic Elegy: An Anthology and Critical Reader* and *Subjecting Verses: Latin Love Elegy*

This insightful new introduction to the study of Roman love poetry offers a highly engaging and detailed primer, guiding students through the complexities and pleasures of reading and responding to Latin love elegy. Focusing primarily upon the Augustan elegists, but taking in the influences of Catullus, Gallus and Sulpicia along the way, *Latin Love Poetry* presents an accessible and articulate roadmap for all undergraduates looking to find their way towards a better understanding of this fascinating body of work.

—Genevieve Liveley, Senior Lecturer in Classics, University of Bristol, author of *Ovid: Love Songs* and *Ovid's 'Metamorphoses': A Reader's Guide*

LATIN LOVE POETRY

Denise Eileen McCoskey
and
Zara Martirosova Torlone

UNDERSTANDING CLASSICS SERIES EDITOR:
RICHARD STONEMAN

LONDON · NEW YORK

Published in 2014 by I.B.Tauris & Co Ltd
6 Salem Road, London W2 4BU
175 Fifth Avenue, New York NY 10010
www.ibtauris.com

Distributed in the United States and Canada Exclusively by Palgrave Macmillan
175 Fifth Avenue, New York NY 10010

ISBN: 978 1 78076 190 9 (HB)
          978 1 78076 191 6 (PB)

A full CIP record for this book is available from the British Library
A full CIP record is available from the Library of Congress

Library of Congress Catalog Card Number: available

Text design, typesetting and eBook versions by Tetragon, London

Printed and bound in Great Britain by T.J. International, Padstow, Cornwall

CONTENTS

Illustrations

INTRODUCTION

I hate and I love

CATULLUS 85

High off of love, drunk from my hate

EMINEM, 'LOVE THE WAY YOU LIE'

OVER TWO THOUSAND YEARS AGO, the Roman poet Gaius Valerius Catullus, commonly known as Catullus, expressed the turbulent experience of being in love in a stark contradiction that has resonated with artists and audiences across the centuries: 'I hate and I love.'[1] At first glance, Catullus' blunt statement seems to give direct access to his emotional state, encouraging readers to connect their own experiences to Catullus' plight. 'I know exactly what Catullus means' is a response shared by many readers. Yet such a rush to identify with Catullus obscures recognition of the ways he has gone about producing such a feeling; in other words, we often take our identification with Catullus' condition as completely natural, when it is a response that has been planned with great care and artistry.

In this book, we want to 'denaturalize' the process of reading Latin love poetry by exposing *how* Roman love poetry actually works – a task akin to looking behind the curtain in Oz. In laying bare some of the devices used by the Roman love poets, as well as the literary and historical contexts that helped shape their work, we do not want to diminish the pleasure of reading Roman love poetry by weighing it down with 'too much analysis'; rather, we strive to make the experience richer and even more satisfying by allowing readers not only the pleasure of their initial reactions to Roman love poetry, but also the satisfaction of seeing the roads that have led them there – as well as the traps they may have fallen into along the way.

Our study of Latin love poetry requires from the outset recognition of the differences between ancient and modern conceptions of literature, for literary genre in antiquity was defined not by subject matter or style, but rather by metre, a recurring pattern of long and short syllables in lines of set length. Love poetry in antiquity was composed in a range of metres before becoming closely associated with the elegiac couplet by the Augustan period (27 BCE–14 CE).[2] Roman love poetry from the Augustan era was thus treated in antiquity as a distinct genre called 'elegy', a form practised by three of the four poets in our study: Albius Tibullus, Sextus Propertius and Publius Ovidius Naso, the last generally referred to as Ovid. Because of his use of a range of metres, Catullus was not, strictly speaking, a Roman elegist, although he played a monumental role in creating the genre of Roman love poetry and so remains essential to our study. We also include in this work poetry that, from a modern perspective, encompasses a subject matter far removed from conventional love poetry: Ovid's poetry from exile. Such poetry fits our approach not only because its metre puts it firmly in the category of Augustan elegy, but also because it extends the emotional turmoil of human love affairs to the poet's longing for Rome itself.

To help situate our study of Latin love poetry, we want to begin by outlining some of the historical and cultural contexts in which it flourished.

The Rise of Augustus

Throughout the early part of the first century BCE, the Roman state weathered a series of brutal conflicts, including what is often called the 'Social War' (91–88 BCE), a war initiated by Rome's Italian allies and resolved only by the extension of Roman citizenship throughout these territories. The Roman poet Publius Vergilius Maro (known to English readers as Vergil or Virgil) references the persistent bloodshed at the close of Book 1 of his *Georgics* by poignantly warning that a farmer may turn up javelins, helmets and even bones as he ploughs, a passage that 'juxtaposes Italian fecundity and Italian death'.[3] Such images serve as a powerful reminder of how unsettled the relations remained between the Romans and other groups in Italy as Roman expansion took hold. Many authors we today consider 'Roman', in fact, were born in other parts of Italy – or later, in other parts of the Empire – and we can often witness in their writings a tension between their pride in Roman identity and their loyalty to their original hometown, a dynamic especially evident in Propertius' love poetry.[4]

Following the Social War, Rome provided the backdrop for two large-scale political rivalries, that of Gaius Marius and Lucius Cornelius Sulla, which ended with Sulla's victory in 82 BCE, and that of Gnaeus Pompeius Magnus (known today as Pompey the Great) and Gaius Julius Caesar, which ended in Munda in 45 BCE following Pompey's shocking beheading on Egyptian shores in 48 BCE. Fearing Caesar's growing power and what they thought was his latent contempt for Republican structures of government, a group of Roman senators assassinated Julius Caesar on 15 March 44 BCE, the famous Ides of March. Caesar's death initiated another decade of violence when a triumvirate including Caesar's young great-nephew Gaius Octavius (also called Octavian) and Caesar's loyal general Marcus Antonius (Mark Antony) joined together to challenge Caesar's assassins, finally defeating the assassins' army at Philippi in 42 BCE. Following this victory, Octavian and Antony soon turned against one another. While Antony headed east, joining forces with the Egyptian queen Cleopatra, Octavian cornered Antony's wife and brother, Fulvia and Lucius Antonius, in a siege at Perusia (modern Perugia) in Italy in 41–40 BCE, a stand-off that ended in the vicious slaughter of some three hundred Perusian senators and massive land confiscations.

The alliance between Antony and Cleopatra became the target of considerable scrutiny back at Rome, and Octavian used it to turn public opinion against his one-time ally, casting Antony as overwhelmed by passion and Cleopatra as the dominant partner of the two.[5] Antony's public liaison allowed Octavian to conceal the civil nature of the conflict, for Octavian progressively framed the internecine feud with his fellow Roman as war against an outrageous foreign queen.[6] In 31 BCE, Octavian met Antony and Cleopatra at Actium, a sea battle from which the two lovers fled. Octavian then pursued them to Egypt, although they both committed suicide rather than surrender. With the demise of Antony, Octavian became the sole inheritor of Caesar's mantle (he is almost always referred to as 'Caesar' in contemporary literature) and he would ever after attribute the origins of his power to his victory at Actium.[7] Assuming the title of *princeps* ('first citizen'), Octavian was later awarded the title 'Augustus' ('revered one') in 27 BCE, the designation by which he remains more commonly known today. During his lengthy time in power – about forty years in all – Augustus would set in motion a gradual, albeit fundamental, transformation of the Roman Republic into what we today consider the Roman Empire.

The Roman poet Quintus Horatius Flaccus (generally known as Horace) uses the phrase 'your era, Caesar' (*Odes* 4.15.4) when praising Augustus' achievements, an idea echoed by Ovid in his later exilic poetry when he writes of 'your times, Caesar' (*Tristia* 2.560).[8] Such terminology underscores the powerful notion that the rise of Augustus had initiated a distinct new era – the rebirth of a veritable 'Golden Age', an age originally associated with the reign of the god Saturn in Roman myth.[9] In Virgil's work, the prediction of a Golden Age appears for the first time in the so-called 'Messianic' fourth *Eclogue* (4–45), written in 40 BCE, a poem that 'came to be considered [...] the quintessential formulation of the aspirations of the [Augustan] age.'[10] Similarly indicative of the optimism of the age, the Romans later celebrated the 'Secular Games' in 17 BCE, a joyful welcoming of the new era or *saeculum* that coincided with the appearance of a comet.[11]

In justifying his authority, Augustus increasingly turned to a series of narratives from early Roman history, a mobilization of ideas about civic origin that reflected the 'need in post-Actian Rome to re-establish the rules for who could belong to the community and identify who was Roman and who was not.'[12] In particular, Augustus associated himself closely with figures like Aeneas, the legendary Trojan whose arduous voyage to Italy is portrayed in Virgil's epic *Aeneid*, and Romulus, Rome's mythic founder.[13]

Augustus apparently even considered taking the name Romulus as a title (Suetonius, *Augustus* 7.2, 95.2), and Romulus himself, as we shall see, appears throughout Augustan art and literature, including love poetry. Yet references to Romulus were risky given that his act of civic foundation involved the murder of his twin brother, Remus, and so might insinuate a disturbing propensity for fratricide from Rome's earliest times, a painful premise for a Roman audience still recovering from its own bouts of civil conflict. Like many Augustan symbols, then, allusions to Romulus stand poised on a razor's edge.

In addition to proclaiming his alleged restoration of peace and prosperity, Augustus also placed considerable weight on his role as a moral reformer, a leader who returned to Rome its traditional values, including piety and respect for the gods. The perpetuation of the next generation loomed large in Augustan ideology, and the *princeps* devoted special attention to the institution of marriage. Indeed, 'family' became a central concept through which the new *princeps* articulated his ideas of religion, stability and statehood[14] – his own familial troubles (as we shall see in Chapter 6) notwithstanding.

AUGUSTAN MARRIAGE REFORM

Attempting to reinforce a population that had suffered considerable losses during the civil wars, Augustus introduced a series of laws specifically designed to regulate marriage within the Roman upper class.[15] One of these laws, the *Lex Iulia de maritandis ordinibus* (*The Julian Law on Marriage*), stipulated penalties for the celibate and the childless, a legal manoeuvre designed to encourage aristocratic families to produce more heirs. The second legislation, the *Lex Iulia de adulteriis* (*The Julian Law on Adultery*), was more to the point: marital infidelity became a punishable crime and people participating in adultery were now subject to severe prosecution with penalties that included *relegatio* ('relegation'), which could involve a partial confiscation of property and enforced removal from Rome. Although making some modifications and concessions, the *Lex Papia Poppaea*, introduced in 9 BCE, was nonetheless still directed towards strengthening Roman marriage by discouraging adultery and celibacy.[16]

Prior to the *Leges Iuliae* ('the Julian laws') adultery had been a private matter, one left to Roman families to deal with on their own. With this introduction of the new laws, there was in effect 'a shift in regulatory power from the family to the state'.[17] Such laws signalled that the *princeps* could now, at least theoretically, apply legal pressure to the lifestyles of individual Romans, and these Augustan incursions on private life presumably provoked a range of responses. Propertius, for example, expresses his delight at the repeal of one such marriage law in poem 2.7.[18] Responding to an interlocutor who protests that, 'still, Augustus is mighty', Propertius answers defiantly that Augustan military power does not matter when it comes to love (5–6). He then rejoices that love for his beloved Cynthia can once again take priority over marriage with a woman of his own class, asserting emphatically that he will produce no children for the state's military machine (13–14).

Even as Augustus was reinvigorating the moral fibre of Roman society, he was also overhauling the city itself, making it a grand showpiece worthy of its place at the centre of a burgeoning empire.

A CITY OF MARBLE

Although Augustus once boasted that he had found Rome a city of clay and left it a city of marble (Suetonius, *Augustus* 28.3),[19] the city had actually begun its remarkable transformations under Julius Caesar. It was Caesar who first tried to change Rome 'into his own personal text' by executing several monumental projects, most of which were left incomplete at his death.[20] Augustus later completed the Basilica Julia and Caesar's forum, and, throughout his lengthy reign, he both restored many earlier buildings and added new structures of his own to the urban landscape with great fanfare.[21]

Crucial both to Augustus' building programme and the early fashioning of his own image was the temple of Apollo on the Palatine, a structure dedicated in 28 BCE and located in close proximity to the *princeps'* own relatively modest house on the Palatine.[22] Augustus' personal identification with Apollo was well known to the Romans; indeed, Antony had allegedly accused Augustus of impersonating the god at a banquet (Suetonius, *Augustus* 70). Augustus' victory at Actium was central to the temple's message, linking 'the Augustan present to the remote heroic past, [and] celebrating Octavian's Actian victory in the guise of the deeds of Apollo'.[23] Propertius' lavish description of the temple complex in poem 2.31 is one of the best contemporary sources for its appearance and visual programme, and we shall look more closely at the temple's important appearances in both Tibullus and Propertius in Chapter 5.

By 20 BCE most of the love poets' careers – and perhaps also their lives – had come to an end; only Ovid would remain to witness the latter stages of the Augustan period. In seeking Augustan monuments to set alongside Ovid's later poetry, it would be hard to find a better example than the forum of Augustus dedicated in 2 BCE, a complex built entirely on the *princeps'* own private property. Augustus' forum impressively promoted the foundation 'of a new national mythology, one that focused both myth and history on Augustus himself'.[24] Insinuating that Augustus' rise to power was the inevitable culmination of Rome's great history, the forum featured on each side a long row of statues of prominent historical figures, a veritable 'Hall of Fame', including Romulus and Aeneas placed prominently in an exedra on each side.[25] At the far end of the forum was the impressive temple to Mars Ultor ('Mars the Avenger'), a temple that had been vowed by the young Octavian at Philippi in 42 BCE, but could now also commemorate Augustus' settlement with the Parthians and the glorious return of the standards in 19 BCE – standards that had been lost with the defeat of Crassus in 53 BCE, an event that had long haunted the Roman imaginary.[26]

Fostered by the relative stability of the Augustan era, it was not only Rome's urban landscape that flourished, but also Augustan literature, which voiced both the great hopes and sizable anxiety associated with the new era.

Augustan Literature

In balancing the glorious claims of the Augustan era against the realities faced by the actual residents of Rome, it is crucial to remember the terror and confusion that characterized those transitional years for many individuals, some of whom, like the Roman statesman Marcus Tullius Cicero (106–43 BCE), would get tragically caught on the wrong side of history. When writers like Propertius or Virgil seek to chart the meaning of the Augustan era in its early years, then, they are not simply reaffirming a set of values and ideas that have been in place for decades, but rather attempting to absorb and at times contest the countless new social and political discourses that were rapidly gaining ground.[27] The poetry of the Augustan Age should thus 'be viewed neither as independent nor as passive in its relationship to political art, but more like participating in a complex interaction'.[28]

In addition to the elegists, the two most important poets of the Augustan era were Horace (65–8 BCE) and Virgil (70–19 BCE). Horace, the son of a freedman, fought on the losing side at Philippi; although, like many combatants, he was granted amnesty afterwards, his ancestral estates were nonetheless confiscated. While Horace's literary voice was shaped to a large degree by his engagement with earlier Greek literature, he remains openly cognizant of his own Roman context throughout his work; perhaps most notoriously, he composes a poem following Cleopatra's suicide in which he calls her a 'deadly monster' (*Odes* 1.37). Book 1 of Horace's *Satires* was published around 35 BCE, followed by his second book of satires and *Epodes* around 30 BCE. In 23 BCE Horace's *Odes* appeared – a work that includes what later scholars have often called the 'Roman odes' (poems 1–6 in Book 3), poems that seem related by style and their focus on Augustus. The *Odes* would exert special influence on Propertius among the love poets, although the two poets seem to have developed a conspicuous rivalry.[29] In any event, Horace wrote a scathing account of the contemporary elegists and what he considered their sycophantic ways with one another in his *Epistles* (2.2.90–102).

Virgil, on the other hand, is most strongly associated with his epic poem the *Aeneid*, which tells of Aeneas' journey from the fallen city of Troy to Italy where he is destined to found a new Roman race. The *Aeneid* was unfinished at the time of Virgil's death and was published posthumously – Virgil's own wish that it be destroyed thankfully having been ignored by his friends. Consonant with other forms of Augustan narrative, the story of Aeneas allowed Virgil's Roman audience to reconsider its own recent struggles through the lens of Rome's earliest history.[30] While Virgil's own views of the Augustan era are today debated,[31] in one of its most famous lines, the god Jupiter presents Rome's future as an 'empire without end' (*imperium sine fine*, 1.279).

Virgil also wrote two earlier poems, both of which influenced Augustan love poetry: the *Eclogues* and the *Georgics*. The *Georgics* (completed *c.*29 BCE) focuses on human cultivation of the land and the taming of wild nature, while the *Eclogues* (or *Bucolics*) was written in the pastoral genre traditionally associated with the singing contests of the shepherds in the countryside. The chronology of Virgil's *Eclogues*, his earliest work, remains hard to pin down when it comes to individual poems, but it is fairly certain that the corpus was written and began circulating between 42 and 35 BCE. The sense of Virgil's pastoral landscape that emerges from these works, often labelled Arcadia, became formative for later writers, providing the 'spiritual landscape' where other poets sought their poetic inspiration.[32]

Especially important for the elegiac sensibility was the last, tenth poem of the *Eclogues*, in which Cornelius Gallus, by some accounts the first elegiac poet of Rome (see Chapter 1), appeared amid pastoral surroundings suffering from unrequited love for his cruel mistress (*domina*) Lycoris.[33] Despite Gallus' attempts to seek refuge in rural solitude, the poem ultimately presents him as unable to forget who he truly is: a poet of unrequited love and the city-dwelling lover of a fickle urban *domina*.[34] In juxtaposing the dangers of the city and the idealized simplicity of the country, *Eclogue* 10 helps set the stage for the elegists' own use of space, a topic that we shall take up at greater length in Chapter 5.

As the example of the *Eclogues* suggests, the Augustan poets were manifestly aware of one another's writing and they responded to each other throughout their work, a literary conversation facilitated to no small degree by the custom of literary patronage.

PATRONAGE

Patronage as a concept is usually applied to explain the networks of social and economic dependency (i.e. the asymmetrical relationships between patrons and clients) by which a relatively narrow group of Roman families achieved social prominence and considerable wealth.[35] There was also a parallel system of aristocrats willing to support the arts in Rome, who – in addition to funding their own building projects – demonstrated their largesse by cultivating relationships with individual artists. Although the exact level of dependency between artist and patron is difficult to determine (including whether, for example, individual artists were receiving direct financial support), we find Roman poets routinely addressing their poetry to such figures.[36]

Two men connected to literary patronage in Augustan Rome are especially important to love poetry: Maecenas and Messalla. Gaius Maecenas (70–8 BCE), a wealthy member of the equestrian order – a category in the Roman social hierarchy second only to the senatorial class – was part of Augustus' inner circle and linked to such prominent writers as Virgil, Horace and Propertius.[37] Maecenas' role as patron is especially visible in Horace's work; indeed, one of Horace's *Epistles* 'is as powerful an evocation of the joys and pitfalls of patronage as Horace ever wrote' (*Epistles* 1.7).[38] The fame of Messalla Corvinus (64 BCE–8 CE) – Augustus' close friend who served as consul in 31 BCE and, a few years later, as governor of Gaul – is mostly confined to his status as patron to Tibullus. As we shall see, Messalla appears in Tibullus' poetry as an embodiment of Roman power, one closely connected to Tibullus' dreams of a tranquil life. Notably, Ovid and Horace were also associated with Messalla, and Ovid's attachment to him lasted from his youth until Messalla's death.[39]

Peter White aptly observes that 'in the Roman milieu it was not unusual to solicit favours, including literary favours, on behalf of one's friends as well as oneself'.[40] But the question of how actively literary patrons dictated the actual subject matter of Augustan poetry is not an easy one to answer. Even as he addresses Maecenas with open praise, for example, Propertius' views of his poetic obligations are difficult to pin down, as we shall see in Chapter 4. We need to apply the same caution to our understanding of Augustus' relationship with the love poets, who often incorporate Augustus into their work in terms that seem ambiguous.[41] Augustus was himself clearly invested in the arts, but to what degree we can speak of censorship in this period, either formal or informal, has been widely debated, including whether Augustus himself placed any kinds of restrictions on what could be said about himself or his regime.[42] As we shall see in Chapter 6, Augustus evidently removed Ovid's *Ars Amatoria* (*Art of Love*) from the libraries and exiled the poet himself, but we cannot assume that all literature and art under Augustus operated under excessive political scrutiny at every point throughout his long reign. Indeed, Augustan literature remains a highly refined medium, one intricate in its methods and frequently open to multiple, even at times conflicting, interpretations.

In the chapters that follow we want to unveil at greater length the operation of Roman love poetry; each chapter is based on a series of paired terms or concepts that we believe helped animate love poetry in distinct yet complementary ways.

Structure of the Book

Chapter 1, 'Beginnings and Backgrounds', traces the development of Latin love poetry, including its relation to earlier Greek and Hellenistic literature. We then give a short account of the works and lives of each of the love poets, including the elusive Gallus. Finally, we consider love poetry's relationship to the politics of its era and its related promotion of a unique set of values and terminology.

Chapter 2, 'Author and *Ego*', examines the form and function of the 'I' voice in Roman love poetry, including the use of the 'I' (or *ego*) in building a false sense of intimacy between author and reader. Looking first at the striking emotional intensity of Catullus' *ego*, we then discuss the role of 'sincerity' in Augustan elegy. Finally, we look at the incorporation of the female voice in Roman love poetry, including the role of the female *ego* in poetry attributed to Sulpicia and in Ovid's *Heroides*.

Chapter 3, 'Power and Play', explores the role of gender in Latin love poetry, querying first how love poetry conceptualizes female subjectivity. Noting the potential opportunities for female empowerment in the text, we also consider the means by which the female beloved (often called the 'girlfriend' – in Latin *puella*, or *puellae* in the plural) is constricted and physically dominated in the work. Next, we consider the role of male homo-sexual desire, as well as the importance of male communities more generally. We conclude with discussion of whether, given its seeming disruption of conventional Roman ideas about gender, love poetry should be considered a feminist genre.

Chapter 4, 'Readers and Writers', focuses on love poetry as a specifically literary enterprise, including the love poets' keen awareness of their posi-tion within various literary traditions. We also explore the *puella's* role as a primary reader of the text (a role often framed by her status as a courtesan), as well as her embodiment of the poet's own literary programme. Finally, we trace the evolution of ideas about love poetry and elegy itself in the works of both Propertius and Ovid.

Chapter 5, 'Country and City', emphasizes the importance of place in love poetry, especially the recurring opposition of *rus* and *urbs*, countryside and city. After situating Virgil's *Eclogues* and Catullus' poetry as important antecedents, we examine the work of Tibullus, whose elegies are full of melancholy ruminations about an idealized country landscape. We next document the ways that Propertius presents the city as essential to his amorous pursuits in Books 1–3 before turning, in Book 4, to the rapidly changing topography of Augustan Rome. Finally, we demonstrate Ovid's ardent preference for the city over the countryside – contrasting *rusticitas* ('the country bumpkin's lifestyle') with *cultus* ('refinement' or 'sophistica-tion') – while coyly presenting specific sites in Augustan Rome as ideal locales for seduction.

Ovid's transformation of the elegiac *ego* from erotic lover to displaced exile is the focus of Chapter 6, 'Love and Exile'. We address first the tantaliz-ing mystery of Ovid's exile to Tomi, which he credits to *carmen et error* ('a poem and a mistake'). Since readers today generally presume that the *carmen* was Ovid's *Ars Amatoria*, we look closely at that work to see why it might have caused offence. While in exile, Ovid continued to write elegy, and we ultimately argue that Ovid's exilic poetry provides the closing chapter of love poetry's development in Rome.

Finally, Chapter 7, 'Death and Afterlife', addresses the reception of Roman love poetry in antiquity and beyond. We offer a brief survey of the textual transmission of all four poets and then examine a number of sites of later literary reception, including Catullus among English writers, Propertius in the work of Ezra Pound, and Ovid's exilic poetry in Romania and Russia.

While each of our chapters takes a different tack, cumulatively we seek to highlight the ways Latin love poetry self-consciously explores the art of writing even as it presumes to document the 'actual' experience of love itself. In this way, Roman love poetry continues to invite lively scrutiny of the tenuous lines between reality and representation, between the ways we experience 'love' and the complex manner in which our experiences and desires acquire meaning in language and against diverse literary and historical backdrops.

I

BEGINNINGS AND
BACKGROUNDS

*Like everything else, like clocks and trousers and algebra,
the love poem had to be invented. After millenniums of sex
and centuries of poetry [...] the true-life confessions of the
poet in love, immortalizing the mistress, who is actually
the cause of the poem – that was invented in Rome in the
first century before Christ.*

TOM STOPPARD, *THE INVENTION OF LOVE*

ANY ATTEMPT TO DESCRIBE the standard features of Latin love poetry –
its style, subject matter, audience or narrative voice – raises perhaps more
questions than it answers since each of these elements has a complexity that
defies generalization. The actual content of Latin love poetry, for example,
often shows greater variety than we might expect. So, too, Roman love
poetry addresses multiple audiences with supreme self-awareness.[1] Love
poetry ostensibly emanates from the poet's desire to confess his love for his
puella, yet many poems are explicitly addressed to other men, friends with
whom the poet wishes to share his experiences and feelings. To that, we

could add the poet's awareness of an audience external to the poetry (the reader or listener) and also the poet's attempt to respond to a range of other writers both past and present. Given its distinct qualities, we want to begin our discussion with an important – albeit much disputed – question: where did Roman love poetry originate?

The Origins of Latin Love Poetry

The origins of Augustan elegy have presented an especially pressing problem for classical scholars over the past century, and it remains difficult to identify a single foundation, much less trace its clear linear progression into the Augustan era.[2] Our goal here, then, is to identify earlier literature that shares many of the same features as love poetry, especially its distinct adoption of a first person voice (a voice often called the poet's 'persona'): it is emphatically an 'I' who loves in Roman love poetry, not merely 'he' or 'she', or even a 'Catullus' in the third person. The scope and purpose of first person narration was developed over time in antiquity, so we turn first to the Greek poets.

GREEK LYRIC AND EPIGRAM

Poetry composed in the first person in ancient Greece, often called lyric because of its presumed performance with a lyre, emerged in pointed contrast to the most authoritative of all early literary genres: ancient epic.[3] While there is considerable doubt today that Homer's *Iliad* and *Odyssey* (epic poems dated roughly to the eighth century BCE) can be attributed to a single historical personage, the ancient Greeks took Homer's existence for granted and his enormous influence over cultural and literary life lasted well into the Roman period. When the poet Sappho (*c.*625–*c.*570 BCE) professes in a famous fragment that 'Some say an army on horseback, some say on foot, and some say ships are the most beautiful things on this black earth, but I say it is whatever you love' (16), she coyly acknowledges the authority of Homer but also advocates a world very different from that of epic, shifting from the public sphere of war to a more private sphere defined by personal experience and emotion, one dramatically articulated through the first person.[4] Archilochus (c.680–c.645 BCE), another Greek lyric poet, likewise presents a humorous refusal of Homeric values and militarism when he claims in one poem that he abandoned his shield on the battlefield while trying to save his own life (fragment 5).[5]

Ancient epic employed its own characteristic metre – dactylic hexameter – yet Greek lyric poets like Sappho and Archilochus experimented with a range of metres. The *elegos* metre – known today as the elegiac couplet or 'distich' – originated in Ionia and from the seventh century onwards spread throughout Greece. Although, by the fifth century, Greek writers assumed that the term '*elegos*' had originally referred to cries of mourning, the elegiac metre was used for a wide range of purposes, such as exhortations for courage in battle, moralizing pronouncements and political ruminations, appearing in the work of authors like Callinus, Tyrtaeus, and Archilochus.[6] Surviving fragments from Greek poets like Mimnermus (*fl.* 630–600 BCE), however, point towards what would eventually become the prominent association of the elegiac metre with erotic themes; later, Antimachus of Colophon (*fl.* 400 BCE) would write an elegiac poem, *Lyde*, about the death of the woman he loved.[7] Greek epigram, a genre that originated with short verses inscribed on votive offerings at sanctuaries and on funerary monuments, also employed the elegiac metre. Epigram later became a distinct literary form during the Hellenistic period (c.323–30 BCE), and the Alexandrian poets – a group that flourished in Alexandria in Egypt during the Hellenistic era – utilized epigram at times for specifically erotic scenarios.[8]

Roman writers frequently acknowledged their debt to earlier Alexandrian poets, especially Theocritus of Syracuse (*fl.* 260–240 BCE) and Apollonius of Rhodes (born c.260 BCE). However, no Alexandrian author was more formative for Latin love poetry than Callimachus (c.305–c.240 BCE), an intellectual born in Cyrene, who made his way to Alexandria where he pursued a range of occupations, including poet, literary critic and even librarian at the famous Library.

THE SHADOW OF CALLIMACHUS

Callimachus was said to have written over eight hundred books during his lifetime, but little of it survives.[9] Callimachus' *Epigrams* presumably exerted considerable influence over the Latin love poets,[10] but two other works seem especially crucial to their sense of poetics: Callimachus' 'Hymn to Apollo' and the preface to his *Aetia*, a work that survives only in fragments.[11] In his epilogue to the 'Hymn to Apollo', Callimachus famously shows Envy criticizing the 'smallness' or limited scope of his poetry. Apollo, however, brushes the criticism aside, responding that big rivers, while they may carry a considerable flow, nonetheless convey mainly 'silt and garbage'; it is only the water from a sacred spring, 'pure and undefiled', that bees (a common symbol for poets) take to Demeter.[12] As this scenario suggests, Callimachus generally 'rejects the long-windedness of traditional epic', advocating smaller poetic forms instead.[13]

Written in the elegiac metre, the *Aetia* (a name that means 'Causes' or 'Explanations') was presumably put into its final form *c.*240 BCE, including the addition of the 'Lock of Berenice' at the end of Book 4 as well as a prologue and epilogue to the work. In the prologue to his *Aetia*, Callimachus relates a dream in which he encounters the Muses while tending his flocks on Mt. Helicon, a scene calling to mind the Greek poet Hesiod, who derived poetic inspiration from the Muses on Mt. Helicon in his *Theogony*. Callimachus then asks the Muses a series of questions about the causes of different things, such as the rituals or customs attached to individual places, questions the Muses proceed to answer in Books 1 and 2.

The prologue of the *Aetia* has attracted particular attention because of the ways in which Callimachus uses it to define his poetic style. His critics, Callimachus claims, 'snipe at me, because it's not a monotonous uninterrupted poem featuring kings and heroes in thousands of verses that I've produced, driving my song instead for little stretches, like a child, though the tale of my years is not brief'.[14] Praising the shorter works of Philetas and Mimnermus, he responds to his critics by asserting:

> To hell with you, then, spiteful brood of Jealousy: from now on we'll
> judge poetry by the art, not by the mile. And don't expect a song to
> rush from my lips with a roar: it's Zeus' job, not mine, to thunder.[15]

Callimachus then recounts the instructions he received from Apollo himself, who urges that the poet keep his Muse 'on slender rations', while avoiding the common road 'even if it means driving along a narrower path'.[16]

We can witness the influence of Alexandrian poets like Callimachus, Philetas and Euphorion on Catullus and his contemporaries through the literary styles they emulated, models 'characterized by metrical and formal experimentation, oblique and *recherché* treatment of myth, and, in general, an avoidance of epic'.[17] The Augustan elegists, in turn, frequently adopt Callimachean terminology in defining their own craft,[18] with Propertius taking direct inspiration from the *Aetia* in turning to aetiological themes in his fourth book.[19] But although Latin love poetry has characteristics that derive from such predecessors (and more, such as pastoral poetry and even New Comedy),[20] it clearly possesses its own unique impulse, one with no exact equivalent in earlier literature. So while a quest for precursors provides a useful beginning to our discussion, it is necessary to turn now more fully to the Latin love poets themselves.

The Inventors of Love

As is the case with many ancient authors, biographical information about the love poets comes primarily from their own poetry. While we need to use caution in relying on any poet's account of him- or herself, we nonetheless want to present a brief overview of the presumed life and work of each of our poets, beginning with Catullus.

CATULLUS: LOVE AND HATE

Beyond Catullus' own poetry, we have only scattered and often contradictory references to his life, including conflicting dates of his death.[21] Catullus was evidently born in Verona (then part of Cisalpine Gaul) in 87 BCE, and references to contemporary events in his poetry indicate that he lived until at least 54 BCE. Significantly, these references can all be dated between 56 and 54 BCE, which suggests Catullus' relatively brief involvement in public life at Rome, even if it does not discount a lengthier period of literary activity.[22] We know from Suetonius that Julius Caesar was a frequent guest of Catullus' father (Suetonius, *Julius* 73), indicating that Catullus' family possessed a certain level of social standing. According to Catullus' poetry, he himself served in Bithynia under Gaius Memmius, a sojourn he does not hesitate to criticize bitterly, as we shall see.

The most notorious aspect of Catullus' life is his alleged affair with Clodia Metelli, a married aristocratic woman generally identified as the 'Lesbia' of Catullus' poems – 'Lesbia' being a pseudonym derived from the Greek island of Lesbos, in homage to Sappho.[23] Clodia enjoyed a scandalous reputation during her lifetime; Cicero presents a damning portrayal of her alleged greed and lasciviousness in his infamous *Pro Caelio*, a speech ostensibly in support of his client Marcus Caelius Rufus, but which hinges rhetorically on his relentless demonization of the Roman noblewoman.[24]

During his lifetime, Catullus seems to have been associated with a group of writers who were prominent at the end of the Republic, a group we today call the 'New Poets' or 'Neoterics', terms taken from Cicero's attacks on them.[25] Catullus' relatively small collection of poetry – which he himself calls a *libellus*, a 'little book' – touches on a range of themes, but probably does not survive today in the form he intended.[26] As we have it, Catullus' corpus can be broken into three parts: the polymetric poems (poems written in a range of metres) (1–60); the longer poems, some in the elegiac metre (61–68); and the elegiac fragments (69–116). The most famous of Catullus' poems are clearly those involving the unpredictable Lesbia, who makes an appearance in all three sections. Because of the emotional intensity of his narrative voice, most scholars see a profound connection between Catullus' poetry and later Roman elegy, as do the elegists themselves, as we shall see in later chapters. Two of Catullus' longer poems are also often singled out for their influence on later Augustan elegy: poems 68 and 76.[27]

Between Catullus and the Augustan elegists falls the tantalizing figure of Cornelius Gallus. Although very little of his work survives, he clearly merits consideration, since Gallus' work 'seems to be the most important link between neoteric poetry [Catullus] and the love poetry of the Augustan age.'[28]

EXCURSUS: CORNELIUS GALLUS, ELEGY'S PHANTOM

Almost everything that was said about Gallus until 1979 was sheer conjecture given that, until that point, only one line from his work survived: *'uno tellures dividit amne duas'* ('divided with one river two lands'). To some critics, this line suggested that Gallus was a skilful poet who composed a perfect 'golden' line with the verb in the middle and an interlocking pattern of adjectives and nouns.[29] Given the paucity of his surviving work, however, other classicists were often harsh in their treatment of Gallus,[30] and, over time, Gallus would become for many 'the poet to whom all can be attributed since nothing is known.'[31] Yet an important new fragment of Gallus' poetry was discovered in Qasr Ibrîm in Egypt and subsequently published in 1979, giving us six full and five fragmentary lines to use in evaluating his contribution.

According to Jerome's *Chronicle*, Gallus was born around 70 BCE, although this date is widely disputed. We know that during his lifetime Gallus achieved a certain amount of political prominence, including Augustus' appointment of him as the first Roman prefect of Egypt in 30 BCE (Suetonius, *Augustus* 66.1). Yet Gallus' relationship with Augustus eventually became more fraught, tension between the two perhaps arising when Gallus ordered for himself a self-aggrandizing inscription praising his own military achievements in Egypt.[32] To this alleged mistake some minor offences were apparently added,[33] causing Augustus to renounce his 'friendship' with Gallus in 27 or 26 BCE, an act that led to Gallus' suicide (Suetonius, *Augustus* 88; Ammianus Marcellinus, 18.4.5).

Gallus is credited with a collection of four elegiac books entitled the *Amores* (*Love Poems*), which were most likely written before 50 BCE. The *Amores* presumably consisted of poems dedicated to a woman named Lycoris, generally identified as the freedwoman Volumnia, who herself used the stage name Cytheris. Much of our understanding today of Gallus' place in the Roman literary landscape comes from Virgil's *Eclogues*. Within this short collection Gallus appears in two poems, the sixth and the tenth (the latter we discussed previously), and the prominent position of Gallus seems puzzling. Franz Skutsch, however, proposes that the tenth *Eclogue* serves as a catalogue of various erotic motives developed by Gallus in his elegiac poetry, and that the sixth *Eclogue* incorporates mythological themes developed by Gallus in his other non-elegiac works.[34]

The fact that Gallus' achievements – before his precipitous downfall – combined political ability with poetic talent was central to his renown and influence among later Roman poets, including the Augustan elegists, a group to whom we now turn.

Augustan Elegy

When scholars define Roman elegy as a genre, they generally focus on three major practitioners of the form: Tibullus, Propertius and Ovid. This canon of three, along with Gallus, is the precise group identified by Marcus Fabius Quintilian (35–95 CE), a Roman rhetorician active in the generation after the elegists, in his *Institutio Oratoria* (*Institutes of Oratory*). Evaluating the main representatives of Augustan elegy, Quintilian proposes that 'in elegy we also challenge the Greeks, of which genre Tibullus seems to me the most terse and elegant author. There are those who prefer Propertius. Ovid is more playful than both of them, just as Gallus is harsher' (*Institutio Oratoria* 10.1.93). Quintilian's brief observations about elegy bear further amplification. First of all, his assessment suggests that the Romans could consider amatory elegy a genre in which they might compete with, if not surpass, the rival Greeks.

Similarly, we find confirmation in Quintilian that Gallus was firmly associated with the genre of elegy in antiquity, even though Quintilian labels him 'harsh' (*durus*), a term that, as we shall see below, might also suggest the most 'manly' of the love poets. Quintilian's pithy attempt to characterize the style and quality of the three surviving elegists has been suggestive for modern critics, with many finding Quintilian's curt dismissal of Propertius especially unfair;[35] on the other hand, Quintilian cites Ovid for his lascivious humour and he singles out Tibullus as the pinnacle of elegiac achievement, a poet who has often been undervalued by later generations of readers.[36]

TIBULLUS: THE LOVER IN PASTORAL RETREAT

Not much is known about Tibullus' life. His death is variously dated to the same year as Virgil's (19 BCE) or to the beginning of 18. Based on this date, his birth in Latium (probably in Pedum or Gabii) has been estimated as taking place between 55 and 50 BCE.[37] Tibullus apparently belonged to a relatively prosperous family of the equestrian class; thus the motif of poverty, which we often encounter in his poetry (and which he shares with the other elegiac poets), should be taken with a grain of salt. Although the Roman elegists after Gallus generally turned away from public service, Tibullus reluctantly followed his patron Messalla on his Aquitanian campaign.[38]

Tibullus survives for us in a single collection of elegies, the so-called *Corpus Tibullianum*, which consists of three books, although the last book was divided into two during the Renaissance.[39] Modern scholars, however, attribute only the first two books of the poetic corpus to Tibullus with any certainty, a debate we shall return to in our discussion of Sulpicia in Chapter 2. The start of Tibullus' first book is dated to around 32 BCE with publication in 26 or 25 BCE.[40] Book 1 is primarily concerned with the capricious *domina* Delia, who, in the second book, is replaced by another woman, Nemesis, a name which signals her unscrupulous and treacherous nature. As we shall see later, despite his use of many elegiac themes and conventions, Tibullus' poetry is concerned to a large degree with the ideals of rural peace and it relies on a persistent juxtaposition of city and country.

PROPERTIUS: THE LOVER IN AUGUSTAN ROME

We know very little about the life of Propertius, who was born in Umbria (most likely in the region of Assisi) to a family with significant land holdings. Lawrence Richardson, jr has placed the poet's birth sometime between the years 55 and 45 BCE – a range suggested by the fact that Ovid speaks of Propertius as older.[41] When Ovid writes of Propertius in the past tense in the *Remedia Amoris* (*The Cures of Love*) (764), written in 2 CE, he likewise provides our only means for estimating the date of Propertius' death. In his *Tristia* (*Poems of Sadness*), Ovid places Tibullus before Propertius in his ordering of elegists following Gallus (4.10.41–53), but Propertius may have begun publishing his work a few years before Tibullus.[42] The content of Propertius' poetry strongly suggests that he began his work in the early years of the Augustan era (around 29 BCE) and completed the fourth and final book in 16 BCE.[43] Despite his persistent engagement with the emerging Augustan Age throughout his poetry, Propertius' own experience of the earlier Republic and its violent demise breaks through on a number of occasions. Two short poems at the end of Book 1 reference the Perusine War (1.21 and 1.22), a traumatic event that seems to have had very personal consequences for Propertius, including the loss of his family's land in the confiscations that followed (see 4.1b.127–130).[44]

As his work developed, Propertius clearly altered the overall themes and methods of his poetry. The changes in Propertius' fourth and final book are perhaps the most dramatic, involving Propertius' partial turn from amatory poetry to the political form of poetry he earlier seemed to disavow. The shift between Book 1 (known as the 'Monobiblos') and Book 2 is also noteworthy, even though interpretation of Book 2 is hampered by serious textual problems.[45] Generally speaking, the realism that seems to define Book 1's account of Propertius' erotic adventures gives way in Book 2 to greater interest in the process of literary production itself, documenting Propertius' growing self-consciousness about the demands of both literary genre and the new Augustan era. While Propertius' poetry continues to treat a number of literary and political questions in Book 3, if Ovid's later recollection of Propertius 'singing his fires' (*Tristia* 4.10.45–46) is any indication, his poems portraying Cynthia were already the most popular part of his corpus at the time of his death.

OVID: THE TEACHER OF PLAYFUL LOVE

Ovid was born on 20 March 43 BCE in the city of Sulmona (in what is today the region of Abruzzo); like Tibullus and Propertius, he belonged to a prosperous family of equestrian rank. Only twelve at the time of Actium, Ovid is often considered the most solidly Augustan of all poets of this period in his point of view. After receiving a thorough education, Ovid eventually abandoned his political career and turned to poetry as his primary occupation. In 8 CE, at the height of his prosperity, Ovid was mysteriously and unexpectedly exiled (or relegated) to the Black Sea, to the region of Tomi (today's Constanța in Romania), an event we shall discuss in greater detail in Chapter 6. Ovid died in exile in 17 or 18 CE.

Among the Augustan elegists, Ovid was the most prolific, experimenting with a range of literary genres over the course of his life. Ovid's first work of elegies, the *Amores*, was published in five books some time after 20 BCE and then in three books during its second edition between 7 BCE and 1 CE.[46] After the *Amores*, Ovid published the *Epistulae Heroidum* (*Letters of Heroines*), also known as the *Heroides*, a work in elegiac couplets that artfully combines the theme of love with Ovid's extensive knowledge of classical mythology. Ovid also wrote a now-lost tragedy *Medea*, which enjoyed great success. Elegy, however, remained a lasting interest and Ovid later produced the *Ars Amatoria*, the poem that may have contributed to his exile, and then the *Remedia Amoris* and the *Medicamina Faciei Femineae* (*The Cosmetics of Women*), in which he inverted and even mocked the conventions of the elegiac genre.

Ovid's lofty poetic aspirations are especially apparent in his attempt at epic poetry in the *Metamorphoses*, a poem in fifteen books in dactylic hexameter, written between 2 and 8 CE. This work was followed by the *Fasti*, a verse version of the Roman calendar in which Ovid once again employed the elegiac couplet. Ovid's *Fasti* notably followed the example of Propertius' Book 4 in using the elegiac metre to treat serious, even civic themes. The years of exile returned Ovid to elegy as a means for expressing his personal anguish. In Tomi, lonely and sad, Ovid penned two melancholy poems *Tristia* and *Epistulae ex Ponto* (*Letters from the Black Sea*), which obliquely and vaguely mention his transgressions and openly beg for Augustus' mercy. *Ibis* – an invective poem named after a bird and modelled on the lost poem of the same name by Callimachus – was most likely Ovid's last work penned in 11–12 CE.

As these short biographies suggest, the tumultuous political events of the first century had a manifest impact on our poets' lives; does their literary work accordingly express their individual views of the emerging Augustan era and its *princeps*?

Pro- or Anti-Augustan?

Writing some twenty to thirty years before the rise of Augustus, Catullus uses his poetry at times to present a lively critique of prominent contemporary political figures. He pens a number of vicious attacks against both Julius Caesar (e.g. 29 and 93) and various individuals associated with Caesar such as Mamurra, the governor of Gaul, whom Catullus refers to by the pseudonym 'prick' (*mentula*) in a number of epigrams (29, 94, 105, 114 and 115). In poem 10, Catullus complains about the stinginess of the *praetor* – a type of Roman magistrate – Memmius, whom he served under in Bithynia;[47] later, in poem 28, he asks whether his friends Veranius and Fabullus have received any profit from their similar service under Piso,[48] eventually pronouncing the verdict that Piso and Memmius are a 'disgrace' to Romulus and Remus (15). To paraphrase Catullus' general feeling: everyone working for the Roman government eventually gets screwed.

While Catullus' attacks are titillating for modern readers, they may have seemed fairly unexceptional during a time when cutting political rhetoric was par for the course.[49] Caesar may have been stung by the ferocity of Catullus' verbal assault, but according to Tacitus he managed to ignore Catullus' insults and, according to Suetonius, Caesar even sought out Catullus' company (Tacitus, *Annales* 4.34.8; Suetonius, *Julius* 73).[50] Unlike Catullus, Augustan authors faced the increasing consolidation of power in the hands of a single leader, and modern scholars have often devoted considerable energy to determining the precise 'politics' of literature from this era, asking whether a particular work or author should be considered 'pro-' or 'anti-Augustan', a question that can be illuminating in some respects, but also at times reductive and simplistic.[51]

J.P. Sullivan, for example, argues that Propertius is at one point 'subtly but unmistakably critical' of the 'imperial conquest and further wars, which were so much in the air at the time of his writing';[52] yet elsewhere in his work Propertius presents the Augustan city and its *princeps* more positively. Miller captures well the potential duality in Propertian thought (i.e. Propertius' ability to be both 'pro-' and 'anti-Augustan') when he proposes that in certain poems Propertius 'displays newfound closeness with the imperial regime and a refusal of its embrace',[53] a stance that may characterize many Augustan artists. In this way, although we may think that we are doing an 'obvious and straightforward thing' by labelling a text pro- or anti-Augustan,[54] we need to allow for a complexity of attitudes towards society and politics across the breadth of Augustan artists, who should be seen as actively advancing and molding – rather than merely reflecting or passively recording – newly emerging ideas of self and state during this period.

Still, as many critics have argued, the very subject matter of love poetry seems uniquely poised to challenge conventional values. Lyne points out that in the *Pro Sestio* 'Cicero vilifies an idle society of pleasure in terms that sound very like a jaundiced and malevolent representation of the world we see reflected in Catullus' poems.'[55] Augustan elegy would go even further in establishing its own 'alternative social creed', 'explicitly advocating a life of leisure, love, and pleasure to the exclusion of conventional masculine pursuits – law, politics, and the military'.[56] In effect, by elevating love over traditional occupations, elegy seems to challenge the very ideals of Augustan Rome, including the demands it placed on the male citizen, thumbing its nose at Augustan moral reform and treating the pursuit of desire as an opening for civic dissent. In doing so, love poetry raises fundamental questions about the very nature of Roman masculinity.

Gender Trouble?

The Latin term *virtus* ('manliness' or 'excellence') was derived from the term *vir* ('man') and was 'a term heavy with moral significance for Roman writers'.[57] In fact, 'Roman men and ancient Roman custom' were considered the 'foundations of the *res Romana* ("the Roman state," or perhaps "Romanness")',[58] furnishing the elements that supposedly made Rome superior to its rivals. Among upper-class Roman men especially, the links between masculinity and self-control were crucial since the 'capacity for self-control legitimated the control they exercised over others who were, it was implied, unable to control themselves'.[59] Notably, such assumptions about domination were used to construct parallel hierarchies in Roman thought pertaining to both gender and imperial relations.

The 'failure' of masculinity was often linked to specific allegations of *mollitia* or 'softness' in Roman discourse,[60] and 'soft' or 'effeminate' Roman men were considered dangerous precisely because they were thought to demonstrate 'political, social and moral weakness'.[61] Like Octavian, Cicero damaged Mark Antony's reputation in Rome by accusing him of a range of effeminate behaviours, not least that he allowed the women in his life to dominate him.[62] Not content to single out only one wife, Cicero alleged a long habit of subservience, professing memorably that Antony's earlier wife, Fulvia, had 'broken him in' (Plutarch, *Antony* 10) for Cleopatra.[63] Yet sources also suggest that Maecenas was considered effeminate by his contemporaries,[64] so that the male performance of gender, reliant as it was on the perception of others (not to mention its intersections with class) could be both unstable and ambiguous.

As Greene observes, 'the instability of Roman "masculinity" is perhaps nowhere more evident than in the amatory texts of Roman poets',[65] works that often celebrate the male *ego*'s patent loss of control in love. Catullus' poetry presents 'a multifaceted and complex performance of "Roman manhood"',[66] while Propertius' embodiment of masculine subjectivity seems at times ambivalent and, at others, wracked by insecurity. *Mollitia* and its related vocabulary, such as *mollis* ('soft'), abound in love poetry; in fact, the terminology of 'softness' and 'lightness' is often used to describe love poetry itself, drawing a strong correlation between the male poet and his 'soft' poetic style. Conversely, references to the *puella* as *dura* or 'hard' (e.g. Propertius 1.15.1) signal a dangerously complementary inversion of traditional gender roles, a topic we shall explore further in Chapter 3.

Beyond challenging traditional ideas of gender, the love poets manufactured a distinct vocabulary for representing erotic relations, one that at times appropriated and redefined major concepts in Roman life. Such manoeuvres display the love poets' at times paradoxical relation to conventional Roman values, for as one scholar writes of Propertius, 'he poses as an anti-establishment figure, but is only able to express himself in the language of the society he claims to distance himself from.'[67]

Setting New Terms

Throughout his poetry, Catullus appropriates a series of terms that were loaded with significance for the Romans, terms such as *fides* ('trustworthiness'), *foedus* ('pact'), *officium* ('duty') and *pietas* ('dutifulness');[68] his inventive use of *amicitia* ('friendship'), in particular, has garnered scholarly attention given that it seems to equate Catullus' erotic bond with Lesbia to that of the obligations between upper-class men.[69] The elegists, in turn, actively promoted leisure over employment, *otium* over *negotium*. Tibullus in his opening poem, for example, expressly admits that he wants to embrace an idle life without *negotium*, leaving it to others (namely Messalla) to pursue wealth or military glory (1.1.1–4). In the same vein, the Augustan elegists embraced the idea of *nequitia* ('worthlessness'), a life of degradation and deviance that repudiated the civic duty of a freeborn citizen. Thus, in the opening poem of the second book of the *Amores*, Ovid proudly calls himself 'a poet of worthlessness' (2.1.2; see also Propertius 2.24.6).

The Augustan elegists likewise reclaimed the role of soldier by using a literary figure known as the *militia amoris* ('the military service of love'), a trope that was both powerful and malleable. For one, the elegists used it to declare both their preference for the role of lover over soldier and their related preference for writing about love rather than war, often casting love itself as a kind of warfare. In his programmatic opening poem, Tibullus declares that in the brawls of love he 'is a general and a steadfast soldier' (1.1.75); Propertius similarly announces that he is not worthy of glory or weaponry (1.6.29–30) but that love is his battlefield (see also 2.1.45–46). Adopting an even more loaded framework, Propertius asserts in another poem that a night with Cynthia provides a 'greater victory than the Parthians' (2.14.23).[70]

Ovid eventually takes the figure of *militia amoris* to its limits, demonstrating the many parallels between lovers and soldiers with an elaborate and showy series of comparisons in *Amores* 1.9.[71]

Much like Stoppard in the epigraph that opens the chapter, Conte has suggested that there is an 'elegiac ideology' that underlies Augustan love poetry, one that distinguishes it from other forms. At the centre of that ideological system stands 'the conception of the love-poet as a slave – of his beloved, his passion, his incurable weakness, and ultimately his own poetry'.[72] We want, then, to conclude our chapter with a final trope that illustrates love poetry's complex engagement with its Roman historical context: love as a form of enslavement.

EXCURSUS: 'SLAVES OF LOVE'

Although Greek literature uses the idea of slavery, the condition generally does not derive from a romantic attachment. When slavery is used to illuminate erotic desire in classical Greek and later Alexandrian literature, 'it connotes primarily the power of love, rather than the lover's humility and abasement.'[73] The Latin love poets subsequently adopted and expanded the notion of *servitium amoris* ('slavery of love') in ways that were unprecedented, using it in large part to communicate a 'state or sense of degradation'.[74] In effect, by casting themselves as slaves to love – or to the *puella* herself – the love poets erode the privileges of their own masculinity by assigning themselves to the lowest possible rung of society while forfeiting the rights of a freeborn Roman citizen. Moreover, since the male body was generally inviolate in Roman law and custom, the male *ego*'s role-playing as a slave – a role defined by the complete loss of control over one's own body[75] – allowed him to extend even further his departure from the norms of masculinity.

Catullus refers to the idea of love as slavery on a number of occasions,[76] but it appears much more prominently in elegy. Summing up his life, Propertius gloomily requests that his epitaph read: 'the one who now lies as horrible dust was once the slave of a single love' (2.13.35–36). Ovid, on the other hand, gleefully proposes that 'if there is anyone who thinks it disgraceful to be the slave of a girl, I will be judged disgraceful by that person!' (*Amores*

2.17.1–2), while Tibullus despondently proclaims 'here I see slavery and a mistress well-prepared for me; goodbye, then, that freedom of my fathers. Sad slavery is given to me; I am held in chains and Amor never releases wretched me from shackles' (2.4.1–4). As Murgatroyd points out, the emphasis on slavery's physical restraints was a 'novel idea' of the elegists,[77] and there is no question that the literary device acquires its potency and, indeed, its density of meaning from the fact that Rome was itself a slave-holding society, one that utilized brutality and violence as a primary method of control.[78]

But we might go even further by considering how the encounter with *real* slaves in love poetry sheds light on the love poets' use of the device to showcase their own ostensible powerlessness. Faced with Cynthia's fury in 4.8, Propertius markedly refuses to intervene on the slave Lygdamus' behalf, claiming he is no less captive (70), but the hollowness of this conceit is soon revealed by the respective punishments Cynthia dictates for each man.[79] Lygdamus also appears in 3.6 as Propertius begs him for an account of what he saw and heard from Cynthia, a request that highlights what William Fitzgerald has called the 'symbiotic relationship of master and slave',[80] one in which Lygdamus is asked literally to stand in for Propertius' eyes and ears. Reminding Lygdamus of his own limitations, the poem concludes with Propertius' dubious claim that he will help Lygdamus obtain his freedom if the two lovers are reconciled (41–42). In the *Amores*, Ovid similarly addresses a slave named Bagoas in two adjacent poems (2.2 and 2.3), a eunuch who, Ovid accuses, guards his mistress Corinna much too closely. Seeking to prevent Bagoas from telling Corinna's husband, the slave's master, about Corinna's infidelity, Ovid at one point brutally reminds the slave of the disparate punishments that await any disclosure: 'Why would you enter an unequal contest? Caught out, there are lashes for you, while she sits in the lap of the judge' (2.2.61–62).[81]

As these scenarios indicate, despite any pretence that they stand as slaves in the arena of love, the love poets do not hesitate to exercise their authority over real slaves, dangling promises of freedom or, conversely, threatening torture and punishment. So, too, *ego*'s relationship to slaves is often triangulated through the *puella*,[82] and Ovid exploits the tension between all three subject positions – *ego*, *puella* and slave – in *Amores* 2.7 and 2.8 when he presents Corinna's maid, Cypassis, as her sexual rival. Having denied that he had any sexual contact with Cypassis in 2.7, Ovid proceeds in 2.8 to demand as 'price' for his 'service' (his denials to Corinna) that Cypassis have sex with him again (21–22). Professing that 'it is enough to have pleased one master', Ovid threatens to tell Corinna everything if Cypassis does not submit (23–28).[83]

Such representations of slavery underline the serious stakes involved in love poetry for many of its participants. Yet, in responding to Ovid's verbal coercion, one scholar writes:

> Taking advantage of a slave's vulnerability is not a very pretty kind of intimidation, and that we are not offended by it in either Amores II.3 or II.8 indicates how skilfully Ovid's wit and humour have removed both encounters from the stereotyped reality of the literary love affair.[84]

Such reaction testifies well to the propensity among modern scholars for treating Ovid's poetry as predominantly 'playful' or 'light-hearted'. That certain readers are 'not offended' by such a passage reveals well the painstaking ways in which Ovid builds trust with his audience, encouraging the reader to identify with his *ego* and so unconsciously accept the values and attitudes he promulgates. Such a tight bond between narrator and audience clearly requires further unpacking – and so we turn now to the question of love poetry's *ego*, exploring more fully the myriad ways that first person narration encourages identification and even collaboration from the reader.

II

AUTHOR AND EGO

Believe me, my life habits differ from my verse;
my life is chaste, my Muse is playful.

OVID, *TRISTIA* 2.353–354

ANY ENCOUNTER with Roman love poetry requires close scrutiny of the relationship between the author writing the poetry and the 'I' or *ego* whose feelings and experiences inhabit the work. Thus, when Catullus professes 'I hate and I love', we need to query what the actual relationship is between the Catullus who wrote that line and the *ego* who ostensibly speaks and feels it within the poetry. Are the two entities the same? Or is there a space that opens between author and *ego*, as what seem like very private thoughts are translated into publicly circulated literary expressions? In the passage above, Ovid explicitly cautions his reader that his life outside the poetry is quite different from what he presents within it. Likewise, in an earlier poem – one whose sexually graphic vocabulary long made editors and translators avoid it – Catullus is even more aggressive when trying to distinguish the activities of his poetic persona from his own, warning two male critics that he will sexually assault them in multiple ways if they continue to assume that his 'soft' poetry with its uncontrolled passion for Lesbia means that he is less of a man outside the work (16). Using a formulation that Ovid and other later Roman writers would echo, Catullus calmly explains that while a virtuous poet might be chaste, there is no need for his verses to be (16.5–6).[1]

We should, of course, be cautious in taking such clarifications at face value, given that both Catullus and Ovid pointedly use the authority of the *ego* to 'correct' the deceptive nature of that very voice, urging, in effect, 'believe me when I say I am not who I said I was' – an injunction that, when followed too closely, threatens to lead one down a rabbit hole. Yet, such passages show well the love poets' own awareness of the assumptions generated by use of the first person, including readers' frequent tendency to conflate author and *ego*.[2] In more modern eras, the love poets' use of the first person has led classical scholars to treat love poetry as testimony of the poets' real lives, a practice often called 'biographical criticism'. This approach to love poetry, however, has been strongly challenged in recent years. In this chapter, then, we want to explore how the distinct narrative voice of Latin love poetry has both encouraged and defied a range of critical approaches. We shall then examine a provocative form of first person narration in love poetry, that of the female *ego*.

'False Confidences'[3]

In the second century CE, the Roman author Apuleius identified the 'real' names of the women featured in most of the major works of Roman love poetry; it is from Apuleius that we learn Catullus used the pseudonym 'Lesbia' to mask Clodia Metelli, while Tibullus used 'Delia' as pseudonym for a real woman named Plania, and Propertius 'Cynthia' for a woman named Hostia (*Apologia* 10). Such identification undoubtedly helped foster the biographical reading of love poetry, for what could be a better explanation of the striking subjectivity of Roman love poetry than its reliance on the experiences of real lovers? Catullus' poetry in particular, given its overtly confessional nature, has often been viewed as transparently recording the vagaries of Catullus' daily life and his tortuously unstable affair with Clodia Metelli. Any attempt to reconstruct the 'real life' of Catullus from his poetry, however, eventually encounters significant barriers.

2.1   *Catullus at Lesbia's* (1865) by Sir Laurence Alma-Tadema.

READING THE CATULLAN *EGO*

Catullus' poems about Lesbia have tended to attract the greatest attention, yet his poetry actually portrays a number of other kinds of relationships, including lively and often hostile exchanges with various friends and enemies – poems that convey a strong impression of real frustration or anger behind the work. As we have seen in poem 16, Catullus threatens to assert his 'manliness' through various sexual acts unless his critics stop presuming that his masculinity has been compromised by his poetry. In equally obscene terms, Catullus accuses Lesbia of engaging in sexual acts with other Roman men in poem 58. Such poems can seem shocking to an unsuspecting reader,[4] and, perhaps unsurprisingly, they often have been perceived as 'a scandal and an embarrassment' to later critics.[5]

Catullus forges a perhaps more sympathetic connection with his reader when he tries to articulate his tortured feelings for Lesbia. In his famous poem 85, the poet fiercely states, 'I hate and I love'. He then ruminates:

'You sometimes ask why I do that. I do not know, but I feel it happening and I suffer' (1–2). While this short poem begins with a blunt expression of opposing emotions, Catullus thus immediately records the presumed reaction of an interlocutor, who ostensibly asks him about the source of such feelings; Catullus answers only that he experiences such suffering, not that he can explain it in any way. Earlier, in poem 75, also written in elegiac couplet, Catullus explicitly diagnoses Lesbia's behaviour as the cause of his fractured mental state and describes the paradox it creates:

> Lesbia, my mind had been reduced to this because of your crime,
> and by its own devotion it destroyed itself.
> It is not able to like you any longer, even if you are on your best behaviour,
> nor is it able to cease loving, even if you do your worst. (1–4)

In both poems, as if looking in from the outside, Catullus exhibits clear insight into his condition, even though he considers a remedy hopelessly out of reach.

Poems 5 and 7, two of the most famous poems in Catullus' corpus, are also written in the 'confessional' vein and express great excitement and good tidings for his love, beginning with the exhortation to Lesbia that they 'live and love each other' (5.1). Urging her to disregard the opinion of 'severe old men', Catullus requests that she give him a thousand kisses, then immediately demands more and still more – so many, he finally says, that they themselves will lose count (5.7–13). Shortly after, Catullus mocks his own greedy exuberance, coyly beginning poem 7 with Lesbia's alleged retort to such a request: 'You ask, Lesbia, how many kisses are enough for me and more than enough?' (7.1–2), then responding that only a number equal to the amount of sand on a beach or stars in the sky will satisfy 'mad Catullus' (3–10).

Taken together, these poems portray a Catullus who gleefully lacks self-control. In the very next poem, however, Catullus responds to his prior zeal: rather than indulge in countless kisses, Catullus orders himself to 'stop the foolishness', to 'buck up', as it were – emphatically using a form of the verb *obduro* ('to harden' or 'persist') three separate times – and accept the demise of his love (8). Noteworthy is Catullus' change from the second person to the third (12) and then back again (19), reiterating the kind of self-consciousness and split perspective we saw above by once again adopting a narrative voice that is constantly both self-aware and trying on new guises.

In seeking to elucidate the workings of Catullus' *ego*, modern scholars have placed his poetry firmly within the lyric tradition,[6] a mode that, as we have seen, originated in ancient Greece. For Miller, Catullus' work is 'the first extant example of a true lyric collection', since Catullus' production of a written collection of poems (as opposed to the oral performance of Greek lyric) elicits a very specific 'responsive understanding' from his audience, one that Miller finds critical to lyric consciousness.[7] It is thus the reader's task, in Miller's view, to build a Catullan *ego* in the course of his or her reading – one that can accommodate all sorts of turns, contradictions and possibilities of ambiguity (even a change of opinion in a later reading) – rather than Catullus' task to present 'himself' as a single coherent narrating subject.[8] Micaela Janan, going even further, sees the Catullan *ego* not as an entity or an identity *per se*, but 'as a site through which social, cultural, institutional and unconscious forces move'.[9]

While perceptions of Catullus' 'immediacy' tend to dominate reactions to his work, another way to challenge the presumption that the Catullan *ego* grants unmediated access to the author's 'real' self is to recognize the ways in which, on closer inspection, Catullus' poetry divulges his considerable literary skill. Catullus' famous sparrow (*passer*) poems present a good example of where we might find deeper artistry at work (poems 2 and 3). In poem 2, Catullus portrays the sparrow as a beloved and envied plaything of his mistress, while in poem 3 he presents an elaborate poem of mourning, marking the sparrow's death. As Richard Thomas writes, both poems can be read as responses to literary forms found elsewhere, poem 2 a seeming parody of the ancient hymn, and poem 3 'working within [...] a tradition of epigrams to dead pets'.[10] Even more since the Renaissance, scholars have debated whether the activities ascribed to the bird, including its preference for its mistress's lap, indicate a kind of mischievous double entendre, that is that Catullus is using the sparrow as a stand-in for the male penis.[11]

In poem 11, Catullus seems to make a more self-consciously literary gesture when he appropriates a poignant image reminiscent of Sappho, one of a flower struck down by a plough.[12] This scenario is at times used to illustrate male penetration of a young girl or bride and so often appears in wedding poetry.[13] Here, however, Catullus provocatively employs the image to describe the end of his love for Lesbia, which, 'by her fault', has fallen 'just like the most remote flower after it has been touched by a passing plough' (21–24). Such appropriation of Sapphic imagery opens many possible interpretations, not least that, consistent with other strategies in love poetry, the Catullan *ego* is pointedly adopting a feminine perspective in documenting his painful loss; however, any embracement of femininity cannot be evaluated without considering the broader context, including the fact that the poem opens with Catullus' plans to depart the city with his male friends as well as his quite graphic wish that Lesbia subsequently indulge her sexual appetite with hundreds of other men.[14] Catullus' entry into Sappho's emotional terrain at the end of the poem is surely signalled by his use of the sapphic metre throughout, and the only other poem in sapphic metre in Catullus' collection is poem 51, an even richer conversation with Sappho's lyrics, which we shall examine later in the chapter.

For now, it is time to turn to the Augustan elegists who have been subjected to their own versions of biographical criticism.[15]

'SINCERITY' AND THE AUGUSTAN ELEGISTS

The basic aim of biographical criticism is to reconstruct the real events and real people ostensibly residing behind the artifice of ancient poetry. Armed with Apuleius' identification of the 'real' Cynthia, scholars beginning with F.G. Barth in the eighteenth century thus sought to reconstruct from Propertius' poetry a chronological account of his actual, if convoluted, romance.[16] Despite concerted efforts by such scholars, Propertius' work persistently defies any attempt to produce a single or coherent romantic narrative, for contradictions and inconsistencies in his account of life with Cynthia abound. To take just one example, Propertius claims that he was faithful to Cynthia for five years in one poem (3.25.3), but in another poem extols the advantage of having two mistresses at the same time (2.22b). Such hurdles, however, did not seem initially to faze the adherents of biographical criticism, who adopted creative methods for making Propertius' poetry conform to biography, even, at times, simply omitting the poems that could not be made to fit.[17] That 'Propertius did not intend his elegies should be read as a story' was generally not considered.[18]

Ovid has traditionally garnered the most scepticism when it comes to asserting a connection between 'real' life and poetic persona. In the words of one nineteenth century critic, 'His [Ovid's] calm surface is most rarely disturbed by genuine feeling. With Tibullus and Propertius love was at any rate a passion. With Ovid it was *une affaire de cœur*.'[19] This recourse to 'genuine feeling' in 'diagnosing' Latin love poetry demonstrates well that any attempt to draw the line between 'real life' and 'literary invention' frequently relies on quite subjective judgement, requiring the reader to determine which feelings are 'authentic' and which are 'merely' feigned or exaggerated for effect. In the mid-twentieth century, Archibald Allen thus dealt perhaps the first major blow to biographical criticism by seeking to unpack the meaning of 'subjectivity' itself, focusing his attention on what had previously seemed a straightforward criterion for evaluating the elegiac *ego*: 'sincerity'.

Insisting that we distinguish between ancient and modern perceptions of sincerity, Allen argued that although in modern times 'the real personality of the artist is an essential factor in the concept of sincerity',[20] in ancient poetry no such construct existed. Turning to ancient rhetorical theory, Allen proposed that an ancient orator was required to *make* people believe in his arguments. The word *fides* (from which we derive our word 'confidence') in Latin therefore combines in itself the ideas of both 'sincerity' and 'persuasiveness', so that the '*fides* of an orator depends on the conviction which he arouses that he possesses the qualities which he claims'.[21] Sincerity, in short, was not viewed in antiquity as a passive quality of the orator's character or personality (his innate possession of certain traits), but rather an impression or conviction about his character, created by his own skill and performance. So what we regard today as 'sincerity' in Roman love poetry is not, in fact, the author's 'real' personality coming through, but rather the effects of his literary style: we view Propertius as 'sincere' not because of *who* he is (or was), but rather *how* he presents himself in the poetry. Allen explains further: 'The question we should ask is not "Did the elegists really feel this?" but rather "Is it reasonable that the lover whose character appears in the elegies should speak in this manner?"'[22]

In the decades following, classical scholars continued to probe the line between life and art in Roman love poetry, with some still insisting that the virtue of Latin love poetry derived from its expression of genuine experiences and emotions[23] and others contending that the Roman love poets seek to construct the very idea of 'romantic experience' in their writing. Marking the growing domination during the 1980s of a more literary approach to Roman elegy – one that saw love poetry as highly sophisticated in terms of both generic conventions and the reading practices it required – Paul Veyne's influential *Roman Erotic Elegy* unveiled the reader of elegy and the author's *ego* as supremely literary constructs.[24] Since that time, critics of love poetry have increasingly shifted their focus from the role of Roman love poets as lovers to their role as writers or poets;[25] love poetry's *puella* has similarly been interpreted as a supremely literary invention rather than a mask for any 'real' flesh-and-blood lover.[26]

In delving further into the literary rather than biographical dimensions of the *ego* or 'I', we want to explore next a revealing phenomenon: the incorporation of a female *ego* in love poetry, a topic that brings us first to the tantalizing figure of Sulpicia, a *scribens puella* or a *puella* who writes.

SULPICIA: *SCRIBENS PUELLA*?

Given the overwhelming bias towards male authorship in our surviving sources, the women of Rome seem mostly silent today, a silence that derives in large part from their relative absence from public life.[27] Yet Propertius' Cynthia is referred to as writing her own poetry (2.3.21–22), suggesting that female authorship was, if not common, at least not unheard of. And, indeed, we know about a number of female poets in Rome, such as Cornificia, who wrote epigrams, and Perilla, a woman to whom Ovid addresses some of his exile poems.[28] There is also evidence for other kinds of women's writing in the Roman era, such as the letters of the virtuous Cornelia (the mother of the Gracchi brothers) and the memoirs of Agrippina the Younger.[29] Unfortunately, none of this writing survives. Given such a meagre record of female authorship, Sulpicia's love poetry seems to offer unprecedented access to a female writer of the Roman period.

Still, the critical reception of Sulpicia's work has been divided; given that it is preserved as part of Tibullus' corpus, serious questions have been raised about both Sulpicia's actual authorship and the relation of her writing to Tibullus' work as a whole. Until the end of the eighteenth century it was believed that Tibullus' manuscripts – the two most important of which are the *Ambrosianus* and the *Vaticanus*, dated to the fourteenth century – contained only poems by Tibullus; in more recent times, however, scholars have come to believe that some of the poems in the third book were actually written by Tibullus' contemporaries. Among the contested poems are six short elegies that have been attributed to a young woman named Sulpicia (3.13–18).

Much uncertainty surrounds the identity of this Sulpicia. One of the elegies that names her also refers to her as the 'daughter of Servius' (3.16). Another elegy addressed to Messalla (3.14) alludes to the fact that Messalla is seemingly in charge of the young woman. Basing their conjecture on these two poems, scholars have concluded that Sulpicia's father was most likely Servius Sulpicius Rufus, a prominent jurist who served as consul in 51 BCE and died eight years later. The later author Jerome (dated to the fourth and early fifth century CE) suggests that Servius Sulpicus was married to Valeria, Messalla's sister, thus making Messalla Sulpicia's uncle and guardian after her father's untimely death; indeed, Sulpicia's kinship with Messalla might help explain why this collection of poems would include her elegies.

The mystery of Sulpicia's identity is further compounded by two epigrams of the later Roman poet Martial (40–*c.*104 CE) that praise a contemporary of his named Sulpicia for her conjugal devotion as well as for her explicitly erotic poetry.[30] To one classical scholar, that 'the only two Roman poetesses we know much about should be named "Sulpicia" is too much a coincidence to be accidental'; he proposes that in later times the name Sulpicia was employed precisely because the earlier Sulpicia 'seemed to provide a precedent for Latin verse in a feminine persona'.[31] This could mean that the name Sulpicia connoted not a specific woman, but rather a tradition of composition in the female voice, a convention that may already have been in use during Tibullus' era.

In the Tibullan corpus, Sulpicia's poems are preceded by the poetically unimpressive *Panegyric to Messalla* (3.7) and the five so-called 'Amicus' poems (3.8–12); often called the 'Garland of Sulpicia', the 'Amicus' poems are sometimes attributed to Tibullus himself and written about, as well as in, the person of Sulpicia. The Sulpicia poems that follow are written as brief love notes in the voice of Sulpicia to a young man named Cerinthus (3.13–18). The opening poem, which calls pointed attention to the act of writing itself, consists of ten lines detailing the joyous emotional state of a young woman who has found a man worthy of her love and does not wish to hide it or entrust it to the 'sealed tablets' (3.13.7). The next two poems in the collection pertain to Sulpicia's birthday: in the first she expresses disappointment at being taken away from the city and from Cerinthus, while in the second she rejoices in the cancellation of the trip.[32] In the following poem Sulpicia is angry at Cerinthus' indiscretions with a prostitute and expresses pride in her own aristocratic parentage; in the next, Sulpicia is ill and seeks to recover with the help of her beloved. In the final poem she apologizes for leaving Cerinthus the night before in an attempt to hide her passion. These six poems are then followed by two short love poems of debated authorship (3.19–20).

There are two schools of thought that differ dramatically on the authorship of the forty lines attributed to Sulpicia. One view – the so-called 'naive' or amateurish reading of the poems – was initiated by Otto Gruppe in 1838, a polymath of the German Romantic era.[33] Key to this reading is the idea that Sulpicia's authorship could be demonstrated through various stylistic qualities, in short, that a 'feminine Latinity' or 'ladies' Latin' could be detected throughout the poems. Such a hypothesis, one based on the notion that sexual difference can be readily identified in patterns of writing, is highly speculative – not least because we have very few instances of female writing in Latin to compare with these poems.[34] Moreover, such a theory often emanates from a distinctly pejorative view of the work; thus, many scholars following Gruppe have emphasized the allegedly artless and unrefined nature of Sulpicia's poetry, crediting female authorship to the verses precisely because they were felt to be inferior in quality.[35]

More recently, scholars have started to recast the meaning of female authorship in relation to Sulpicia's poetry, departing from the previous notion of 'female Latinity' by analysing the themes and poetic imagery explored in it rather than its stylistic features. Kristina Milnor, for example, argues that Sulpicia's poems are not merely written in a woman's voice, 'but as a woman poet [...] quite distinct from her male counterparts'.[36] In one passage, Sulpicia pointedly uses 'an image of disrobing to describe the act of writing her love poetry', equating the revelation of the nude female body with the disclosure of her love story.[37] The use of the female body is not altogether new for elegiac discourse; as we shall see in Chapter 4, both Ovid and Propertius use their beloved's appearance and clothing as a stand-in for their poetic programme. In Sulpicia's poem, however, the meaning of the female body becomes closely linked to female self-expression, to female poetic agency rather than female objectification.[38] In similar ways, Sulpicia's poetry discusses female desire and female sexuality quite explicitly, a forthrightness that has caused some consternation among critics.[39]

Against these interpretations, a different school of thought proposes that the poems were written not by a young woman named Sulpicia, but rather a male poet 'consciously imitating the style and emotions one might expect from a teenage girl'.[40] The prospective identity of the author on this side of the argument is open to debate.[41] One possibility is Tibullus himself, who, being close to Messalla, would have known Sulpicia. Tibullus might thus have adopted Sulpicia's style and voice in order to celebrate her pending marriage to a man whom he calls Cerinthus.[42] In this view, the poems attributed to Sulpicia can be read as Tibullus' poetic gift to a young girl, 'a playful epithalamic tribute'.[43]

Despite continuing debates, most scholars today conclude that Sulpicia herself wrote poems 13–18 and some scholars contend that she also wrote 8–12 (or perhaps a portion of these poems in the so-called 'Garland').[44] But we want to turn in the final part of this chapter to other examples of the female *ego* in Latin love poetry, voices explicitly adopted as a kind of narrative cross-dressing.

Writing as a Woman?

As the various sides taken in debates over Sulpicia's poetry indicate, the intersections of gender and writing are complex; even as we are anxious to identify more fully the extent of women's writing throughout history – Virginia Woolf's unforgettable adage 'anonymous was a woman' challenging the limits of some of our conventional assumptions – the prospect of the female author raises important questions for any critic. For one, how can we actually identify women's writing when we encounter it? What, if anything, makes it different or 'stand out' from male writing? Seeking to disentangle such questions from the actual physical makeup of an author – that is to say, from the notion that women and men inherently write a certain way because of their biological sex – some feminist critics have argued that women's writing should be classified by a range of social rather than biological factors, such as whether the writing reflects a position of structural or systemic powerlessness or presents itself as 'marginal to the symbolic order'.[45] Taken to its logical conclusion, such arguments presume that male authors can themselves conceivably write 'as women'.

Given that, as we discussed in Chapter 1, the love poets often seem to identify as 'feminine', what then is gained by their writing 'as women' and, even more, their adoption of a specifically female narrating voice? With even greater complexity, Ovid adopts not just the voices of various women, but of various women in the act of writing and, ultimately, Sappho herself. Why? We begin first with an important antecedent to Ovid's *Heroides*, Catullus' self-conscious play with Sappho's voice in poem 51.

EXPERIENCING SAPPHO'S DESIRE?

While little is known about Sappho's life, her work, which today survives only in fragments, employs not only a distinctive 'I' voice, but also a rich range of imagery in its attempts to articulate what seem to be her most intimate desires, desires primarily directed at various female counterparts.[46] She was without question the most famous female poet throughout antiquity; while continuing interest in Sappho may have been partially due to the rarity of female poets in the classical world, later audiences clearly considered her poetry some of the finest of the Greek era. Her poetry influenced many later authors, but in poem 51 Catullus goes one step further by explicitly reworking one of Sappho's most famous poems: poem 31.

Scholars have long been intrigued with Catullus' 'strong dash of the feminine',[47] and have raised many questions about the precise choices he makes in this poem, including how we should read the obvious imposition of his own male *ego* onto Sappho's unique expressions of female desire. Sappho herself seems to have written predominantly in the genre of epithalamia, or 'wedding songs', a genre Catullus also attempts in his own work (poems 61, 62 and 64.323–381). Some scholars accordingly classify Sappho's original poem as a nuptial hymn intended to serve a more communal and less individual purpose, meaning that while Catullus' poem embodies 'a complex meditation on the ambiguities and contradictions of subjective experience', Sappho's poem 'seeks to reintegrate that experience within the bounds of communally accepted forms'.[48] Similarly, the differences between the two poems can be said to derive in part from the differences between 'a lyric designed for oral performance and a lyric of the book'.[49]

In her poem, Sappho presents a notable fracturing of perspective; the audience is hearing a poem in which Sappho's *ego* is watching a man talking with an unnamed woman. Key to Sappho's scenario is the role of speech, reflecting its connections to oral performance: the man hears both the other woman's conversation and her laughter, while, in the second part of the poem, Sappho describes the destruction of her own capacity for speech (her tongue 'breaks'). Sappho then lists a further series of physical responses provoked by her envy (a fire burns under her skin; her eyes go out of focus; she sweats and shudders), culminating in her sense that she is on the verge of dying. Throughout, Sappho's 'symptoms' are uniquely – and many feel stunningly – conveyed by her unconventional language choice and the density of sensation she communicates.[50]

Catullus' subsequent poem consists of four stanzas, three of which correspond closely to Sappho's poem, although his choices yield certain changes in its overall impact. For one, Catullus explicitly names Lesbia as his object of desire in line 7, a name that not only documents the poem's place in Catullus' larger corpus but also alludes back to Sappho herself.[51] So, too, while the 'other man' remains in many ways peripheral to Sappho's poem, Catullus focuses his attention on him by placing *ille* ('that man') at the start of his first two lines.[52] This emphasis placed on the other male party suggests that Catullus' relation to other men remains a pivotal frame for the scene, and indeed the public world of male obligation drives Catullus' final stanza, which has no parallel in Sappho's work. We shall examine the meanings of the gendered body in love poetry in the next chapter; however, it is significant here that Catullus also describes his physical reactions in ways subtly different from Sappho. While Sappho performs a kind of 'dismemberment of her own body', achieving a 'disintegration' of self, Catullus' account suggests 'at most, only partial disintegration', as from the outset he insists on perceiving his body as a totality and only then records the reactions of its individual parts.[53]

It is with the fourth stanza of the poem that Catullus seems to depart most radically from Sappho, as he adds his own coda to the experience through a moralizing address to himself. As T.P. Wiseman points out, this use of self-address (a tactic we have seen elsewhere in weighing the many sides of the Catullan *ego*) forces the reader to 'distinguish the persona, Catullus the lover, from Catullus the poet'.[54] Moreover, Catullus' placement of *otium* ('leisure') at the beginning of two consecutive lines in the last stanza – giving it the emphasis he gave *ille* earlier – reminds us of the weight of that idea throughout Latin love poetry, especially as a counterbalance to conventional Roman pursuits like *negotium*. In effect, throughout the final stanza, Catullus is able to turn 'abruptly away from his interior world of poetic images and back toward male public culture.'[55]

In his *Heroides*, Ovid pursues a much more in-depth experimentation with female writing, composing a series of letters written in the voices of famous mythological women. While the *Heroides* offers Ovid an opportunity to probe the narrative voice as it relates to gender more broadly, it ultimately allows him not merely to speak *like* Sappho but effectively to speak *for* her.

OVID'S *HEROIDES*

Letters between lovers recur as a trope throughout Roman elegy. Propertius suggests the exchange of letters between his *ego* and Cynthia in numerous places (e.g. 3.16 and 3.23), and, as he instructs different audiences about the appropriate modes of conduct in love, Ovid also asserts the importance of written communication. In the *Ars*, in fact, Ovid discusses at length the practice of writing love letters (1.459–468 and 3.469–498); at one point he even warns men and women about the different kinds of errors they might fall victim to in such letters (3.482–483).[56] Although Ovid claims in the *Ars* that the literary letters of the *Heroides* introduced an entirely new literary form (3.346),[57] Propertius actually includes a lengthy poem in Book 4, written as a letter from a woman named Arethusa to her husband Lycotas, who is off campaigning in the east (4.3).[58]

Ovid's *Heroides* consists of twenty-one letters, although the final six actually function as three sets of pairs – Paris and Helen, Leander and Hero, and Acontius and Cydippe – with the male hero in each pair providing his own letter.[59] Scholarly evaluation of the *Heroides* has fluctuated over the centuries, with critics often citing a paramount tension in the work: while the epistolary form suggests a certain spontaneity and emotional intimacy (especially given that in most of the letters the abandoned female writers profess to be experiencing extreme anguish), the letters are themselves highly literary, even 'artificial' in tone.[60] Moreover, if we judge the letters according to their presumed function – each writer aims to get her errant lover to return – the reader knows only too well from the myths evoked that they are doomed to failure and that they will ultimately be unsuccessful as forms of seduction or persuasion. Much of the richness of the *Heroides* therefore lies in Ovid's assumption that the reader is aware of the relevant myths that define each woman.

As a distinct genre of writing, letters have numerous conventions, as does the associated tradition of literary letters.[61] Duncan Kennedy has proposed that one way of evaluating the *Heroides* is thus to assess its actual use of the epistolary format – does Ovid make full use of the letter as a literary form in the *Heroides* or does the format seem merely a superficial device?[62] Kennedy himself points to two key factors that help to evaluate the effectiveness of literary letters: their relation to time and to their own dramatic context. In the former case, it means assessing something like the alleged moment of the production of the letter; in the latter, how the writing of the letter both emerges from the plot and how it contributes to it in turn.[63] If, as readers, we are distracted by wondering how a letter will ever be 'delivered' to its addressee, given the heroine's distance from him, or even how it was produced in the first place – how did Ariadne actually find writing material on her deserted island? – then the format might in the end undermine its own impact.[64] On the other hand, Kennedy points to the considerable pleasure added to reading Penelope's letter (*Heroides* 1) when we realize that Ovid is relying specifically on Homer's version of her myth in his *Odyssey*, for Ovid makes Penelope compose a letter to the long-absent Ulysses (Odysseus in Greek) just prior to her reunion with him, at a time when he has already returned home in disguise; even more, Penelope's letter states that it will be given over to this very 'stranger' for delivery to her husband (1.59–62).[65]

Penelope's letter clearly acquires much of its meaning from the reader's ability to 'insert' it into the frame of Homer's earlier epic poem; many scholars have therefore argued that the primary achievement of the *Heroides* is precisely this engagement with other ancient literary texts, a kind of literary conversation that is often called 'intertextuality'. 'Intertextuality' or literary allusion characteristically functions 'backwards': authors write in response to earlier authors. Yet Alessandro Barchiesi points out that in the *Heroides*, Ovid is also able to employ allusions to future time, allowing a much broader terrain for the reader's imagination, not to mention opening greater opportunities for irony.[66] In the case of Penelope, then, Ovid may look back to Homer's version of her tale, but he also encourages his readers to balance Penelope's words against what we know her future entails after the completion of her letter.

Adding to the richness of his project, when Ovid uses his heroines to 'talk' to earlier literature, he seems to probe the limits of literary genre itself, including what might happen when certain material crosses into a new genre. Is Medea – a figure most widely known from the Greek playwright Euripides' version of her myth – still 'Medea' when her plight is 'translated' from Greek tragedy into elegiac couplet? Or, as Barchiesi succinctly phrases it, what happens when Medea 'attempt[s] to write [her] own story in terms of a new and different code'?[67] Similarly, when Sappho asks at the opening of *Heroides* 15 whether the reader 'recognizes' her writing, she jokingly admits that the lyric mode is more suited to her – coy acknowledgement of the different metre Sappho used in her original poetry (1–6). As we shall see below, Sappho proves to love very differently in elegiac couplet.

With the exception of the men in the paired letters, the internal writers of the *Heroides* are all pointedly female, meaning each woman serves as her own story's *ego*. By taking the pen, it is not merely that female writers enable Ovid to respond to a previous literary tradition, but that their feminine perspective threatens to shift its very axis.[68] Barchiesi poignantly elaborates:

> The heroines' struggle for control over their own destinies in the face
> of adverse or even impossible conditions is dramatic for the very reason
> that these destinies have already been recorded and written down: the
> women are in fact writing against the grain of the classical authorities.[69]

The act of writing, therefore, helps assert and establish female agency, but can we go further still in witnessing the unique subjectivity of each woman through the actual account she gives?

Because of Ovid's heavy reliance on earlier literary texts, scholars have often puzzled over the apparent discrepancies between the letters in the *Heroides* and Ovid's source material. Kennedy, for example, lists a series of claims made by Ovid's Penelope that run counter to Homer's poem. But rather than approaching such deviation as a source problem – did Ovid get his Homer wrong? was he perhaps relying on a different version of the myth? – Kennedy encourages us to see such gaps as central to Ovid's method of characterization. In other words, it is only in 'deviation from an established source' that the reader can 'recognise and penetrate the subjectivity of the "writer's" viewpoint'.[70] In effect, Ovid's heroines emerge from the changes they make to the previous 'record'.[71]

The narrators of the *Heroides* frequently reference the process of writing in ways that draw attention to the complexities of language as well as the letters themselves as material objects. In the opening of her letter to Achilles, Briseis, for example, refers to her halting ability in Greek (3.1–2), a conceit containing no little irony given that the letter itself, of course, is written in Latin. She then professes that her tears may have blotted the letter, but that they, too, have the 'weight of words' (3–4). Such blurring of corporeal functions with the materiality of writing is provocative, and eventually Ovid gives similar expression to his own language deficiency and physical erosion as he writes of his experiences in exile; the many connections between the *Heroides* and Ovid's writings from exile are explored later in Chapter 6.[72] Finally, the epistolary format allows the writers in the *Heroides* to allude to the precarious lines between love poetry's multiple readers, at times playfully juxtaposing – even blurring – the 'internal' and 'external' audiences. When Oenone's letter emphatically begins with the word *perlegis* (5.1) – 'are you reading this through?' – she thus seems to address not only the letter's presumed recipient, Paris, but also us as 'outside' readers, since we are 'eavesdropping' on the exchange and so also caught in the act of reading her letter.

But does such an elision of readers suggest that Ovid's literary letters seek not to align the reader with the narrating *ego* (a bond commonly constructed by love poetry), but rather to create a kind of disturbing collaboration between the 'external' reader and the abandoning male lover?[73] Perhaps, but as Erfossini Spentzou notes, while a reader might find her- or himself unconsciously aligned with the absent man and against the writer, the potentially disruptive nature of the letters 'is also open to rescue by readings which refuse to cooperate'.[74] Taking a different approach, Laurel Fulkerson has explored the ways in which the *Heroides* function as 'intratextual' and not just 'intertextual', in the sense that the letters and their female authors respond to one another as a community and not merely to their male lovers or external literary sources.[75] In this way, the work of Fulkerson and others places important emphasis on understanding the women of the *Heroides* as active readers and not merely writers.[76]

In interrogating the specific consequences of Ovid's appropriation of the female voice, it is worth considering Sappho's letter to Phaon (*Heroides* 15), a clear anomaly among the letters. For one, Sappho is the only letter writer associated with a real woman as opposed to a mythological one; so, too, she is the only figure explicitly associated with poetic authorship in her own right.[77]

TAKING SAPPHO'S PEN

Given its unique position within the collection, scholars have split over whether the Sappho letter should be considered authentic. It is mentioned in a passage from Ovid's *Amores* (2.18.26), which lists many, but not all, of the writers in his *Heroides*; however, Richard Tarrant, deeming the Sappho letter spurious, has argued that these lines were merely inserted later into the work.[78] Surviving manuscripts show that the Sappho letter was itself added belatedly to the collection we have today, but whether that means it was restored to Ovid's text at that time – having been removed previously for unknown reasons – or was an entirely new addition lies at the heart of the debate.[79]

Sappho's letter has many interesting qualities, including the explicit juxtaposition of lyric poetry and elegy, opening a conversation with Sappho's original poetry that allows commentary on two distinct metres of ancient poetry. Perhaps most notoriously, Sappho, a poet well-known for her ardent desire for other women, writes her letter to a male lover, Phaon. The character of Phaon appears briefly in the limited fragments of Sappho's work, and also in Greek New Comedy, but this letter introduces an entirely new premise to their relationship, for, in appealing to Phaon, the Sappho of the *Heroides* explicitly repudiates her 'earlier' mode of same-sex passion (15.15–20).[80]

Such a major turnabout in Sappho's erotic object choice has caused considerable comment by classical scholars. One interpretation proposes that Sappho's newfound desire serves simply to make her consonant with other conventions in Ovid's text.[81] Other scholars, however, have suggested that an overt homophobia is evident by the Roman period, especially in relation to female homosexuality, and that this led Ovid (or the later author) to make a radical change to Sappho's professed desires.[82] The important question of homosexuality (albeit primarily male) and its place in Roman love poetry will be addressed in the next chapter. What is of interest here is a much more targeted issue: how perceptions of female same-sex desire may have informed the construction of Sappho's *ego* in the *Heroides*. In other words, given the reader's knowledge of Sappho's self-presentation in her original poetry, is there an even more intricate game in Sappho's letter pertaining to gender, desire and voice?

Reviewing earlier theories about Sappho's role in the *Heroides*, Pamela Gordon argues that the voice of the letter 'fits a pattern that emerges when we view the treatment of female homoeroticism in Roman literature in general'; more succinctly, she proposes that Sappho in the letter writes 'like a man'.[83] As Gordon recognizes, it is crucial not to discount the potentially negative connotations of such a trope – she discusses modern stereotypes of 'mannish lesbians' and the Roman poet Horace's own reference to 'masculine' Sappho suggests that questions about Sappho's gender identity in relation to her desires went far beyond the *Heroides* (*Epistles* 1.19.28). Yet, in the *Heroides*, 'writing like a man' seems to accord with Sappho's ability to seize an active rather than passive role in pursuing Phaon, a stance that generally sets her apart from the other female writers in the *Heroides*, and it is a role Gordon finds parallel to that of male narrators throughout Ovid's writing.[84]

Sappho's letter thus reminds us of the manifest complexity of the experiment Ovid has undertaken with the female voice; as Victoria Rimell dramatically expresses it, *Heroides* 15 'stag[es] a power struggle between Ovid and Sappho, whose poetic voices wrestle for visibility in a vacillating hierarchy',[85] and in the end it may be impossible to determine the precise gains made here or in the work overall – that is, who or what eventually emerges from the melee. For one, it remains difficult to determine whether the text ultimately seeks to explore the relationship between female subjectivity and female authorship or rather the capacities and limits of Ovid as an author. In other words, do the women of the *Heroides* exercise anything akin to an independent voice or are they merely vehicles for Ovid's literary play? Is it indeed the case that, as one critic memorably phrased it, 'although Ovid for the time being succeeded in disguising himself in silken petticoats, he did not succeed in ceasing to be Ovid'?[86]

Sarah Lindheim has gone further in suggesting that Ovid's narrative appropriation may in fact be driven by an anxiety or fear of women's 'uncontrollable, indefinable diversity and otherness'. In this view, Ovid's narrative cross-dressing becomes an attempt to tame the threatening nature of women by making all of his female narrators conform to a single type. Lindheim writes: 'The self-representations of the heroines demonstrate the powerful drive to circumscribe women by means of a single, universal definition, to achieve some sort of control over women by turning them into Woman'.[87] If Woman (or in love poetry, the *puella*) is a kind of threatening chaos, can order be imposed on her by making her write in a specific way? Can her threatening difference be contained within letters that make her subject to both earlier literary traditions and the hand of a male author? In seeking to understand the intricacies of such dynamics more fully, it is time to undertake a broader investigation of gender and power in Latin love poetry.

III

POWER AND PLAY

The girl whose boyfriend starts writing her love poems
should be on her guard.

W.H. AUDEN

ALTHOUGH LATIN LOVE POETRY centres around the exploits of
the male *ego*, it remains predicated on the erotic failures of that narrating subject: Latin love poetry is emphatically not a genre of 'happily ever
after'.[1] Despite the fact that the male *ego* rarely – or only briefly – 'gets
the girl', Paul Veyne insists nonetheless on the carefree nature of elegy, its
status as a 'pleasing falsehood'.[2] Ovid, in particular, seems to reinforce the
image of love as a blithe game; in *Amores* 1.4, for example, he instructs a
married woman as to how she and Ovid can use special gestures to communicate secretly with one another (18). In his *Ars*, he goes even further
with this conceit of love as a set of signs or learned behaviours, outlining
at considerable length the appropriate methods for pursuing love, as we
shall see in chapters 4 and 6.

However, other scholars have taken Latin love poetry much more seriously. Noting the popularity of Catullus' tenth poem – a poem in which
Catullus is caught out by a friend's girlfriend when he brags about the alleged

wealth he has brought home from Bithynia – Marilyn Skinner calls attention to the hostile language Catullus levies against the young woman when she exposes him, proposing that Catullus' humour and aggression are actually vehicles of power and control.[3] So when Catullus seeks to put the woman 'in her place' (a phrase that reveals well the hierarchy Catullus attempts to reassert), 'she becomes a point of convergence for a variety of other tensions provoked by class and gender difference.'[4] Augustan elegy also 'presents gender roles and constructs as revolving around a power struggle,'[5] so we attempt in this chapter to unveil more fully the role of gender and female subjectivity in Latin love poetry.

Readers of love poetry have long been intrigued by the genre's ostensible willingness to grant power to the *puella*, for she exercises, at least on the surface, an autonomy and control over her male pursuer that makes her role distinctive among female characters in Roman literature. It is the *puella*, after all, who seems to dictate the terms and longevity of her love affairs. Yet in weighing power and its possessors, we might want to distinguish two distinct, albeit related forms: 'power to' and 'power over'. The first suggests the 'power of an individual or group to affect their outward environment', a capacity that at times overlaps with the second, which is a form of power expressed against others, allowing a person 'to manipulate, to persuade, or in extreme cases to force'.[6] In the case of the *puella*, then, we should assess not only whether she indeed exercises 'power over' her lover, as the poets would have it, but also whether she possesses the 'power to' affect her environment, including the ability to influence the situations in which she appears or even the storylines themselves. As this latter criterion suggests, power in love poetry remains entangled in questions of narrative and authorship; indeed, Auden's wry quotation which serves as our chapter epigraph reminds us from the outset to be constantly on the alert when it comes to the *puella* and her literary representation.

Just as questions of biography have attended the interpretation of love poetry's *ego*, the representation of the *puella* has also been subjected to speculation about its connections to Roman 'reality'.

The Puella *at Rome*

In trying to assess the transformations in Roman society wrought by the chaos of the civil wars and the rise of Augustus, historians have sought to determine whether the relations between Roman men and women, including what was expected of each group, were substantially influenced and, if so, how. J.P. Sullivan, for one, sees in Propertius' Cynthia the reflection of new opportunities for women's empowerment in this turbulent era. Relying primarily on literary evidence, Sullivan proposes that 'in the last century of the Republic and beyond, it is evident, there were women of strong character who did not follow the traditional pattern of dutiful daughter and patriotic wife', concluding that 'the social turmoil of the civil wars had for some its compensations'.[7] For Sullivan and other like-minded critics, such changes specifically entailed 'the growth of a recognizable demi-monde', one in which 'ex-slaves, lower-class free (or freed) women, actresses [...] [and] even women of some family and independent means' were able to engage in '*concubinatus* or more casual liaisons'.[8]

While appealing at first glance, such theories of female 'emancipation' in the first century are often problematic, not least because they rely so heavily on literary sources and derive almost exclusively from speculation about Roman women's sexual activities.[9] Indeed, in the latter case, as Maria Wyke points out, reconstructions of ancient female sexuality often themselves draw precariously on 'elements of moral turpitude transferred wholesale from the writings of the Roman moralists'.[10] In other words, modern critics often infer the increasing sexual liberation of Roman women from contemporary accusations of their sexual promiscuity.[11]

The women of Latin love poetry share one main feature when it comes to their sexual activities: their inability to enter into permanent relationships with the poets who pursue them.[12] Thus, the love poets generally present their *puellae* as either already married, making the relationship pursued adulterous (adultery being an act not without considerable social stigma and legal risk in the Roman world), or as courtesans, a pact that is presumably more formal and longer-lasting than the one-night arrangement between a

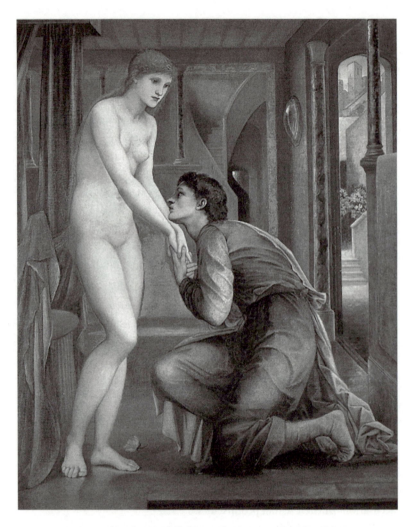

3.1 *Pygmalion and Galatea IV: The Soul Attains* (1878)
by Edward Burne-Jones.

Roman prostitute and her client, but that nonetheless presumes an economic
foundation and difference in social class. Further underlining the elusive
status of the *puella*, some of the love poets depict their lovers alternating
between the roles of Roman wife (*matrona*) and courtesan (*meretrix*).[13]

Given such indeterminacy, any concrete attempt to link the *puella* to social attitudes or social revolutions outside the text remains a thorny proposition, and we shall return at the end of this chapter to the pressing question of love poetry's treatment of gender and its possible relation to contemporary Rome. For now, we want to explore what Alison Sharrock has called 'womanufacture', meaning the process by which love poetry 'creates its own object, calls her Woman, and falls in love with her – or rather, with the artist's own act of creating her'.[14] Setting aside for now the desires attached to her, how is it that love poetry creates Woman, and, for our starting point, is Woman (or the *puella*) ever constructed as a subject in her own right?

The Puella *as Subject*

One way of probing the *puella*'s subjectivity is through the dichotomy of active versus passive: does the *puella* take shape through the actions that she herself performs or through those that are performed on her? In her study of female subjectivity in Homer's *Odyssey*, Ingrid Holmberg adopts a slightly different emphasis by positing desire – a term that charts not merely a character's sexual urges, but also her capacity for constituting a will of her own more expansively – as a means for tracing subjectivity in literature.[15] When Homer acknowledges the desires of women like Penelope in his epic poem, for example, Holmberg argues that he also attributes to them a form of independent subjectivity. Yet Holmberg also observes that such female desires are generally presented negatively, often as a serious threat or obstruction to the overall narrative.[16] While Homer may open the possibility of female subjectivity, then, any self-sufficiency the female characters attain is ultimately repudiated and their desires are forfeited to larger narrative forces, forces often explicitly dedicated to the ongoing development and eventual 'success' of the male hero.[17] Central to Holmberg's argument is her assertion that the *Odyssey* 'employs control over narrative production itself' as a means of constructing gender difference.[18]

Male alignment with narrative power remains a key feature of Latin love poetry, despite the occasional presence of a female *ego*. So we might add to our distinction of 'power over' and 'power to' a series of related questions suggested by Holmberg's treatment of female subjectivity: does the *puella* possess her own mind, as it were, or is she simply a projection of the needs and desires of others, including the reader? If the *puella* does attain her own distinct subjectivity, can it withstand narrative pressures, even when they seem set against her? Finally, is the *puella* ever able to take control of the narrative or – as we might phrase it – does she ever have the 'power to' dictate the terms of her own participation in love poetry? We can begin to discern the *puella*'s capacity to be a subject by looking more closely at how she is actually constructed, including the problems raised by her very name.

NAMING NAMES

Already in antiquity, many Roman writers identified individual love poets closely with their *puellae*, while also tracing a literary genealogy of the *puella* herself. Thus, in one poem, Propertius compares Cynthia directly to Catullus' Lesbia, arguing that 'Lesbia did all these things with impunity before her, surely she who follows is less to blame' (2.32.45–46). Earlier, Propertius positions Cynthia among the women made famous by Roman love poetry, proclaiming in one poem that his books will make her beauty the most famous of all and asking only Calvus' and Catullus' pardon (2.25.3–4). In 2.34, Propertius defends his own choice to write love poetry by listing the poets who have previously been successful in such work; citing specifically the pairings of Catullus and Lesbia, Calvus and Quintilia, Gallus and Lycoris, he concludes: 'Cynthia too will live, praised by the verse of Propertius, if fame wishes to place me among these poets' (93–94). In Book 3 of *Ars Amatoria*, Ovid, in turn, connects the *puella* to literary reputation when he lists the number of women who have been made famous by poets, notably omitting Catullus' Lesbia, while adding one of Tibullus' girlfriends (535–538).

In *Amores* 2.1, signalling his emphatic repudiation of epic for love poetry – an act of poetic self-definition that we shall consider more fully in the next chapter – Ovid bids farewell to 'the distinguished names of heroes', urging instead that *puellae* turn their beautiful faces towards his song (35–39).

Through such phrasing, Ovid strongly implies that male heroes can be located by name, while *puellae* are identified instead through their physical appearance. Indeed, on closer inspection, the name of the *puella* proves to be elusive. For one, all the names of the *puellae* have strong roots in the Greek tradition: Catullus' Lesbia, as we have seen, derives her name from Sappho's island Lesbos, while the name of Ovid's Corinna comes directly from an early Greek poetess. Both Cynthia and Delia's names can be linked to the Greek god Apollo (as well as, in the case of Cynthia, Apollo's twin, Diana), and Nemesis is itself a Greek word, one often personified as the goddess of retribution.[19] Moreover, as we discussed in Chapter 2, the name of the *puella* is often presumed to be a pseudonym, a cover for some 'real' woman outside the work. So we might say that the name of the *puella* both focuses our attention and, at the same time, deflects it elsewhere.[20]

Our difficulty in pinning down the *puella* of love poetry, a feature we have already encountered in her uncertain social status, is made even more acute by the challenges the reader often faces in simply recognizing her in the work. For the poet's act of giving his *puella* a name creates an expectation of presence and consistency that is not always actively maintained.[21] Most obviously, the *puella* remains often unnamed in individual love poems, requiring a conscious decision on the part of the reader about whether to assume that, say, Corinna is meant even when Ovid avoids naming her.[22] Moreover, Veyne characterizes Cynthia and Delia themselves as 'so vague and so incoherent that we may draw nothing from them';[23] Corinna's presence in Ovid's poetry is equally tenuous,[24] giving all three *puellae* a fluidity or 'lightness' (*levitas*) of character that serves to define them. Such inconsistency is enshrined in love poetry's recurring reference to the *puella* as *levis*, a term often rendered as 'fickle', but potentially connoting more fundamental changeability.[25] Not coincidentally, the *levitas* of the *puella* is set against the apparent solidity and consistency of the male *ego*.[26] A powerful bond between reader and poet can thus be forged as the reader's inability to grasp the *puella* with any confidence parallels *ego*'s frustrations with her sexual inconstancy.[27] In short, the *puella* seems at times as impossible to read as she is to love.

But what other demands or strategies – beyond her name and her at times exasperating indeterminacy – circumscribe the *puella*'s subjectivity in love poetry? We want to turn now to two other features vital to the 'womanufacture' of love poetry's *puella*: the body and the voice.

Reading the Body

Because it is so often defined by its biological properties, it is tempting to see the body as a completely natural entity. Indeed, Propertius professes a strong preference for Cynthia in her 'natural' state, one in which her body is unmarred by cosmetics or elaborate adornment (*cultus*). Dismayed at the prospect of her carefully made-up hair and dress in 1.2, Propertius asks why she would ever 'destroy the grace given by nature with purchased adornment' (5).[28] While Propertius' predilection for an unadorned Cynthia might seem commendable, his *puella*'s elaborate preparations prove to be troubling in another poem precisely because they rouse his suspicions about her interest in attracting other men (1.15.5–8). Not surprisingly, Propertius turns out to have a very specific definition of 'sophistication': 'if a girl is pleasing to one man,' he proclaims, 'she is refined enough' (1.2.26). Although, as we shall see, Ovid later enthusiastically endorses the notion of *cultus*, Propertius in 1.2 exposes the tenuous lines separating nature and culture when he paradoxically uses artworks to illustrate nature's beauty (1.2.21–22).[29]

Gillian Rose has argued that 'far from being natural [...] bodies are "maps of power and identity"; or, rather, maps of the relation between power and identity'.[30] The residents of Augustan Rome were witness to a very potent display of the female body when an effigy of Cleopatra, 'opened and eroticized by the snakebite', was displayed in Roman triumph in 29 BCE,[31] a spectacle Propertius exploits in poem 3.11 (53–54). Traversed by an array of social anxieties, female bodies take on many meanings in Latin love poetry, even serving at times as 'metaphors for the poetic projects and political interests of their authors',[32] an idea we shall return to. Here, we want to examine how gender and power intersect on the body in love poetry, including how male and female bodies are respectively imagined and represented.

CORINNA'S ABORTION

The female body is often distinguished specifically by its reproductive role, an emphasis that – despite its prominence in contemporary Roman thought – is actually quite rare in love poetry, given that the genre insists on the impossibility of permanent bonds between the lovers.[33] Propertius in 2.7, as we have seen, explicitly denies any prospect of children with Cynthia. In another poem, he proclaims Cynthia's childlessness a physical advantage (2.15.21–22). A pair of poems in Ovid's *Amores* (2.13 and 2.14), however, goes further in actually acknowledging the risk of female pregnancy by responding to an action Corinna has allegedly undertaken without the poet's knowledge: an abortion.

Abortion was a complex issue both medically and ethically in antiquity, just as it is today,[34] and even though Ovid's poems are often taken as an important source for discerning ancient attitudes about the act, his viewpoint remains subject to his own designs as author and *ego*.[35] Ovid begins by informing us that Corinna is dangerously close to death following an abortion (2.13.3–4). In a malicious jab, he casts his own paternity as mere speculation, professing that 'nonetheless either she conceived from me, or so I believe it, for often I take as fact that which is possible' (5–6). The bulk of the poem then presents a prayer for Corinna's recovery to Isis and Ilithyia, the latter a goddess of childbirth invoked with perhaps intentional awkwardness. In the following poem, Ovid 'treats abortion as an abstract question, denouncing the practice in the *persona* of a stern satirist'.[36] Utilizing the recurrent imagery of warfare, Ovid begins by asking why, when women are not made to participate in warfare, they choose to 'suffer wounds from their own weapons' (2.14.3–4). He then bitterly charges that 'she who first instituted the plucking out of tender foetuses deserves to die in the battle of her making' (5–6). Ovid finally concludes the poem by requesting that although such women often pay with their lives – a punishment, he notes, that is approved by observers – Corinna should be spared for now, albeit punished if she tries again (43–44).

This pair of poems has presented many obstacles to interpretation, not least because Ovid's overall tone seems highly inappropriate given the seriousness of Corinna's condition;[37] so, too, a general 'asymmetry' of male and female viewpoints pervades the poems. For one, Ovid fails to present Corinna's side of the story; not once does he reveal the considerations essential to any understanding of her act, such as her reasons for undertaking the abortion or even her actual methods.[38] Pointing out Ovid's relentless 'attempts to keep the focus on himself', Mary-Kay Gamel proposes that Ovid's treatment ultimately betrays an anxiety about women's power, including the fact that 'it is they who take action, while he only talks'.[39] We seem, then, to encounter a significant conundrum, for although Corinna's actions ostensibly drive the poem, her own perspective remains out of reach as Ovid invites us to experience the episode entirely from his point of view. So how are we, as readers, invited to witness such events; or to phrase it another way, how do things come into focus in love poetry?

THE GAZE

Just as the *puella*'s body is often the source of poetic composition, it is continually offered up in patently visual terms for the reader's consumption; we do not merely hear about issues that pertain to the *puella*'s physical self – such as the role of adornment or her dangerous abortion – but are invited quite explicitly to look upon her. Many debates about the distribution of power in Latin love poetry therefore centre around the 'gaze', a concept that highlights the difference between who is doing the looking and who is being looked at in various forms of story-telling.[40] Latin love poetry often calls attention to the role of the eyes and vision (e.g. Propertius 1.1.1), and many different physical features of the *puella* are designated as the source of her beauty.[41] Taken together, such passages seem to support the proposition that men always take the active role and 'see', while women, conversely, are passively 'seen'. Yet just as the love poets undercut other terminology that defines Roman gender roles, they at times purposely refuse to adhere to a stringent distinction in acts related to viewing, and so it might be better to envision love poetry as both interrogating and reinforcing such a dynamic.[42]

In her reading of Propertius 2.15, Barbara Flaschenriem argues that 'insofar as she is associated with narrativity, Cynthia either eludes spectacle or subverts it'. On the other hand, in Ovid's *Amores* 1.5 – a poem Flaschenriem calls a 'reductive but revealing parody' of Propertius' poem – she finds something very different: 'a more purely fetishistic use of the female body'.[43] Ovid's description of Corinna's body in 1.5 is, indeed, infamous both for what it displays and where it abruptly stops.[44] The poem begins with Ovid calling attention to the time of day (around noon) and the attendant lighting of his bedroom. Next Corinna arrives only to have Ovid quickly tear away her clothing (13–16) and scan her body from the top down (17–22). When he reaches the thigh, however, he suddenly stops, asking coyly, 'why should I detail each part? Everything I saw deserved praise' (23–24). Soon after, Ovid announces: 'who does not know the rest? Exhausted we both lay quiet. Would that midday often turn out this way for me!' (25–26).

Joan Booth has called this poem 'a near-cinematic sex scene',[45] but although it offers an unabashed view of Corinna's body, Ovid's poem constructs power relations that are not entirely straightforward. For one, the poem seems to pit Ovid's sexual desires against those of the reader rather than Corinna. Building our anticipation as he approaches her midsection, Ovid plays with the reader's desire to see her body fully exposed, including what modern editors often primly call her pudenda, the very site at which he brusquely halts. But does Ovid set out to feed the reader's voyeurism or to parody it, purposely leaving the reader's desire to see Corinna unsatisfied in contrast to his own exhausted sexual state? Of course, Ovid's attempts to vie with the reader do not discount the fact that the relationship between poet and reader has been articulated through varied access to Corinna's body. So is Ovid himself all talk and no body? Does he ever open his own physique to similar scrutiny?

THE MALE BODY

As we have seen, the male body remains an important site for illustrating the degradation of the figure of the *servitium amoris*, slave bodies being manifestly open to physical penetration and punishment. On the other hand, protection of the male citizen body was a major tenet in Roman law,[46] making it both a site of authority and one closed to incursion of any kind. Ovid, like many of the love poets, seems to take this prerogative for granted, holding his own body mostly above the fray. When he laments Corinna's love for a former soldier over himself, in fact, Ovid evokes a mind and body hierarchy by pointedly using the soldier's reliance on his body as a sign of his inferiority: 'look at the scars,' he says with scorn, 'the remains of old battle. Whatever he has, has been attained with his body' (3.8.19–20).[47] Yet in the poem immediately preceding, Ovid calls attention to his own body by revealing its moment of shameful failure: his impotence.[48] Sharrock calls Ovid 'a poet renowned for his self-esteem' and 3.7 'a poem about power and manhood'.[49] How, then, can we account for this apparent revelation of his own physical shortcomings? The answer may lie in the demands of authorship itself, meaning that the poem provides 'a reflection on the nature of elegy, doomed as it must be to perpetual "failure" through which it achieves success'.[50] Ovid's poem thus exposes a paradox: he becomes a good elegiac poet precisely in his failures as a lover.[51]

Propertius seems even more willing to place his body before the reader's gaze. From the very outset, Propertius cites Milanion, an emphatically wounded figure, as his model (1.1.9–16), and he subsequently exposes his own body to both examination and punishment. In 1.5, for example, Propertius advises his friend Gallus that when Gallus falls in love he will no longer be surprised by Propertius' pale colour, or 'that I am nothing when it comes to my whole body' (21–22). On the other hand, Propertius confronts an interlocutor who thinks his limbs are emaciated, urging him to consult with a *puella* who has experienced Propertius' ability 'to do his duty the whole night through' (2.22b.21–24). Other love poets likewise draw on the idea of physical performance as a sign of power. Despite claims to impotence in 3.7, Ovid gives an accounting in the same poem of the number of times he was able to make love to various women in a single night, culminating with the claim that Corinna once demanded it nine times (3.7.23–26), a seeming echo of Catullus 32, where Catullus, playing on the idea of a dinner party, asks Ipsithilla for 'nine courses of sex' (8).[52]

AGGRESSION AND ASSAULT

Despite such boasts and ribaldry, Latin love poetry markedly avoids any description of the actual sexual acts between the *ego* and the *puella*. Indeed, Kirk Ormand makes a useful distinction between the sexual and the erotic in Catullus' poetry, noting that while 'eroticism [...] suggests a mutual give-and-take and the apparent elevation of the beloved to a position of power', 'sex is nearly always an expression, not of love, but of physical and political domination'.[53] We have already seen the use of such terminology in Catullus' attacks on his friend's girlfriend in poem 10; similarly, in poem 41 he ridicules the mistress of Caesar's colleague Mamurra, who, he says, offered to sell herself to him for ten thousand sesterces.[54] Such poems display a distinct nastiness directed at other women, but many of Catullus' attacks on Lesbia herself, as well as his various male associates, are even more shocking in their coarseness and use of obscenity.[55]

Actual acts of violence against women, including rape, recur throughout ancient myth and Roman literature.[56] The rape of women or boys – 'intercourse by force' or *per vim stuprum* – was punishable by law in Rome,[57] and the prospect is present in love poetry, albeit generally relegated to the mythic past or treated as unfulfilled fantasy in the present. This does not mean the idea of rape does not hold serious repercussions in love poetry; indeed, it would be difficult to find a more savage and repugnant justification for rape than that articulated by Ovid in the *Ars Amatoria*, 'advice' that can be summarized in modern parlance as 'no' means 'yes' and, even more, that a woman's feelings will be hurt if she is not taken by force (1.673–680; see Chapter 6). Critics, however, have varied in their response to the tone of such sentiments; Ovid, after all, is the poet who seemed to show such compassion for rape victims in his *Metamorphoses*.[58]

Yet although love poetry deliberates the potential for violence in intimate settings, rape does not generally seem like the most appropriate framework for interpreting such acts. More often, the Augustan elegists describe physical altercations with their *puellae*, encounters that pointedly leave marks on the surface of the body, suggesting that, for some love poets, violence is beneficial precisely because of its ability to enter private passion into the public record.[59]

BRUISES AND BLOWS

The representation of the *puella*'s body alternates between an emphasis on its perfection – or beauty – and its degradation.[60] When weighing the intensity of physical violence in love poetry, however, Sharon James advocates distinguishing between *rixae* (quarrels), 'a form of sexual play', and outright assault.[61] In 1.1, as Tibullus outlines the features of his modest life, he registers his expectation that 'quarrels' are central to love affairs when he proclaims that since old age will come, now is his time to pursue *levis venus* ('light sex'), that is, while it is not shameful to 'break down doors' and is pleasing to 'enter into quarrels' (71–74). Even as the elegists allude to physical fights with their lovers, they frequently seek to define its 'appropriate' limits. In 1.10, Tibullus describes the actions of the *rusticus*, meaning a man of the countryside (a more pejorative term in Propertius and Ovid), who 'barely sober' goes home where the 'battles of love heat up' (51–53). Having recorded the brutality of the scene and its impact on the man's wife, Tibullus offers his own commentary, calling anyone who would beat his *puella* 'stone and iron', since this is like 'ripping the gods from heaven' (59–60). He then proposes that it is enough to tear the *puella*'s garment and disarrange her hair, making her cry (61–62), since 'four times blessed is he, who in his anger, can make a *puella* cry' (63–64). But the one who is fierce with his hands, Tibullus urges, should go to war and stay far away from 'tender Venus' (65–66).[62]

In 2.15, Propertius excitedly recounts the *rixa* he and Cynthia once had. Delighting in the initiative she seems to take (5–6), Propertius nevertheless threatens at one point that if she will not disrobe, she will experience his hands and a ripped gown; perhaps even 'show bruised arms' to her mother (17–20). Yet, in an earlier poem, Propertius pointedly disavows such violence (2.5.21–24). 'Let some *rusticus*,' he says, 'seek these disgraceful battles': one who does not, like the poet, have ivy on his brow (25–26). Reaffirming his own status as poet, Propertius makes his attack instead in verse, threatening his *puella* with a damning epitaph: 'Cynthia, mighty in form, Cynthia, light in word' (27–28).[63]

Scenes of violence against the *puella* draw at times on the figure of *militia amoris*, and Leslie Cahoon proposes that 'the love of the *Amores* is inherently violent and linked with the Roman *libido dominandi*'; it is this 'appetite for domination' that provides 'a domestic manifestation of the same impulses that have motivated both civil war and military aggression abroad'.[64] Ovid references the injury of his *puella* in a number of poems (e.g. 2.5.45–46), but it is his full-out assault on her in 1.7 that best illustrates this correlation between imperialism abroad and control at home. Ovid begins 1.7 by proclaiming his *furor* ('madness') in attacking his mistress; his wounded *puella* cries and her tears no longer seem a virtue.[65] Ovid later decries his deed, noting that he would have been punished if he had struck the least of Roman citizens. 'The one I professed to love has been wounded by me,' he concedes (33–34). He imagines Corinna in the context of an imagined triumph, one in which she would be paraded as a captive and he, he sarcastically notes, would be celebrated as her victor (35–40); later, Ovid urges her to attack him back, or, at the very least, to hide the signs of his assault (63–68).

Amores 1.7 has elicited different reactions from its readers. Saara Lilja, for one, believes that 'Ovid is as shocked at his violent fit of jealousy as if he had committed an atrocious crime.'[66] Other critics, however, are not as persuaded by Ovid's alleged remorse and self-disgust,[67] especially since he himself callously flashes back to the scene in the *Ars Amatoria* (2.169 ff.). Calling attention to Ovid's extensive use of myth (a feature of love poetry that we shall examine in the next chapter) and other literary devices, Ellen Greene contends that he 'metaphorizes the woman right out of sentient existence and again diverts attention from his violent behavior to his poetic virtuosity'.[68] Ovid's use of imperatives in demanding that Corinna seek revenge likewise points to his continuing attempts to control her,[69] a control unmasked as well by the cold final request that she at least clean herself up.

Like Cahoon, Greene argues that Ovid's poetry depicts the life of the lover not as an alternative to the demands of the dominant culture at Rome (a main pretence of elegy, as we have seen), but rather its complement; or, as she phrases it, in Ovid '*amor* often reiterates the mercantilist and imperialist values in Augustan culture'.[70] Fredrick, on the other hand, finds in elegy's violence a quite different relation to contemporary Roman society, namely that it records Roman men's 'vanishing capacity for political action' under the new Augustan regime rather than their propensity for domination.[71] In effect, for Fredrick, the *puella*'s body presents a site for documenting contemporary male frustration (a thesis that may, of course, be of little comfort to the *puella* herself) – a broader social and political disempowerment that, as we shall see, is potentially reenacted on the male body itself in Catullus' Attis poem. In charting gender and power in terms of physical force, however, it may be important to determine whether violence is ever reciprocal: does *ego* ever suffer abuse at the hands of the *puella*, as Ovid demands of Corinna?

In 1.6, Tibullus accepts for himself 'harsh laws', namely that if he praises another woman, he may be attacked in his eyes or by his hair, even thrown into the street (69–72); but Propertius goes the furthest of all the love poets when he makes Cynthia the aggressor in two important poems. In the first, Propertius claims to be thrilled by a night-time brawl (*rixa*) with his enraged lover (3.8). Recounting the event, Propertius dares Cynthia to go beyond simply throwing things at him by directly assaulting his body (5–8). All these marks of violence, he asserts, will furnish him with 'signs' of her deep passion (9). Calling himself a 'true interpreter' (17), Propertius excitedly hopes that his male contemporaries will witness his 'wounds' (21–22), and so understand Cynthia's 'real' feelings. James Butrica notes that 'violence as proof of sincerity was well established in ancient erotic lore, but Propertius here hammers at the theme with an intensity and exaggeration unparallelled elsewhere'.[72] Moreover, we should underscore two points of contrast with Ovid's attack on Corinna: firstly, Propertius places his own wounded body in the reader's gaze, and secondly, he believes that its public display will elicit envy rather than shame.

The contrast between the abused Propertius and the abusive Cynthia is taken to its extreme in poem 4.8 when Cynthia assumes almost superhuman powers in seeking revenge on the poet who foolishly holds a dinner party in her absence.[73] Cynthia appears in only two of the poems in Propertius' final book (4.7 and 4.8), and her presence there confounds the oft-repeated dictum that Propertius wishes to move away from Cynthia and elegy itself in his fourth book (an idea that will be discussed further in chapters 4 and 5). Propertius begins 4.8 in dramatic fashion: 'listen to what put the well-watered Esquiline to flight and sent the peoples living near by scurrying'

(1–2). He explains that Cynthia had departed for Lanuvium and in response to her abandonment he decided to hold his own party with two young women. Suddenly a loud sound issues from the gates: Cynthia has returned (49–50). The next twenty lines describe the havoc Cynthia wreaks on the party-goers (51–70), a scene Propertius compares to the spectacle of a city being sacked (56).[74]

Cynthia first goes after the two women (57–62), then, 'like a conqueror', she attacks the poet himself, striking his face with the back of her hand and bloodying his neck by biting it (63–66). Cynthia eventually turns to Lygdamus, the slave we saw in Chapter 1, who pleads in vain to Propertius for help (67–70). In the final part of the poem, initiated by Propertius' own act of supplication, the two lovers settle their terms, a scenario meant to resemble a formal surrender (73–74). Forbidding Propertius the sites and activities that will put him in contact with other women (such as Pompey's colonnade, the forum during festivals and the theatre), Cynthia also demands that Lygdamus be shackled and sold (75–80). Propertius immediately accepts her conditions, leaving Cynthia to laugh rather ominously, 'made arrogant with power [*imperium*] handed over to her' (82). The two then purify the house, ultimately 'laying down their arms on the well-known couch' (88).

As Richardson notes, 'the tone throughout the poem is mock-epic'[75] and its rich play with the idea of *militia amoris* is evident. Propertius, however, subverts the usual expectations by making Cynthia rather than the male *ego* the soldier or, here, conquering general. Cynthia's acceptance of *imperium*, the specific power or authority granted to Roman military leaders, affirms the superiority of her position for contemporary Romans, meaning that if Roman imperial power indeed serves to structure the *amor* of love poetry, Cynthia is clearly its beneficiary in this poem. So, too, by making Cynthia humorously re-enact Odysseus' homecoming and revenge on Penelope's suitors, Propertius effortlessly slides Cynthia into the role of one of the most famous male heroes of myth.

In a celebrated poem from Book 1, Propertius seems to do the precise opposite, using myth instead to enshrine Cynthia's passivity (1.3); as the poem progresses, however, any inherent alignment between gender identity and the active role in love is brought seriously into question.

CYNTHIA WAKES

Propertius begins 1.3 by comparing his sleeping lover to a series of mytho-logical women: Ariadne resting after Theseus' abandonment, Andromeda sleeping after her rescue and a maenad worn out by her 'incessant dance' (1–8).[76] While each woman has a different source of slumber, Propertius' descriptions cumulatively call attention to female inactivity. Many critics have argued further that, by drawing on these specific moments from myth, Propertius is intentionally referencing popular scenes in Roman art, creat-ing an over-determined tableau of female flesh as he enthusiastically invites the reader to join with him in gazing on Cynthia's inert form.[77] In addition, Propertius' use of myth serves to establish an elevated tone for the scene, a means of idealizing Cynthia.

Having set the stage, Propertius then recounts his own drunken approach, a depiction of male action as ineffectual and inappropriate. Compelled by desire, he thinks to act upon Cynthia's supine body, that is, 'to take up kisses and arms' (16), a phrase that signals his potentially violent intentions; how-ever, he admits that he is afraid to disturb her (17–18). As Propertius phrases it, he instead merely looks upon her like Argus, who guarded Io with his one hundred eyes (19–20). The objectification of Cynthia continues as Propertius attempts to arrange and decorate her static body (21–26); he claims that he himself froze every time she stirred, fearing that she was dreaming about an aggressor who wanted to force her against her will (27–30), a mirror of his own initial reactions to her vulnerable state.

But the moon soon falls across the window, and it wakes Cynthia, whose rebuke of Propertius fills the remainder of the poem. As one critic writes of the turn the poem takes,

> Cynthia's dream-shattering speech that concludes the poem is made to reuse elements of the wording of the elaborately idealistic open-ing section. The ironical effect of this is clear: Cynthia, crushingly and conclusively, flings back in Propertius' face his own idealiza-tion of her.[78]

Or, as another critic phrases it, 'When she begins to speak, Cynthia seems to wrest control from the narrator and take over her own focalization.'[79] A similar dynamic occurs in 2.29b, when Cynthia punctures Propertius' rapturous description of her sleeping form by voicing her own perception of the scene; perhaps most significantly, she ridicules Propertius' pleasure in watching her by calling him a *speculator* or 'spy' (31), an insult that casts watching (or possessing the gaze) not as a position of power, but as one deserving contempt.

In both these poems, Cynthia has the final word and Propertius seems to be offering his readers a glimpse of what it might look like (pardon the pun) for the *puella* to 'speak back' to the events taking place.[80] So if the female body is often presented as passive in love poetry, as an object of the gaze or even abuse, does Propertius' poem suggest that speaking grants the *puella* greater access to power and subjectivity?

The Puella *Speaks (*Puella Loquens*)*

Female speech is, of course, not the only means for unsettling dominant male narratives. When Dido refuses to respond to Aeneas in Book 6 of Virgil's *Aeneid*, her silence serves as a powerful form of resistance, a refusal to validate Aeneas' version of events.[81] Yet, as one scholar has remarked, 'the representation of speech is commonly conceived as one, if not the only, way for a literary text to represent something beyond itself.'[82] So can the *puella* locate herself beyond the bounds of love poetry through her speech?

In examining the role of the female voice in Catullus' poetry, Judith Hallett provides a helpful list of passages in which women are cited in direct quotation, a list that includes the deflating comments that so provoke Catullus in poem 10, as well as the many allusions Catullus makes to the work of Sappho.[83] Significantly, while Catullus refers to Lesbia's conversation seven times in his text, he never records her actual speech.[84] The most famous example of female speech in Catullus' poetry falls outside his love poetry *per se*, although the poem provides an important model for later Latin love poetry.

ARIADNE'S LAMENT

Written as what is often called an 'epyllion' or mini epic, Catullus 64 features two interlocking stories: that of the wedding of Peleus and Thetis (Achilles' parents) and that of Ariadne, who helped the hero Theseus navigate the Minotaur's labyrinth only to be subsequently abandoned by him on a deserted island. Moreover, the poem incorporates the story of Ariadne and Theseus through an ingenious device: the description of a coverlet on Peleus' and Thetis' marriage bed which is decorated with the scene of Ariadne standing distraught on the beach as she watches Theseus sail away.[85] As one critic notes, 'Looking, gazing, watching – *seeing* – is Ariadne's most characteristic activity' in the poem,[86] and the reader's first encounter with Ariadne plays openly with the idea of vision, since even as the reader's gaze is directed towards Ariadne, she herself is shown actively watching Theseus. Although Ariadne seems to claim a kind of subjectivity through her vision, the narrator constantly reminds the reader that Ariadne is simultaneously the object of our gaze, describing her hair in disarray and her body exposed, her clothes falling off as she forlornly wades into the water (63–67).

Temporarily digressing to explain Ariadne's plight (76–115), the poem soon records her famous seventy-line reproach of the absent Theseus (132–201). In her speech, Ariadne expresses her considerable bitterness towards Theseus, while also reminding him of his earlier dependency on her. She concludes with a curse that Theseus bring death to himself and his family with the same mindset that allowed him to abandon her (192–201), namely his 'forgetfulness' or 'carelessness' (cf. 248). Ariadne despairs of the futility of her speech, but, in fact, her words hold considerable power since the narrator tells us that the ruler of the heavens nods assent. The poem then shows the fulfilment of her wishes as Theseus, arriving home, forgets to change his sails, making his own father believe he is dead. Despondent, Theseus' father hurls himself from the rocks, causing Theseus, as the poem states, to feel the same grief he brought to Ariadne (246–250).

As a formidable piece of female self-expression, Ariadne's speech resonates throughout later literature; Catullus' Ariadne provides a model for Virgil's Dido, and Ovid imports her directly into his *Heroides* (7). Critics have also identified the poem's influence on Propertius 1.3, which begins with a kind of ecphrasis of the sleeping Cynthia (one that compares her explicitly to the abandoned Ariadne), but soon yields to her voice.[87] Cynthia even gives an Ariadne-like curse when she calls for symmetry between male and female experience, specifically that Propertius endure nights like hers (39–40). Gardner links Ariadne to love poetry's *puella* in even more fundamental ways, suggesting Ariadne 'represents a disruptive force'; she expands that Ariadne 'anticipates the *puella*'s marginalized position and thus better identifies the elements of female subjectivity that Catullus hands down to his elegiac successors.'[88] For Gardner, Ariadne's isolation epitomizes women's distinct relationship to space and time.[89] We would like, however, to continue emphasizing the specific links between female voice and subjectivity by returning once again to Propertius' Book 4.

CYNTHIA AND CORNELIA

Ovid records only brief glimpses of the *puella*'s voice in his *Amores* (e.g. 2.18.8 and 3.7.77–80, the latter chiding him for his impotency), although he personifies the genres of tragedy and elegy as women who speak in 3.1, a poem that we shall look at in the next chapter. Propertius, as we have seen, gives Cynthia a voice in 1.3 and 2.29b, but there are only two other passages in the first three books that record her voice directly (2.15.8 and 3.6.19–34). On the other hand, Propertius occasionally plays with the spectre of Cynthia's voice: in 2.8, he accuses her of never saying 'I love you' (12), casting not her speech, but its withholding as sadistic;[90] in 2.24b, he conversely (and self-servingly) puts words into her mouth, fantasizing that she will praise him in elaborate fashion when he is dead (35–38).

Propertius' most extensive experimentation with the female voice, however, occurs in Book 4, where he presents an unprecedented series of speaking women. The dramatic changes of Propertius' fourth book have long produced divided opinions over how it pertains to the rest of his work: is Book 4 a departure from his earlier love poetry or a means of expanding its boundaries? Maria Wyke proposes that 'the range of women who speak in the fourth book [...] contribute[s] to an innovatory, bipolar poetics' creating 'a range of elegiac tones that oscillates between the aetiological and the amatory, the public and the private, the grand and the sorrowful'.[91] Among its other devices, Book 4 features the return from the dead of that most loquacious of all *puellae*: Cynthia, who most definitely has more to say.

Cynthia appears in a dream to Propertius in poem 4.7, a poem that has elicited immense scholarly interest.[92] Puzzling through the difficult juxtaposition of a poem pronouncing Cynthia dead (4.7) with one showing her very much alive (4.8), Wyke suggests that the pair intentionally responds to epic models, balancing an allusion to the *Iliad* and the appearance of Patroclus' ghost in 4.7 with the return of Odysseus from the *Odyssey* in 4.8.[93] Writing about the poem in 1949, William Helmbold focuses on the ways that Propertius seeks in the poem to find a pointed kind of closure with his *puella*, observing wryly: 'It is clear that Propertius is uneasy about his treatment of his former mistress, both before and after her death, and hopes to clear his conscience by making her posthumously exonerate him [...] This, in modern jargon, is called Wishful Thinking.'[94] Others have taken the poem as an ending not with his *puella*, but with the genre of elegy itself.[95] However, beyond the questions of poetics (to which we shall return in the next chapter), what does it mean that Cynthia does not merely return from the dead, but so emphatically speaks?

In a striking reversal of 1.3, the poem begins with Propertius rather than Cynthia in sleep; Propertius is a passive participant throughout: 'things happen to him. He is lying in bed, the "dream" appears, speaks, vanishes.'[96] When Cynthia materializes before him, Propertius describes first how ravaged her body is; she appears as she was in burial, no longer possessing the idealized body of the *puella* (7–10). Cynthia's voice has patently 'outlasted' her body (11–12) and she proceeds to deliver an impassioned speech of eighty-two lines. Still, she alludes to the corporeality of the two lovers' relationship before she departs, ominously laying claim to Propertius' own body by boasting that she will eventually grind his bones with her own (93–94).[97]

Earlier in the speech, Cynthia emphatically inverts the standard accusations of female 'levity' by accusing Propertius of being inconstant and using 'deceitful words' (21) and later insisting on her own faithfulness (51–54). But it is Cynthia's self-consciousness about her own place in Propertius' poetry that perhaps best indicates her potential power, for Cynthia forcefully states that 'long was my reign in your work' (50). Soon after, she commands the actual destruction of his poetry: 'And whatever verses you have made in my name, burn them. Stop taking honours through me' (77–78), thus attempting to wrest her representation from his control. She orders him instead to tend her grave near the Anio River, and even dictates a song, or *carmen*, to place on it (85–86). The destruction of Propertius' poetry – demanded, of course, within that poetry – remains a complicated injunction,[98] but as Flaschenriem asserts, 'when she "composes" her own grave monument [...] Cynthia adopts a polemical, and highly authoritative, mode of discourse, one that was reserved in Books 1–3 solely for the male speaker. She becomes an authorial figure in her own right, a rival narrator within the text.'[99] In essence, Cynthia seems to acquire at least temporarily the 'power to' dictate her own role in – and departure from – Propertius' love poetry.

Propertius uses another reanimated female voice to narrate the very final poem of his collection: that of Cornelia, a figure whose status as an upper-class wife (indeed, we can identify her as Augustus' stepdaughter) brings sharp contrast with Cynthia. In 4.11, 'a formal piece in good rhetorical tradition,'[100] Cornelia addresses her husband Paullus, while also presenting a 'defence' of her life to the gods of the Underworld, a life distinguished by its connections to noble ancestors, her blameless conduct, the survival of her children and marriage to a single husband (29–68). 'This is the highest wage [*merces*] of a woman's triumph,' she says, 'when free opinion praises her well-deserved marriage bed' (71–72). Readers over the centuries have praised the poem's depiction of Cornelia as a faithful and self-sacrificing wife;[101] Richardson, however, detects darker themes at work, suggesting that it

> is not only indictment of the cruelty of the untimely death of a much admired young woman of the highest Roman aristocracy, but more significantly it amounts to an indictment of the life Rome required of the women of its nobility.[102]

Cornelia's voice, then, seems to function as a kind of reproach to the conventional values attached to marriage, provocatively presenting her virtue in economic terms (as a 'fee' or *merces*), a characterization that might suggest her similarity to the courtesans of love poetry, who, as we shall see, are located through their own set of material relations.

The female voice, then, seems to allow the *puella* a means of self-expression that places female experience in the spotlight, but what about the possibility of desire as a basis of female subjectivity? Another woman in Propertius' Book 4 gives voice to female desire more directly, presenting it as a serious challenge to both the state and male order.

VOICING FEMALE DESIRE

Although love poetry pivots on *ego*'s alleged attempts to ensure that the *puella* is faithful in loving him, her actual desires are rarely considered.[103] When female desire is evoked, it is generally presented as either dangerously misplaced or excessive, the lack of female self-control being a common trope in ancient writing. Presumably responding to Cynthia, Propertius decrees in 3.19, 'You always throw my desire [*libido*] back at me; believe me, yours orders you around even more' (1–2).[104] Catullus is much more blunt in his attack on his *puella*'s desire when it is ostensibly directed elsewhere, sending a message that she 'live and be well', while 'busting the balls' of her three hundred lovers (11.17–20). Ovid's *Ars Amatoria* also presents female desire as a manifest threat,[105] although in one passage he seems to perceive it more positively when he implies that sexual union with women, as opposed to boys, is advantageous precisely because it satisfies both parties (2.681–684) – a passage we shall return to.

But there are also occasions in Latin love poetry that seem to contemplate female desire and its relation to oppressive social structures more sympathetically. Sulpicia's poetry, for example, gives direct voice to the desires of a female *ego* thus 'reveal[ing] an acute sensitivity to the transgressive role of female sexuality in Roman society and literature, while [...] deftly articulat[ing] a far less restrictive vision of female passion'.[106] When Ovid turns to address his female readers in Book 3 of his *Ars Amatoria*, he casts them as Amazons, a mythical group notoriously emblematic of female power and self-sufficiency.[107] Propertius mentions Amazons four times in his poetry (including 3.11.13–16, 3.14.13–14, and 4.3.43–44), but it is his use of the Amazons as a model for Tarpeia in Book 4 that announces well her role as a 'spokesperson' for the dangerously disruptive nature of female desire (4.4.71–72).[108]

TARPEIA'S FATAL PASSION

The myth of Tarpeia is distinctly Roman. As the story goes, the Sabine forces were besieging Rome in response to the rape of the Sabine women (see Chapter 5); Tarpeia agreed to open the Capitoline citadel to them and their leader Titus Tatius in exchange for what was on their arms, presumably meaning the gold bracelets and other jewellery they wore. Having gained access to the Roman fortress, however, the Sabines rewarded Tarpeia by offering an alternate interpretation of her request and instead crushed her to death with their shields.[109] Tarpeia's story, set in Rome's distant past, became a kind of paradigmatic account of civic betrayal for the Romans,[110] and evidence suggests that images of Tarpeia were especially resonant in the Augustan era with its growing focus on public morality.[111]

Propertius begins his own version of Tarpeia's story with conspicuous focus on the topography of Rome, a focus characteristic of the entire book, proclaiming that the poem will explain the 'Tarpeian grove and the shameful grave of Tarpeia' (4.4.1).[112] Propertius calls attention to Rome's appearance in former times and draws heavily on the meaning attached to various spaces in the city. Indeed, Tarpeia's problem ensues in part because she is caught symbolically between two prominent sites: the Roman forum, where the Sabines are based, and, above that, the Capitoline, where the Roman fortress stands.[113] Like the Roman writer Varro (116–27 BCE), Propertius makes Tarpeia a Vestal Virgin, 'a public role that emphasizes her duty to the state and raises the heinousness of her treason'.[114] In assigning her an office that was both sacred and civic – one that required, among other things, the chastity of women holding the position[115] – Propertius conceives Tarpeia's desires as subordinated to, even the property of, the Roman state. Thus, her status as Vestal Virgin complicates the main motive Propertius attributes to her betrayal, for Propertius makes love for Tatius the basis for Tarpeia's traitorous act.

As a Vestal Virgin, Tarpeia descends the Capitoline hill daily to collect her ritual water, and it is when she is drawing water for Vesta that she catches sight of Tatius and falls instantly in love, ominously dropping her urn in the process (15 ff.). Once Tarpeia falls in love – and feigns reasons for going down to seek water – Propertius reports that on her climb back up the hill, her arms are now torn by brambles (27–28), using the scars on her body as a physical record of her growing incompatibility with both the city and her sacred task. It is from the slope of the Capitoline that Tarpeia gives her lengthy monologue,[116] and it is from here that Tarpeia laments, as the narrator phrases it, the 'wounds [of love] that were not endured by nearby Jupiter' (29–30).

Tarpeia begins her speech by proclaiming her willingness to serve as a captive of the Sabines (31–34), then bids goodbye to Rome and Vesta (35–36). Musing that Tatius is more deserving of power than Romulus, 'who, orphaned, was nurtured by the harsh breast of the animal she-wolf' (54–55), Tarpeia adamantly appropriates the idea of marriage, calling Rome's betrayal 'her dowry' (56). Later, after she has betrayed the city gate (87), Tarpeia asks Tatius to name the day of their wedding (88); he responds by telling her to 'marry and climb my royal bed' (89–90), the word 'climb' meant to recall their treacherous ascent of the Capitoline. He then crushes her beneath the shields of his companions. Echoing Tarpeia's earlier language, the narrator professes that 'this, maiden, was the fitting dowry for your deeds' (92). The poem closes with the reminder that the hill thereafter took its name from Tarpeia, notifying a 'watcher' (presumably Jupiter) that 'you have the reward of an unjust fate' (93–94), a sentiment that, while it may refer to the undue capture of the citadel, may also signal that Tarpeia's end is undeserved.[117]

The poem raises a multitude of questions as Tarpeia struggles unsuccessfully to 'reconcile the irreconcilable: her private passions and the needs of the state'.[118] Her attempt to redefine marriage, one the narrator throws back at her in reuse of the idea of a dowry, seems barbed in the context of Augustan marriage law, but, as Propertius shows us in his final poem of Book 4, even involvement in a marriage that satisfies the demands of the state does not ensure a happy outcome. By allowing Tarpeia to express her own perspective and desires, many scholars maintain that Propertius' poem ultimately shows clear sympathy for her plight and, in so doing, presents a fundamental challenge to the structures of power that order Tarpeia's world.[119] We might even say that in Propertius' poem Tarpeia is 'an example not of how the individual threatens the state, but rather how the state threatens the individual.'[120]

Traces of Tarpeia resurface in Book 4 when Propertius associates one of the women at his impromptu dinner party with the 'groves of Tarpeia' (4.8.31–32). When Ovid evokes Tarpeia in the *Amores*, however, he returns to the more familiar motive associated with her: her alleged desire for financial reward (1.10.49–50), an accusation often levied against love poetry's *puella*, as we shall see next chapter. In deliberating the intersections of gender and state power, however, Propertius employs another crucial figure in Book 4: the mythical Hercules. And for Hercules the dilemma is not so much the contingencies of female desire, but rather the very boundaries of gender itself.

Gender and Cross-Dressing

Elegy undertakes an important examination of gender boundaries on the few occasions when it depicts acts of cross-dressing or transvestitism. Unlike some of Shakespeare's memorable heroines, the *puella* herself never appears in men's or boy's clothing; the possibility is imagined entirely from the male perspective and features two prominent figures from Greek myth: Achilles and Hercules.[121] According to myth, as a young man, Achilles was dressed in girls' clothing at his mother's behest and hidden on the island of Scyros to avoid being identified and taken along to the Trojan War. Ovid labels Achilles' act of 'disguising his manhood' 'shameful' in the *Ars Amatoria* (1.689–696), but, by chance, Ovid continues, there was a young girl in the bedroom, and 'she discovered he was a man through his rape of her' (698). Ovid then pronounces the foul sentiment that Deidamia wanted to be raped and begged Achilles to stay (*Ars* 1.703–706). Beyond its skewed notions of female consent, what seems most significant in this passage is Ovid's attempt to repudiate any ambiguity in Achilles' gender-bending disguise: the line between 'man' and 'woman' is firm for Ovid despite any surface role-playing;

Achilles ultimately shows (or rather confirms) his 'true nature' in his sexual domination. Propertius, on the other hand, is much more open-ended in his portrayal of Hercules (4.9), exposing rather than fortifying the tenuous boundary separating masculinity and femininity.

HERCULES ON THE EDGE

Hercules is not the only character in Book 4 associated with cross-dressing; the narrator of poem 2, a statue of the god Vertumnus, demonstrates his shape-shifting abilities by claiming his suitability for both the garment of the *puella* and the toga worn by men (4.2.21–24), a duality that epitomizes the view of many scholars that the entire book probes the line between 'masculine' epic (epitomized by Rome or *Roma*) and 'feminine' elegy (love or *amor*).[122] The myth of Hercules was prominent in the Augustan era, connoting both Hercules' strength and his role as a civilizing force; he was at various times appropriated by both Mark Antony and Octavian.[123] As one of the book's many aetiological poems, poem 4.9 specifically recounts the origins of the Ara Maxima in the Forum Boarium, a story involving the theft of Geryon's cattle by Cacus and Hercules' subsequent punishment of him, a story also told in Virgil's *Aeneid* (8.185–275). Although Hercules does not speak in the *Aeneid*, Propertius expressly gives him a voice in 4.9, and while this Hercules speaks 'with Vergilian grace and dignity', 'what he says is something else again.'[124]

Propertius' poem is meant to explain the origin of the Ara Maxima, but he departs from that story to focus on a subsequent event: Hercules' attempts to quench the thirst he acquired from killing Cacus at the sanctuary of the Bona Dea. While worship at the Ara Maxima was limited to Roman men, the celebration of the Bona Dea was pointedly restricted to upper-class women.[125] In the Augustan era, the restoration of the sanctuary of the Bona Dea was attributed with great fanfare to Augustus' wife, Livia, suggesting its prominence within the Augustan programme of moral reform.[126] Propertius' allusion to both these rites, then, provides the crux of the argument that the poem is strongly invested in responding to the Augustan regime by dismantling contemporary ideas about gender.

As Hercules first approaches the sanctuary of the Bona Dea, Propertius calls attention to its seclusion and the secrecy of its rites in regard to men (4.9.23–26). Hercules nevertheless approaches the doors and gives a speech requesting entry, one meant to mirror the pleas of the excluded lover in the stock *paraclausithyron*.[127] While extolling his accomplishments, Hercules urges that if anyone inside is frightened by his appearance, they should remember that he wore a 'Sidonian gown' and worked the distaff; 'a soft [*mollis*] band,' he says, 'bound my hairy chest and even with rough [*duris*] hands I was a fitting girl' (45–50). In claiming the identity of a *puella*, Hercules refers to his time as the slave of Omphale, Queen of Lydia, service that involved their explicit exchange of gender roles.[128] Far from disavowing that episode, however, Hercules seems to embrace the 'authenticity' with which he managed both genders; his careful use of language claims mastery of both 'softness' and 'hardness'.[129]

In response, the priestess of the rites denies Hercules entry, reminding him that the site is forbidden to men and that water flows only for girls (53–60). Hercules, in turn, breaks down the door violently, drinks his fill, and issues a proclamation that the Ara Maxima, won so gloriously by him, subsequently be closed to *puellae* 'so that the thirst of the outsider Hercules not go unavenged' (67–70). Given Hercules' own claims to a fluid or plural gender identity, this 'resolution' has invited considerable debate: does Hercules, to borrow Ovid's phrasing, ultimately 'prove' his manhood by crashing down the doors and imposing his own restrictions on worship?[130] Or is Hercules' vigorous 'reassertion' at the end unable to dissolve all the uncertainty that has been introduced? Does 'the perfumed scent of the god's feminine boudoir [linger] in the Roman monument'?[131] Janan argues that Propertius' poem, in the end, seeks to expose the conceptual failings of gender itself as a system, for even though Hercules may try to bar women from his altar, his own experiences suggest the futility of any attempt to demarcate a precise boundary between women and men.[132]

Perhaps the most shocking violation of gender boundaries occurs in Catullus 63, a poem outside the main body of Catullus' love poetry, which begins with the self-castration of a young man named Attis during a ritual frenzy provoked by the goddess Cybele. The lengthy poem portrays an anguished Attis trying to come to terms with his act, while also carefully exploring the meaning of his bodily loss on gender identity and even language itself.[133] Skinner suggests that the poem portrays 'the personal and social consequences of an aborted ephebic transition': that is, Attis' failure to leave behind his boyhood in socially appropriate terms.[134] Reading the poem 'as a response to political conditions', while also adhering to Michel Foucault's insistence on 'a causal connection between changes in Roman political conditions and new modes of subjectivity', Skinner further contends that Attis' abject relationship to the powerful Cybele 'reflects elite alarm over perceived restrictions on personal autonomy and diminished capacity for meaningful public action during the agonized death throes of the Roman Republic'.[135] In contrast to earlier ideas about violence and the *puella*'s body in the Augustan Age, then, Skinner sees Attis' disenfranchisement as a Roman citizen being performed through the mutilation of his own (male) body.

The possibility of male loss written exclusively on the male body invites us to turn to another critical feature of Latin love poetry: its recurring reference to the world of men.

In the Company of Men

Although Latin love poetry clearly places the romantic pursuit of the *puella* at centre stage, it persistently references the role of other men in witnessing these affairs; as we saw earlier, Propertius delights in the bruises Cynthia gives him precisely because he can show them off to other men (3.8.21–22). Even more, the love poets frequently address various male friends or acquaintances, situating them, in effect, as the internal audience or ideal reader. In Propertius' Book 1 alone, over half the poems are addressed to other men, including some that are otherwise seemingly 'about' Cynthia.[136] By making men the arbiters of one another's affairs, love provides the means for establishing not merely an erotic bond with the *puella*, but also social bonds within a wider male community; as one critics phrases it, in Propertius' poetry 'a relationship with Cynthia is a shared relationship between men', one 'that even rivalry can reinforce'.[137] In similar ways, when Ovid negotiates with Corinna's husband in *Amores* 2.19 and 3.4, the *puella* becomes simply a tool 'in the process of establishing male relationships of mutual interest and solidarity'.[138] Scholars have often termed such male-centric networks 'homosocial', and Eve Sedgwick, in her seminal study, writes that 'in any male-dominated society, there is a special relationship between male homosocial (*including* homosexual) desire and the structures for maintaining and transmitting patriarchal power'.[139]

A man named Gallus is addressed in four poems in Propertius' first book (poems 5, 10, 13 and 20), while an epitaph is given to someone of that name in 1.21 and a seeming reference made to the dead man in 1.22, the latter two part of Propertius' contemplation of the Perusine War in the closing of Book 1.[140] Gallus is perhaps the most intriguing of the many male figures evoked in Propertius' poetry, with critics divided over whether he should be read as the earlier love poet Cornelius Gallus.[141] Moreover, there is not even consensus as to whether all of these references to 'Gallus' should be taken as the same man given the numerous inconsistencies across the poems.[142] As Miller points out, one of the 'problems' with Gallus' representation in Propertius is his seeming association with homosexual desire in 1.20, a form of passion that is otherwise unattested in the surviving writings about and by the poet Gallus.[143]

Miller argues, however, that this shift in Gallus' object-choice is, in fact, part of 'a complex yet consistent system of relations that on the manifest level substitute heteroerotic relations for homoerotic ones, while maintaining the affective and erotic valorization of the homoerotic subtexts'.[144] In other words, just as the male community 'shares' in *ego*'s romantic plot, the ties between men, at times erotic, continue to ground love poetry, even if they are at times incompletely concealed behind heterosexual passions. To give just one prominent example, the opening of Propertius' entire corpus (1.1.1–6) echoes an epigram by Meleager, an epigram that originally extolled the attractions of a male beloved and would presumably be known to Propertius' Roman audience.[145] And although Propertius does not himself openly pursue young men in his poetry, he does profess at one point that 'if ever someone is an enemy to me, let him love girls,

but let him delight in a boy [*puer*], if that one is a friend' (2.4.17–18),
a formulation that suggests hetero- and homosexual passions are equally
conceivable to the poet, yet destined for different ends. So what role
does same-sex desire play? How does the *puer* compare to the *puella* as
an object of pursuit?

LOVE POETRY'S *PUER*

It is essential to historicize briefly the meaning of sexuality before we
embark on any discussion of same-sex desire in Latin love poetry, for historians have drawn a series of important distinctions between modern and
ancient notions of homosexuality.[146] Most significantly, ancient thought did
not classify people as 'homosexual' or 'heterosexual', but rather viewed individuals according to their presumed type of participation in sexual activities,
primarily whether they assumed the active or passive role in any encounter
(the active role understood as the one penetrating),[147] a distinction that cor-
relates closely with attitudes we witnessed about gender in Chapter 1. While
Catullus' *ego* may construct a sexual identity based on being the penetrator
of others, then, 'he does not have clear sexual orientation' in the modern
sense.[148] Roman attitudes thus did not condemn sexual relations between
men *per se*, but rather considered the passive male partner, like all women,
less powerful than the penetrator, and therefore a role that a Roman male
citizen should be unwilling to occupy.[149] Hence, the only socially acceptable
male same-sex relationship was one between a Roman citizen and a partner
of lesser standing, usually a younger man 'who was a slave, an ex-slave, or a
noncitizen', all of whom could be labelled *puer*.[150]

We can witness the force of such ideology in Roman political invective
as accusations of sexually passive behaviours were levelled time and again
at prominent Roman leaders. Sling bullets from the Perusine War have
been found inscribed with graphic accusations of Octavian's alleged passive
sexual practices,[151] and Curio once infamously described Julius Caesar as 'a
man for all women and a woman for all men' (Suetonius, *Julius* 52.3).[152] In
one of his poems, Catullus similarly calls Julius Caesar a *pathicus* ('passive
receiver') (57.2),[153] and in another calls Romulus himself a *cinaedus* (29),

one of the most pejorative Latin terms used of the passive male partner.[154] As we have seen, Catullus threatens various kinds of forced penetration in poem 16, yet such verbal attacks on other men pivot around the prevailing association of power and penetration rather than any negative connotation of homosexuality *per se*.[155]

Catullus does at times place *pueri* in an erotic context, but while he openly articulates his desire for them, he generally avoids reference to explicit sexual acts.[156] In poem 48, addressed to a young man called Juventius, Catullus suggestively returns to the idea of endless kisses, a request he also made of Lesbia in the famous poems we looked at in Chapter 2 (poems 5 and 7). In a lengthier poem, 99, Catullus talks of stealing a kiss from 'honey-sweet Juventius', after which he claims to be tortured by the young man's immediate attempts to wash it off. He expresses jealousy that Juventius prefers someone else in 81, although his tone is noticeably more restrained (and less sexually explicit) than in his attacks on Lesbia.[157] Just as the *puella* helps consolidate the relationships between men, the *puer* also serves as an object of exchange when Catullus gives a boy to his friend Aurelius, begging that he return him untouched and vowing that he will be punished as an adulterer if he gives in to any desire for the young man (15.18–19). Although the *puer* is occasionally situated as the object of desire in Catullus' poetry, some critics have argued that there is nonetheless a difference between Catullus' poetry to young men and his poems about Lesbia, the latter more numerically prominent in the corpus. For one, although Juventius seems able to choose a different suitor in one poem, as well as refuse Catullus' kiss, he does not seem to possess the same degree of sexual agency overall (or perhaps, in Catullus' terms, sexual appetite) as Lesbia.[158]

Tibullus includes in his corpus a number of poems about a young man named Marathus, and the representation of this relationship has led some scholars to suggest that Tibullus was himself more invested in same-sex relationships.[159] Of the ten poems in Book 1, Tibullus devotes five to Delia and three to Marathus (4, 8 and 9), but unlike the seeming imbalance between Lesbia and the *pueri* in Catullus, there seems to be 'parallel power dynamics' in Tibullus' relationships with Delia and Marathus.[160] 'Both in the relationship with Delia and that with Marathus, *amor* leaves the poet/lover in the position of the passive, servile partner, in contrast to the norm.'[161] Poem 1.4 begins with a question to the god Priapus: how, the poet asks, is he so successful with beautiful boys? (1–6) In a stance not unlike that of the later *praeceptor* in Ovid's *Ars Amatoria*, Priapus responds with a lengthy speech of advice, explaining what kinds of boys to pursue and how (9–72). Praising the worth of poetry, Priapus critiques the tendency of boys to sell their favours, wishing that any who are that mercenary become followers of Cybele and commit acts of self-castration (57–72) – a clear allusion to Catullus' earlier poem.[162]

Fredrick suggests that the role of the *puer* in Latin love poetry can be considered generic as well as erotic in that it can be traced back to Callimachus.[163] But there are no representations of love poetry's *ego* pursuing boys after Tibullus' first book, leading some to propose that Latin love poetry, as it developed, increasingly 'found male–female relations a more fruitful ground for its purposes than male–male sexual relations'.[164] Such a tendency does not imply a firm stance against male same-sex desire, only that the *puella* seems to have become the main figure around which desire was contemplated in Latin love poetry; nor did the reliance on sexual difference as a key element of romantic relationships eliminate the power of homosocial bonding in love poetry. As Propertius' above wish for a friend suggests, the prospect of same-sex relations continued to offer a pointed alternative to the *puella*. Ovid, in his own programmatic poem (*Amores* 1.1), treats both options as parallel, noting that he has neither a suitable *puer* nor *puella* for his song (19–20). On the other hand, in a passage we referenced earlier, Ovid professes in the *Ars Amatoria* that he is 'less moved by love with a boy' since he 'hates sexual union that does not satisfy both' (2.681–684), a claim that suggests a range of attitudes about the relative disparity between partner types, but is nonetheless difficult to pin down.[165]

We have come a long way in trying to map out the myriad crossings of power and gender in Latin love poetry and it remains only to consider the ways in which modern scholars have tried to interpret such complex dynamics.

Is Latin Love Poetry Feminist?

Although the term feminism is often used loosely, strictly speaking it denotes a political struggle against patriarchy and sexism; feminism, therefore, does not merely indicate an interest in women's rights or a concern for the status of women, but a commitment to exposing and unseating historically pervasive systems of male domination.[166] Since feminism is at its root a political stance, it is possible for men to be feminist just as it is possible for them to be feminine. As we have seen throughout this chapter, classical scholars have formed diverse views about how power works in Latin poetry and, indeed, what such power relationships connote. Some critics have applied the term 'feminist' to one or more of the Latin love poets:[167] is such a designation appropriate? Does Roman love poetry advocate an ancient form of 'girl power', including a dismantling of longstanding forms of inequality, or is its aim something quite different?

Paul Allen Miller and Chuck Platter divide feminist scholarship on Augustan elegy specifically into two opposing camps: 'the negative view sees elegiac women as completely mastered by masculine cultural discourse, while the positive view detects in them elements of subversion that unsettle received modes of thought.'[168] We can elaborate this distinction in a number of ways. For one, we might ask whether certain poets like Ovid seek to celebrate male privilege or rather to expose its brutality. In more fundamental ways, as critics like Janan have argued in relation to Propertius, we might posit that love poetry attempts to reveal not merely the inequity in – or damage done by – cultural systems like gender, but also the flaws and fault lines in the very ideology that undergirds them. As Janan phrases it, Propertius has a 'special fascination with Woman', and 'aptly so', since 'Woman [...] iconically marks the point at which logical systems break down'.[169]

For many critics, it is impossible to separate the purpose of love poetry from the turmoil of the historical context in which it was produced, periods of both massive uncertainty and dramatic social change. Such instability was already felt at the time of Catullus' writing and, by the next generation, the elegists would need to come to terms with the rise of Augustus and the promise of a new age, one built on the ashes of the Republic and perhaps despite the traumatic memories of some its residents.[170] Sullivan, as we have seen, suggests that 'the social turmoil of the civil wars had for some its compensations', but, whether accurate for some Roman women or not, scholars like Skinner and Fredrick have seen in Catullus and the Augustan elegists a record of the progressive political marginalization of Roman male citizens as a group. Adopting a Lacanian approach, Miller suggests that even greater catastrophe can be witnessed in elegy, proposing that it 'does not so much reflect the lives and positions of a Tibullus or a Propertius as it does a crisis in the categories of the Symbolic',[171] which he defines as 'the world of linguistically constituted norms that allows us to be recognized as subjects within the community'.[172]

But even if love poetry exposes the changing nature of political power at Rome, or more deep-seated structural crises, was it also committed to unseating persistent forms of male domination, the second part of feminism? To phrase it somewhat differently, if the world outside shapes Latin love poetry, did Latin love poetry, in turn, try to reshape the Roman world outside? In a groundbreaking article, Judith Hallett has argued that the elegists were part of a 'counter-culture'.[173] Hallett's article launched an important debate that continues still today, one centred around the question of whether Latin love poetry aims ultimately to sustain the status quo or rather to alter radically the social and ideological structures that defined men and women in Roman society. Contesting Hallett's claim that elegy was actively directed at social transformation, Aya Betensky countered that even if elegy offers new roles for its lovers, they are merely poetic license rather than social statement.[174]

Sometime later, Maria Wyke would revisit the same question, wondering whether Augustan love poetry, 'focus[ing] on a female subject who apparently operates outside the traditional constraints of marriage and motherhood, could [...] constitute the advocacy of a better place for women in the ancient world'.[175] Turning from the larger (and largely unanswerable) question of love poetry's precise impact on contemporary Roman society, she insists that, in any case, the only gains to be found in elegy are those received by the male narrator: 'it is not the concern of elegiac poetry to upgrade the position of women, only to portray the male narrator as alienated from positions of power and to differentiate him from other, socially responsible male types.'[176] In this way, some scholars have argued that the love poets are far more invested in interrogating their own relation to power than in elevating that of the *puella*. Nor is it clear how reliable the poets' frequent claims to disempowerment actually are; as Gardner sees it, 'the poet-lovers of elegy betray a certain satisfaction with their own marginality, as well as the power to return to the familiar territory of symbolic structures.'[177] Is the experience of male vulnerability lauded throughout love poetry, then, a sign of the times or rather a vicarious pleasure, a kind of fantasy or closely controlled means of role-playing that ultimately does not abrogate much authority at all? In the end, is it the *puella* who 'bears all the risks of elegiac love'?[178]

While Barbara Gold acknowledges the manifest risks in love poetry, she nonetheless imagines potential gains for the *puella*, at least in Propertius, by arguing that Propertius attempts to 'show us new ways of organizing and reading sexual difference.'[179] Thus, Gold reads Cynthia's instability or changeability, her 'levity', not as a means for dissolving or denying female subjectivity, but rather for providing its very grounds. In short, it is her very fluidity that animates the *levis puella*, while allowing her at the same time to remain subversive in her refusal to adhere to traditional structures of being and representation.[180] Could Virgil's infamous statement 'woman is a thing ever variable and changing' (*Aeneid* 4.569–570), then, be not an insult, but a call to action?

What does it mean, moreover, for Propertius and the other poets to identify as 'feminine' (a stance beyond simply sympathizing with the plight of women)? Does that strategy provide a way to unsettle gender boundaries, or, as Gold phrases it, a means to 'disrupt the structures of [...] society and to produce in the process a new formulation of gender'?[181] Or perhaps in line with other arguments, we might envision the love poets as being exclusively devoted to rewriting what it means to be masculine. As one scholar maintains, Catullus' *ego* 'carves out for himself a relatively new sexual identity' – that of a lover who 'cannot completely control himself' – yet he carefully distinguishes any such stance from one of passivity.[182] Of course, not all poets (or even poems) need do the same thing. Even as 'the Catullan lover appears to struggle against his own "feminization"',[183] are the Augustan elegists (or perhaps only Propertius) more willing to experiment with and occupy such a position? Is one strategy necessarily 'better' or more productive than the other? Relying on some of the same theoretical groundwork as Gold, Miller deems Propertius a woman, 'because his subject position cannot be precisely located in any one spot within conventional Roman ideological space'.[184] But he adds: 'Unlike other women, however, Propertius, at least theoretically, retains the option of being a man [...] And that is real power too.'[185]

As Miller and Platter observe, in some ways our very approach to love poetry can undermine any sense of the work's radical nature. They ask:

> on what basis can an ethics or politics of gender liberation be propounded, if the category of gender itself is the product of power, so that any strategy that takes this category as its starting point is always already complicit with the ideological structures that make it possible?[186]

Meaning that, if we bring gender to the study of love poetry, do we simply reproduce its authority, its longstanding power as a means for structuring and regulating difference, from the very outset? Perhaps the best way to end our discussion of power and play in Latin love poetry is thus to consider the role of the reader, the person or persons charged with 'making meaning' of these complicated, and at times contradictory, texts. Sharrock argues that the male friends in love poetry serve not only as an internal community for the poet, but also as a stand-in for the reader her- or himself.[187] But what if we refuse to play along?

Vicki Kirby calls reading 'an act of transformation, not a simple retrieval or diagnostics',[188] and Kathryn Gutzwiller and Ann Michelini propose that the feminism of Latin love poetry may ultimately come from how we self-consciously resist its devices. Noting that feminist literary approaches grant one 'the means to escape the elegist's persuasion and to see more clearly his rhetorical techniques', they contend that, by resisting such manipulation, readers gainfully strip the love poet of 'the means by which he uses his subservient pose to seek power and sexual control'.[189] The love poets themselves recognize well the paramount role of the reader, and so we turn next to a consideration of the ways in which both writers and readers are constructed in love poetry, as well as to the poets' evolving views on love poetry itself.

IV

Readers and
Writers

... So, girls, be generous to the poets;
they have divine spirit and the Muses favour them.

OVID, *ARS* 3.547–548

IN THE THIRD BOOK of his *Ars Amatoria*, Ovid prescribes for his female audience an impressive reading programme. On the Greek side, he advocates the works of Callimachus, Philetas, Anacreon, Sappho and Menander, while on the Latin, he calls for Varro, Virgil's *Aeneid* ('a work more famous than any other in Latium'), as well as a 'song of tender Propertius', 'something of Gallus' or of 'yours, Tibullus' (*Ars* 3.329–338). Ovid slyly notes that someone may eventually even recommend his own works, urging that they 'read the sophisticated songs of our master' (*Ars* 3.341). Ovid's list of authors and works is suggestive and includes what we might call a brief synopsis of Roman love poetry, one that omits Catullus and pointedly culminates in three of Ovid's own elegiac works: the *Ars Amatoria*, *Amores* and *Heroides*. As this attention to the education of his female reader insinuates, love poetry's *puella* often serves as a primary reader of love poetry, yet she can also serve as a written artifact herself – a personification of the poet's own literary project. In this chapter, then, we want to examine more fully the role of the poet and his *puella* in terms of both reading and writing. In addition, we shall chart the specific ways in which Propertius and Ovid further extend their own examination of what it means to be a love poet, in the process defining and redefining the boundaries of elegy itself.

We begin with the love poets' attempts to define their own place in the Greek and Roman literary canon, a strategy that underlines their status as close readers of earlier literature.

In the Company of Poets

The love poets routinely present themselves as immersed in a vibrant world of other writers, both past and present. Catullus, for example, presents literary authors and texts in constant dialogue; he dedicates his 'little book' to Cornelius Nepos, a Roman historian and biographer, and, among other writers, Catullus makes frequent reference to his friend Licinius Calvus, the author of elegies (now lost) to a woman named Quintilia. Mocking the work of certain poets sent to him by Calvus in poem 14, Catullus threatens to take his revenge by sending Calvus other 'terrible poets' in return. Conversely, in 50, he expresses delight at the day he and Calvus spent writing poetry for one another.[1] Catullus also twice mentions sending Callimachus' work to others (65 and 116), although his gift in 116 does not seem, he laments, to put an end to his often obscene antagonism with a man named Gellius.[2]

Propertius responds to a friend named Bassus in 1.4, presumably the same iambic poet that Ovid also references in the *Tristia* (see below). In 1.7, Propertius addresses the epic poet Ponticus, warning Ponticus that he will gain new appreciation of Propertius' poetry when he himself has been struck by Cupid's arrow; Ponticus will then seek in vain to write 'soft verse' (19), Propertius predicts. Shortly after, in 1.9, Propertius gloats that Ponticus has indeed been brought low by love. Once again connecting Ponticus' predicament to his literary output, Propertius asks what Ponticus gains from writing epic when 'the verses of the poet Mimnermus are worth more in love than Homer' (9–11). 'Go,' Propertius pleads, 'and set aside those gloomy books of yours and write what a girl wants!' (13–14).

In poem 2.25, Propertius directly names Calvus and Catullus as his predecessors by begging their pardon when seeking to make Cynthia's beauty more famous than those who came before (3–4). Propertius devotes even greater attention in 2.34 to the identification of his extended literary genealogy. The poem begins with an alleged romantic betrayal by his friend and fellow poet Lynceus. Expressing delight that Lynceus is now insane with love (25–26), Propertius urges Lynceus to imitate Philetas and 'the dream of unpretentious Callimachus' (31–32); openly employing Callimachean terminology, Propertius suggests more specifically that his friend 'turn his verses on a narrow lathe' and approach his own 'fires' (43–44). Later Propertius boasts that he himself holds court among a crowd of women because of the very 'genius' Lynceus disparages (57–58).

In the remainder of the poem, Propertius presents a record of notably Roman literary achievement, one that ends with his bid for a place in that canon. Praising the poet Virgil, Propertius includes a couplet that, perhaps not surprisingly, 'enjoyed remarkable fame in antiquity':[3] 'Give way, Roman writers, give way Greek writers! Something greater than the *Iliad* is being born' (65–66). He next praises both Virgil's *Eclogues* and his *Georgics* (67–76), noting Hesiod's influence on the latter (77–80). Finally, in the passage we saw in the last chapter, Propertius references earlier Roman writers who wrote love verse, citing also the names of most of their *puellae*: Varro (who seemingly wrote love poetry after finishing his translation of the *Argonautica*), Catullus, Calvus and Gallus (85–92). He concludes that Cynthia will have similar renown if he is allowed to take a place among them (93–94).

While Tibullus gives little attention to his predecessors (beyond Virgil of the *Eclogues*, a relationship explored in a later chapter), Ovid frequently constructs his own literary lineage. Most notably, in *Amores* 1.15, he lists both his Greek and Roman precursors finding appropriate epithets to describe each: 'Ennius lacking in skill', 'spirited Accius', 'elegant Tibullus' (16 ff.).[4] As we have seen, Ovid constructs a curriculum in the *Ars Amatoria* that terminates with his own love poetry, and in his exile poem alone, *Tristia*, Ovid likewise twice establishes his place in literary history. In the first passage, Ovid lists all the poets who, according to him, sang about love, starting his list with the Greeks and displaying an impressive mixture of epochs and genres. Under Ovid's pen, Homer's *Iliad* and *Odyssey* become nothing but stories about adultery and love (*Tristia* 2.371–380), and Ovid similarly claims that all of Greek tragedy is plainly concerned with love (2.381–408) – claims underlined by his use of both Homer and tragic material in the *Amores* and the *Heroides*. On the Roman side, Ennius and Lucretius are listed as poets who use erotic material and 'can be seen as teachers of immorality if we make up our minds to read them in a certain way'.[5] These poets are followed by Gallus, Tibullus, Propertius and Virgil, whose epic is also seen through the lens of love poetry (2.361–466).

In his second list, Ovid limits himself to Roman poets and, even then, his vision of literary influence has narrowed (*Tristia* 4.10.41–54). While he mentions Macer (an author of didactic verse), Ponticus (the epic poet we just encountered in Propertius 1.7), Bassus (presumably also the one in Propertius), Virgil and Horace, he does not associate himself with their poetic legacy. Instead he observes: 'Vergil I only saw; greedy fate gave Tibullus no time for friendship with me. He was your successor, Gallus, and Propertius his; after them I was fourth in order of time' (50–54). Through this sequence, Ovid classifies himself exclusively as an elegist, and as Peter Knox observes, it is Ovid who essentially 'defined the canon' for later generations, because when Quintilian categorizes the main representatives of elegy, as we discussed in Chapter 1, it is 'these same four whom he names and no others' (*Institutio Oratoriae* 10.1.93).[6] Perhaps most significantly, although Ovid responds to Catullus in a number of poems in the *Amores*, he here omits him from his list of predecessors, a move in clear contrast to Propertius, who continually cites Catullus as a literary influence.

In poem 35, Catullus introduces an important conceit attached to the act of reading love poetry, one that reverberates throughout the love poets: namely that love poetry can produce in its audience the very thing it describes – love.

Poetry and Seduction

That love poetry should incite desire in the reader is also suggested by Catullus 16, a poem in which Catullus infamously proposes that his poetry, when hitting the right balance of softness and shamelessness, should 'rouse an itch' not merely in young men, but in those 'hairy old men' who can barely move their loins (7–11). Similarly, for Propertius, the reading of love poetry both provokes and guides romantic feeling. In considering the appropriate audience of love poetry, Propertius thus hopes that his poetry will 'inflame boys and girls' (3.9.45; see also 3.2.1–2). Ovid likewise underscores the association of readers and lovers in *Amores* 2.1 when he claims that his reader should be a woman warmed to the sight of her lover and a boy touched for the first time by passion (5–6). Reiterating the notion that the ideal reader of love poetry is one on the verge of love, Apollo tells Propertius in 3.3 that his 'little book' is fit for a girl to read as she waits for her lover (19–20). As we shall see, love poetry gradually takes on an emphatically didactic purpose, casting the reader as a kind of student of love, a function that reaches its peak in Ovid's work. But already in Propertius, there is an implied lesson as the poet urges a 'rejected lover' to read his work closely and so learn from Propertius' misfortunes (1.7.13–14).

In 1.7, Propertius brags that his fame should be that he alone has pleased a *docta puella* ('a learned girl) (11) and, in 2.13, he similarly expresses pleasure at being able to lie in the lap of his *docta puella*, reading his poetry, to which she listens with faultless judgement and approves (11–12). Such passages, like Ovid's reading list in *Ars Amatoria*, cast the elegiac *puella* as an educated reader of love poetry (see *Ars* 2.281–286), a status that remains central to her standing throughout.[7] Indeed, love poetry operates at times as a form of persuasion and even seduction directed at the *puella*. Tibullus, for example, openly professes that he seeks not merely his *puella*'s literary approval, but also sexual entrée, that his work may grant 'ready access to his mistress' (2.4.19–20). Yet such reliance on the *puella*'s reading creates frequent tension,[8] for the *docta puella* remains a markedly resistant reader of Roman elegy, in large part because she remains cognizant of the gap between her interests and those of the poet.[9]

Noting that poetry may actually succeed where the lover fails, Ovid bitterly asks in *Amores* 3.8 what reward poetry brings when his work has dutifully gained entry to his beloved's room, even as he remains locked outside (5–6). Acknowledging the inevitable separation of a writer and his or her work (a conceit central to the *Heroides*), the Latin love poets often emphasize the status of writing as a physical object, one passed precariously between the poet and his *puella*. In poem 42, Catullus elides poetic form – hendecasyllabic verse[10] – and content in playing with the idea of poetry's separation from its author. Complaining that his writing tablets have been stolen by some *moecha* ('whore'), Catullus calls on his hendecasyllables to help restore them, then launches a torrent of abuse on the impudent *moecha* who took them in the same metre.

Appropriating Catullus' theme of lost tablets, Propertius later professes that his missing tablets were capable of appealing to girls in his absence (3.23.1–10). Now, however, he can only guess at the message they conveyed from Cynthia, dejectedly imagining them overwritten with some greedy person's financial accounts (11–20). In the *Amores*, Ovid returns to this same scenario, but his experience is emphatically defined by failure rather than loss, for Ovid's eager anticipation of Corinna's response in 1.11 is dashed by her one-word answer, 'no', in 1.12. Threatening the tablets with destruction, Ovid muses that they might more suitably contain the accounts of some greedy man – a conscious echo, and ironic embrace, of Propertius' worst fears.[11]

Playing with the idea of the materiality of writing, the love poets also seek to imbue love poetry with economic value. For the Roman elegists, protesting their own poverty, like to claim that their poetry serves as payment or reward for the *puella*, a commodity that allows the poets to compete against rivals who have more tangible things to offer. But does the *puella* share this view of love poetry's compensations?

EXCURSUS: LOVE FOR SALE?

The love poets frequently castigate the *puella*'s alleged desire for material payment (e.g. Tibullus 2.4 and *Amores* 1.10),[12] and modern scholars often show similar disregard for the economic relations underlying the romantic plot in

Latin poetry.[13] As Sharon James points out, however, greed (or 'avaritia') – a feature the poets paint as a 'character flaw' of the puella – is actually an essential trait of the courtesan, an occupation many of the puellae hold.[14] Hence by insisting – or pretending – that the courtesan can offer 'free' love, the love poets create 'an insoluble tension' or what James calls the 'elegiac impasse'.[15] For the Roman courtesan, lacking long-term financial security, was required to earn money while she could, and the love poets themselves hint at the uncertainty of the courtesan's future when they gleefully predict the effects of ageing on the puella (e.g. Propertius 3.25). Equally indicative of the imbalance between lovers, while the courtesan's livelihood leaves her few options, 'the lover can always return to other activities and careers (as, indeed, he does in Propertius 4 and Am. 3.15)'.[16]

The love poets bring into their poetry a provocative look at the professional demands placed on the puella through the figure of an already aged courtesan or lena ('female pimp' or 'procuress').[17] The character of the lena appears in all three Augustan elegists, but while she is presented only as a figure of opposition in Tibullus (1.5.47–56 and 2.6.44–54),[18] she actually speaks in both Propertius and Ovid. Suggestive of the general hostility directed against the lena, Propertius' lena is named Acanthis (4.5), meaning 'thorn', while the lena in Ovid is called Dipsas (Amores 1.8), the name of a small snake renowned for its thirst, implying her drunkenness.[19] In both Propertius and Ovid, the lena gives important advice to her protégée, the puella, and, by doing so, the lena presents a rival perspective to that of the ego – one that both complements ego's romantic visions with some hard truths and seems to usurp his very narrative authority.[20] Still, while the lena may dramatically hijack the text with her speech, her reign is only provisional, and both Propertius and Ovid end their poems with expressions of rage directed against her, aggressively reclaiming their jurisdiction over the practice and meaning of love.

FIFTEEN MINUTES OF FAME?

As we have seen, ego's control of writing remains an important source of power, and poetry is employed at times directly against the puella. When Propertius tells Ponticus that he is accustomed to writing love poetry, he openly confesses that he seeks in it something to use 'against his cruel mistress' (1.7.5–6). In a passage we looked at previously, Propertius refuses to commit physical violence against Cynthia, threatening her instead with something even more damaging and enduring: his curt written assessment (2.5.27–28). But the poets also insist that their poetry provides a reward for the *puella* by bestowing fame upon her. Thus, Ovid professes in *Amores* 1.10 that his gift 'is to celebrate deserving women in song', which allows him to make 'whomever he wants famous' through art (59–60; see also *Amores* 2.1.33–34). Later, in *Amores* 2.17, Ovid brags, 'many women want to be famous through me,' adding jokingly that he even knows a woman 'who goes around pretending to be Corinna' (28–29). In 3.2, Propertius similarly announces that any woman would be lucky to be celebrated in his book since his poems provide 'monuments' of female beauty (17–18).[21] He nonetheless reverses his opinion later in the book, bitterly regretting the fame he has given his *puella* and claiming his 'exaggerations' of her beauty have made her too arrogant (3.24.1–8).

While announcing their ability to grant literary fame to their lovers, the love poets increasingly point to the status of the *puella* herself as a carefully constructed literary invention, a creation the poet moulds (or 'womanufactures') not so much to extol her special talents as to prove and ascertain his own.

THE *SCRIPTA PUELLA*

In the very first line of his work, Propertius famously opens with the name 'Cynthia', accusing her eyes of being the source of his downfall (1.1.1–2). Propertius' first book was circulated on its own in 29 or early 28 BCE, and the placement of Cynthia's name was key to its reception; in addition to being referred to as the 'Monobiblos' in later eras, the work was presumably also known by its first word, 'Cynthia'.[22] Such a practice creates an ambiguous line between Cynthia the poet's beloved and Cynthia the poetic book; in Book 2, Propertius exploits the potential overlap, quoting an unnamed interlocutor who reminds him that he has become a subject of gossip now that 'his Cynthia is read all over the forum' (2.24.1–2).

Earlier, Propertius opens Book 2 with an elaborate explanation of his standing as a love poet. Responding to imagined interlocutors who ask how he is so prolific at love poetry – that is, from which source his 'soft' (*mollis*) book comes – Propertius denies the influence of Calliope, one of the Muses, and Apollo (affiliations he will later claim in Book 3), professing that it is Cynthia who stirs his efforts (2.1.1–4). Making love poetry and not love *per se* the inevitable outcome of Cynthia's attractions, Propertius asserts that everything about Cynthia inspires him: her Coan dress, her flowing hair, her lyre-playing, even her demeanour as she falls asleep (5–12).[23] With a dig at Homeric epic, Propertius announces that from their night-time struggles 'long Iliads' emerge (13–14).

Propertius eventually amplifies Cynthia's relation to textuality, treating her as not merely the font of his poetry (i.e. the thing that generates his writing), but also its primary product (i.e. the thing generated by his writing), casting her as *scripta puella* or 'written woman'. He himself provides the terminology for such a shift in 2.10, when he ostensibly indicates that it is time to sing the exploits of Augustus – observing that the young poet sings of love, while the older poet sings of battles – and then clarifies: 'I will sing wars when my girlfriend is written [*scripta*]' (2.10.6–7).[24] Propertius' insistence on a contrast between *bellum* ('war') and *puella* underscores the boundaries between elegy and epic,[25] a contrast that remains prominent throughout Propertius' attempts to define his poetic voice. Yet the phrasing of his promise here, as Richardson argues, is 'tantamount to saying that he will not take up the theme of war in the foreseeable future',[26] and indeed *scripta* Cynthia continues to appear throughout Books 2 and 3.

In 2.5, a poem about the induction of Messalla's eldest son into the priesthood, Tibullus likewise casts Nemesis as the source of his verse, noting that she gave him 'words' and 'rightful feet' (2.5.111–112).[27] Later, in *Amores* 1.3, Ovid similarly requests that his *puella* furnish herself as *materies* ('material') for his poetry, poems that will, he promises, prove worthy of her (19–20).[28] Echoing Propertius' use of *recusatio* ('refusal', a rhetorical device that we shall examine below), Ovid goes even further in 3.12 in refuting mythical themes and the deeds of Augustus as the subject of his verse, naming Corinna instead as the sole source of his 'genius' (16). This insistence by the Augustan love poets on the *puella* as the source of poetic composition becomes so associated with their work that poets of the later Empire return to it as they seek to insert themselves into the same tradition. Claiming that Cynthia made 'lascivious' Propertius a poet, and that the other *puellae* – Lycoris, Nemesis and Lesbia – were similarly responsible for their authors' renown, Martial wryly asks only for 'some Corinna' of his own (8.73; see also Juvenal, 2.149 ff.).

Even as the *puella* becomes the source of poetic production, palpable anxiety is nonetheless generated by her extension from a 'written' to a 'read' *puella*. In *Amores* 3.12, the very poem in which he calls Corinna the driving force of his 'genius', Ovid bemoans the fact that through the circulation of his poetic work she has been made an object of widespread consumption, an availability he equates with prostitution (*Amores* 3.12.7–10). In effect, by writing about her, Ovid envisions himself as a kind of *leno* ('pimp') (11), candidly admitting just how closely his role as poet vies with that of the *lena*.[29]

Even as the *puella* becomes enmeshed in literary composition and consumption, she also serves at times as a direct personification of the poet's work. A.M. Keith argues that 'Corinna's bodily perfection corresponds to the stylistic refinement privileged throughout the *Amores*.'[30] Noting Propertius' continuing attempts to define his poetic project, in part by distinguishing it from other possible literary pursuits, McNamee likewise asserts that Propertius' physical descriptions of his lover in 1.2 and elsewhere can be read as allusions to specific aspects of literary style, such as the poet's preference for Cynthia's unadorned simplicity.[31] More generally, McNamee maintains that 'Cynthia is in every detail an allegory for the kind of poetry that Propertius *is* willing to write.'[32] Wyke argues that Propertius establishes Cynthia's status as a literary device especially in Book 2 (especially 2.10–13), associating 'Cynthia so intimately with the practice of writing elegy as to undermine her identity independently of that practice.'[33]

In *Amores* 3.1, Ovid presents an explicit rendering of poetic genre through female flesh, personifying the literary genres of elegy and tragedy as two distinct types of women. While Tragedy enters impassioned with grand strides (11–14), Elegy, presented as a *meretrix*, conveys the central features of her genre through her body, demonstrating not only a 'beautiful form, the thinnest cloak and a face for loving', but also approaching with what seems to the poet 'one foot longer than the other' (9), an allusion to the elegiac metre and 'flaw' that Ovid labels 'the reason for her beauty' (10). As Wyke maintains, the overall appearance and comportment of Elegy reinforces throughout the main tenets of Callimachean style, including the adherence to small poetic forms.[34] At first, Ovid seems to prefer elegy (despite its frivolous nature) to tragedy because 'what she demands requires little time' (68). However, Ovid eventually ends the poem by defining his own poetic agenda in more precise terms: 'Let my "Loves" hurry on while I have time: a grander masterpiece is urging me on' (69–70) – lines that perhaps nod towards his future tragedy, *Medea*, and suggest that at this stage of his career Ovid was not connecting his hopes for longevity with his elegiac verse.

Given such juxtaposition of elegy and tragedy – or love poetry and epic in Propertius – we want now to examine more closely how both Propertius and Ovid consistently redefine themselves as poets, at the same time expanding the boundaries of the genre of love poetry itself.

Propertius: Elegy as Augustan Poetry

As we have seen, Propertius constantly uses earlier writers to help locate his own literary undertaking, and we can discern the concrete influence of many authors throughout his work. In addition to adopting certain general qualities of Catullus' love poetry, Propertius alludes directly to Catullus' exhortation to Lesbia that they 'live and love', ignoring the rumours of jealous old men (Catullus 5) when he writes in 2.30, 'let harsh old men criticize these entertainments of ours, my life, while we wear away our intended path' (13–14). As mentioned in the previous chapter, there is continuing debate over whether some or all of the Gallus figures of Propertius' first book should be read as the poet Cornelius Gallus. Beyond this conundrum, Gallus' influence on Propertius was surely evident to an ancient audience that possessed his entire work; some modern scholars discern Gallus' influence already in Propertius' opening poem.[35] So, too, Propertius' difficult Book 2 may show Tibullus' impact on his work, perhaps leading Propertius to experiment with longer poems.[36]

There are two prominent and interrelated features of Propertius' poetic self-definition, however, that we would like to examine here: his ostensible rejection of epic in defining his poetic programme and his increasing identifications with Callimachus. We begin with Propertius' employment of *recusatio*, a trope that ostensibly allowed a poet to refuse certain literary and social demands,[37] although, as we shall see, the precise meaning of such refusal in Propertius' work often remains elusive.

THE POETICS OF REFUSAL

Epic was the earliest and clearly most authoritative literary genre in antiquity. Attempts to stake out the grounds for other types of poetry – especially those related to love and personal experience – can be traced all the way back to Sappho, as we have already seen. When Propertius in poems 1.7 and 1.9 urges the epic poet Ponticus to embrace love poetry and so better reflect his own experiences in love, he follows a time-honoured tradition of defining love poetry as a distinct genre by showcasing its departures from epic. For the Augustan poets, such a stance also reflected the strong influence of Callimachus, who famously distinguished his poetic style from that of epic.[38]

In poem 2.1, Propertius addresses his patron Maecenas with an elaborate *recusatio*, recounting the topics he deems himself unfit to sing. Propertius' employment of the trope serves as a kind of two-layered denial, since he professes that if Fate had allowed, he would be writing about different themes – not, he hastens to explain, events of myth or even early Roman history, but rather, 'I would sing of the wars and achievements of your Caesar [Augustus], and you would come next, after mighty Caesar' (25–26). Propertius then lists a series of specific sites and events that praise for Augustus might entail, such as Mutina and Philippi – the location of two of Octavian's victories during the civil wars – and also 'the Nile, when, having been dragged into the city, it flowed, diverted, with seven captured waters' (2.1.27–32), an image evoking Augustus' triple triumph of 29 BCE celebrating the defeat of Antony and Cleopatra.

Although Propertius assures Maecenas of his place in all these themes

(35–36), the construction of the actual list potentially undercuts any straightforward idea of glory. For one, Propertius calls Philippi 'the citizens' graveyard', reiterating its ties to the traumas of civil war, and before Actium he names another potential theme: 'the overturned hearths of the ancient Etruscan race' (29), an allusion to the brutal Perusine War of 41–40 BCE which devastated Propertius' homeland. Moreover, Propertius closes the *recusatio* by comparing himself to Callimachus, whose 'slender voice' could not sing of the mythological Gigantomachy, and he ultimately pronounces himself unfit for both *duro versu* ('epic poetry') and for writing about Augustus (39–42). Professing that everyone should practise the craft best suited to their abilities, Propertius explains that his wars are best 'waged on a narrow bed' (45–46).

In poem 2.10, the poem in which Propertius initiates more fully the idea of the *scripta puella*, he also presents an extended list of the themes that he should write about, only to defer such undertakings by the end. He begins:

> Now it is time to traverse Helicon [a site sacred to the Muses] with other dances
> > and time to give the field to the Thessalian steed.
> Now it is pleasing to celebrate troops brave in battle
> > and to speak of the Roman camp of my leader.   (1–4)

Noting his own limits, and that he will turn from his *puella* once she has been 'written', Propertius begs for a loftier voice. He then records his predictions of the future exploits of the *princeps*, beginning with the idea that Augustus will avenge Crassus' loss of the Roman standards at Carrhae:

> Already the Euphrates refuses to shelter
> > the Parthian cavalry behind its back, and grieves
> that it has held Crassus' men. But India yields its
> > neck to your triumph, Augustus, and the
> abode of untouched Arabia trembles before you,
> > and, if any other land drags itself to the ends of the earth,
> that land, captured, soon after will feel your touch!   (13–18)

Propertius' jubilant personifications of the territory waiting to be conquered by Augustus seem to endorse contemporary ideas about the bright future that awaits Rome. Having predicted such unequivocal domination and that, by recording it, he will be a 'great poet' (using the term *vates*, which we shall discuss below), Propertius nonetheless immediately equivocates, admitting he is still held in the grips of love (19–26), seemingly undermining his earlier praise and enthusiasm.[39]

In poem 3.9, Propertius again addresses Maecenas, the only poem – aside from 2.1 – to do so. Asking why Maecenas sends him into 'such a vast ocean of writing', Propertius protests that 'massive sails' are not suitable for his tiny boat (1–4). He goes on to repudiate a series of mythological themes, proclaiming it will be enough for him 'to find favour among the work of Callimachus' and to sing in the strains of Philetas (43–44). But Propertius abruptly seems to reverse himself by suggesting to Maecenas that with Maecenas 'as guide' he will write of grand mythological events and also of Roman history, including the 'walls established by Remus killed' (47–50) and culminating with 'Antony's hand, fatal to himself' (56), a reference to Mark Antony's suicide in Egypt. Propertius then concludes that it is due to Maecenas that he will be praised and be seen as one of Maecenas' cohort (59–60). With such a finish, one infused with unsettling internecine violence, Propertius ostensibly promises to undertake a very different kind of verse for Maecenas, yet in the very next poem he resumes what seems like his standard fare, penning a playful poem about his *puella*'s birthday.

Such contradictions or false turns in Propertius' work have led to ongoing debates about his evolving sense of his own poetic programme and, more specifically, his use of *recusatio* itself.[40] Sullivan sees the *recusatio* as Propertius' 'main shield' against any political pressure.[41] Yet, as Margaret Hubbard points out, 'the recurrence of the Callimachean apology is certainly in itself no evidence for pressure'.[42] And, on closer inspection, the *recusatio* proves to be a slippery rhetorical device since it involves delineating what will not be included in a poet's work and so manages to incorporate the very thing it denies. Gregson Davis, examining the device in Horace, has called *recusatio* a 'mode of assimilation', explaining that it is 'a device by which the speaker disingenuously seeks to include material and styles that he ostensibly precludes'.[43]

The fact that, for Propertius, the *recusatio* often involves not merely a stance against epic, but also a promise that he will, one day, celebrate Augustus means that the trope raises questions about Propertian politics as well, especially given that Propertius' prospective catalogues of refused topics often include events from the civil wars – a complicated emotional terrain, surely, for any Roman reader of the era. So what should we infer from such passages about Propertius' understanding of what it means to be not merely a poet, but an Augustan poet at that? Moreover, what should we make of the fact that Propertius eventually *does* alter his programme in Book 4? Has he given in to relentless pressure and critique or simply extended an ongoing and decidedly unpredictable literary experiment? We can approach such questions from a strictly literary angle by turning to a closely related feature of Propertius' poetry: his emergent identification with Callimachus.

THE 'ROMAN CALLIMACHUS'?

Hubbard helpfully traces the growing presence of Callimachus in Propertius' work, pointing out that although Book 1 utilizes certain Hellenistic models and Book 2 shows 'the influence of Callimachus in a more profoundly assimilated form', it is in Book 3 that Propertius specifically 'asks for initiation into Callimachus' rites',[44] substantially elevating their association. Notably, whereas Propertius opens Book 1 with the name 'Cynthia', he starts Book 3 with the name 'Callimachus', requesting that the 'shade of Callimachus and the rites of Coan Philetas' allow him to enter their grove (3.1.1–2). The replacement of Cynthia with Callimachus marks well Propertius' shift from a preoccupation with the actual experience of love to the more literary idea of the love poet, and the poem as a whole stakes a lofty position for Propertius.

Labelling himself a *sacerdos* or 'priest' from a 'pure spring', Propertius next asserts that he is the first to 'convey Italian mysteries through Greek dances' (3–4). In phrasing replete with Callimachean precepts, he bids goodbye to those who 'delay Apollo in arms' and requests that his own verse go forward polished with 'slender pumice stone' (7–8), noting soon after that a 'broad path' is not given for the Muses to run (14). Promising that others will speak of Rome's future military accomplishments, Propertius proclaims that his own work, deigned for peacetime, was brought down from the Muses' mountain on an 'untrodden path' (17–18). He requests that the Muses award him a 'soft' rather than 'hard' garland (19–20), a seeming contrast with either epic's presumed reward or the standard garland awarded to triumphant generals (perhaps both; for the triumph, see Chapter 5). Referencing an 'envious crowd' of detractors (21), Propertius finally predicts that his fame will increase after his death, just as the reputations of the Trojan War and Homer himself (21–36).

Soon after, in poem 3.3, Propertius presents an even more impressionistic sense of his place in the Roman literary canon, recounting a dream he had 'in the shade of Mount Helicon' at the spring of Hippocrene (1–2), a setting that links the poem both to the *Aetia* and to the *Annals* of the Roman poet Ennius. Suggesting that he drank from the same spring at which Ennius 'thirstily' drank, Propertius is about to follow Ennius by singing episodes of Roman history when suddenly Apollo interrupts him (5–14).[45] Demanding to know who ordered the poet to sing a 'work of heroic song' (15–16), Apollo reminds Propertius of his ties to love poetry, using a by now familiar emphasis on the modest size and weight of such poetry (18 and 22). Calliope later reiterates that Rome's military achievements are not for Propertius, using her own list of themes unsuited to him (41–46). At the poem's conclusion, the Muse now wets Propertius' lips with the very same waters that Philetas once drank (51–52).

Although he evokes Callimachus with greater reverence in Book 3, it is in Book 4 – after proclaiming himself free of love and condemning Cynthia to the ravages of old age (3.24 and 3.25) – that Propertius demonstrates perhaps most dramatically his debt to the earlier poet by undertaking a major shift from his previous poetry. While Propertius, as we have seen, incorporates the voices of Cynthia and other women in Book 4, he also adopts the *Aetia* as a model for many of the poems, offering an account of the origins of various rituals and sites in Rome. The book opens with a request that a 'visitor' look at 'mighty Rome' (4.1a.1), then juxtaposes the present grandeur of the city with its earlier, more humble form. We shall explore in the next chapter the role of this poem and others in Book 4 in elucidating the meaning of the Roman past in light of its present landscape.

For our purposes here, it is enough to note that, after recounting at length the glories of Rome and its history, the poet signals his intention to change poetic modes by announcing that his role is now to 'serve his country' (60). Requesting recognition from Ennius and the god Bacchus, he hopes that his homeland 'Umbria might swell with pride at my work, Umbria home of the Roman Callimachus!' (63–64).

As in earlier books, however, Propertius' connections to love poetry defy any straightforward attempt at literary transformation. For Propertius' claim to Rome that 'this work rises for you' (67) is punctured shortly after by an interlocutor, later identified as the astrologer Horos, who cautions Propertius that Apollo does not approve of such poetry from him (4.1b.73–74). Relaying Propertius' horoscope, during which he briefly recounts the poet's own biography, Horos soon orders Propertius instead to 'compose elegy, a deceitful undertaking [*fallax opus*]' (135), a characterization of elegy that might seem surprising, but nonetheless conveys well the unpredictability of the genre in Propertius' hands. Despite the seeming reinforcement of Propertius' status as love poet, then, Book 4 develops in ways that demonstrate Propertius' serious engagement with new poetic forms, even as he continues to juxtapose, and at times blur, the opposing genres of elegy and epic.

As many critics have argued, Propertius' third book demonstrates patent familiarity with Horace's odes, offering, in many places, a sly rejoinder to them.[46] Horace, in turn, launches a scathing attack on Propertius' claims to the title 'Roman Callimachus' in his *Epistles* (2.2.99–101). Such parries suggest the vibrancy with which Roman literary genres were taking shape – and being contested – throughout the Augustan era. Rome's Greek inheritance in particular provided a malleable resource for the Latin love poets, albeit one with a certain amount of contradiction, especially when it came to their use of myth. In declining epic themes through devices like the *recusatio*, Propertius seems to reject myth as suitable material for his poetry. On the other hand, he frequently incorporates mythical references into his work. How can we reconcile these two opposing strategies, not merely in Propertius, but in love poetry more broadly? That is, given their strong adherence to Callimachean principles, why do the Latin love poets so often integrate myth, the foundation of epic, into their verse?

Excursus: Why Myth?

Myth unquestionably occupied a central place in ancient literature and culture. Inhabiting a time and place categorically removed from everyday experience, myth could shed light on the present precisely because of its distance from it.[47] More specifically, myth provided a repository of well-known characters and stories that poets or artists could adapt to their own needs while still maintaining 'a community of experience' with their audience.[48] Part of the appeal of myth for the love poets was the specific way it allowed them to demonstrate their extensive knowledge of previous literature, while also carving out their own voice by reinterpreting or reimagining individual stories. Ovid, in particular, uses myth to showcase his learning and *cultus*, features clearly evident in Ovid's *Metamorphoses*, an impressive collection of about 250 mythological tales, which remains one of our main sources today for classical mythology.

The careful repurposing of classical myth in love poetry is evident already in Catullus, who artfully turns to myth in his longer poems. In poem 64, as we saw in Chapter 3, Catullus presents his own take on the myth of Ariadne's abandonment, while in poem 68 Catullus treats the myth of Laodamia and Protesilaus' love as a parallel to his own clandestine affair with Lesbia. The widespread use of mythological *exempla* ('examples') in helping to 'explain' the actions or qualities of various individuals – juxtaposing, as it were, the grandiose with the mundane – appears throughout love poetry, as it does throughout ancient literature. As we discussed in the last chapter, Propertius uses a series of mythological women to help describe the sleeping Cynthia in 1.3. In more anguished tones, he compares his own violent desire to die alongside Cynthia to the self-inflicted death of Haemon in Antigone's tomb (2.8.21–24).

Ovid's *Heroides* examines the plight of the abandoned lover exclusively through the lens of mythical characters. Myth, however, also appears in Ovid's other amatory works, where it functions to illuminate both the *puella* and *ego*. Although Ovid uses myth in such situations to offer seeming models of behaviour, he frequently employs it in ways that parody myth's authority or that undercut his own arguments.[49] In *Amores* 1.3, for example, Ovid tries to persuade his mistress to pursue an exclusive relationship with him, promising to make her famous through his poetry, just as former poets made the loves of Io, Leda and Europa famous (21–26). Initially compelling in its learnedness, Ovid's actual choice of mythical women here raises red flags. As Fritz Graf observes, 'the very triteness of the argument directs attention to the underlying incongruity: those relationships did not last very long, nor did they bring happiness to the women.'[50] Like many devices in Ovid's work, then, myth ultimately allows the poet to pay homage to an earlier tradition, while at the same time establishing his own critical distance from it.

Since mythological examples are often used for didactic purposes in love poetry, they accordingly become especially prominent in the *Ars Amatoria*. In the *Ars Amatoria*, *exempla* serve alternately as models to be imitated or as warnings against certain types of behaviour. At times, *exempla* also help Ovid illustrate 'general' or 'universal' truths; thus, in one passage, he recounts the myth of Pasiphae and her copulation with the bull as proof that women are innately libidinous (*Ars* 1.289–326). Similarly, the example of Clytemnestra, the unfaithful and murderous wife of the Greek chieftain Agamemnon, is used by Ovid to exemplify the notion that 'a wronged woman will take her just revenge by committing the act of infidelity on her own part' (2.399–408).[51]

We can perhaps better observe the arresting suppleness of myth in the hands of the Roman love poets by tracing the appearance of a single myth across a number of works: the myth of Atalanta.

ATALANTA TRANSFORMED

Atalanta's myth generally encompasses two main events: her participation as the only woman in the Calydonian boar hunt and her father's use of a foot race to find her an appropriate husband. Having previously vowed to remain a virgin in service of the goddess Artemis, Atalanta is only defeated in the race when Milanion – or, in other versions, Hippomenes – uses golden apples to distract her, after which she is given to him in marriage. Atalanta markedly appears in three lines at the end of Catullus' second poem. Often treated as a separate fragment, the lines avoid naming her and read only: 'it is as welcome to me as they say the golden apple was to the swift *puella*, which dissolved her girdle bound for a long time' (2b.11–13). Alluding to the foot race, Catullus' short fragment mainly seems to celebrate the role of the apple in overcoming Atalanta's erotic reluctance.

Propertius echoes Catullus by also using Atalanta to illustrate his ideas about love in his first poem (1.1.9–16); in Propertius' poem, though, Atalanta's *exemplum* is adapted to demonstrate how much hard work and persistence matter in the pursuit of love, and the poet focuses not on Atalanta, but on her male pursuer. Significantly, Propertius references a lesser-known version of Atlanta's myth, one minus the legendary foot race, in which Atalanta grows up in the wild after being exposed on Mount Parthenius as an infant. As a young woman, Atalanta is pursued by a range of suitors, including Milanion, and, while hunting one day, the two centaurs Hylaeus and Rhoeteus assault her. According to Apollodorus, she kills them herself (3.9.2), but Propertius places Milanion at the scene, where he is wounded defending her; Propertius then credits Milanion's devotion with his ulti-mate conquest of the young woman.[52] Throughout his use of the *exemplum*, Propertius closely identifies with Milanion, casting him as a double for his *ego*, one whose wounds foreshadow well the bruises Propertius' own body will acquire in his dogged pursuit of Cynthia.[53]

Atalanta appears twice in the *Amores*. First, she is evoked – along with Ariadne and Cassandra – in helping demonstrate Corinna's beauty in her dishevelment following Ovid's assault in 1.7. Identified only as 'Schoeneus' daughter', Atalanta is described as equally lovely when she 'disturbed the Maenalian wild animals with her bow' (13–14), an image that pointedly evokes her vigorous hunting activities. In 3.2, however, Ovid coarsely reduces Atalanta to her legs – presumably an outcome of her speed – in urging his *puella* to show more of her own limbs, exclaiming, 'such legs of swift Atalanta Milanion wanted to raise up in his hands' (29–30). Later, in the second book of the *Ars Amatoria*, Ovid returns to Milanion as a model of praiseworthy persistence and masculine prowess (185–196), a passage that recalls Propertius' earlier poem. But, in the third book, Ovid boils the myth down once again to an objectifying focus on Atalanta's legs, instructing his female readers to assume sexual positions using their best physical attributes and offering, as crude illustration, Atalanta's placement of her legs on Milanion's shoulders during the act of love (*Ars* 3.775–776).

As this progression in the use of Atalanta's myth demonstrates, myth allows the love poets to adopt a range of attitudes in alternately prescribing male and female behaviours. Ovid's tone towards myth, however, changes perceptibly in his exile poetry, as he uses it to illustrate the hardships of his banishment. In the *Tristia*, for example, Ovid compares himself to Odysseus, whose fate as a homeless vagabond he presents as similar to his own. Yet Ovid's comparison emphasizes that Odysseus was a tough hero and built for that sort of life, while he, Ovid, is only a 'tender poet' for whom life in exile is deadly (*Tristia* 1.5.57–84). In the stories about Phaeton, who incurred Jupiter's wrath, and Icarus, victim of his own reckless behaviour (1.1.79 and 89), Ovid finds additional templates for his own harsh fate. Throughout his exilic poetry, then, myth loses its frivolity for Ovid and is turned into a poignant and at times bitter discourse. Fritz Graf importantly perceives in this pessimistic recourse to myth an acknowledgement of the limits of love elegy's conventional devices: 'the very exempla that were useful in the world of urbane love [...] are no real help in understanding what is going on.'[54]

As such analysis suggests, in the evolution of Ovid's work from the *Amores* to the exilic poetry, we see the transformation of many of elegy's devices, as well as greater and greater exposure of its tactics and limits. So it is time to turn more fully to Ovid's evolving view of his own poetic programme.

Ovid: Elegy Redefined

At the core of many scholarly treatments of Ovid are assumptions that draw on his final position in the development of elegy as a genre, with many openly suggesting that he brings about the ultimate 'decline' of the form. Barbara Boyd, however, identifies the pitfalls of interpreting Ovid in terms of a progressive and generic fallacy according to which 'Ovid is the last, and so the least good, of the elegists.'[55] As we have seen from his literary lists, Ovid positions himself as part of a longer tradition, so one way to approach Ovid's poetry is to acknowledge that he provides an invaluable manual for reading earlier writers,[56] but that is certainly not the only lens to use in assessing the value of his work. That Ovid's sole claim to immortality was his ability to make people laugh at the shortcomings of his predecessors seems far too unsophisticated an interpretation; Ovid's elegiac output may be seen more profitably as 'not simply a replica of a tradition but rather a contribution to that tradition'.[57]

We can already witness a lively examination of elegy and its boundaries in the work of Propertius, including his evolution from a poet of strictly amatory themes to one drawing on such diverse topics as poetics, politics and even, by Book 4, antiquarianism. Exploration of the flexibility of elegy, as well as the variety of themes it could incorporate, becomes the main characteristic of Ovid's love poetry. Moreover, there is no clear, linear development in his treatment of the elegiac genre. His early work, the *Amores*, was written (in its first edition) during the same period as the *Heroides*. The *Ars Amatoria* and the *Remedia Amoris*, written between 1 BCE and 1 CE, further display Ovid's interest in remapping and reconfiguring the genre, tendencies which find ultimate expression in his poetry of exile. But we turn first to Ovid's *Amores*.

AMORES: LOVE AS A GAME

Ovid first composed the *Amores* (translated literally as 'Loves', but more often known as 'Love Poems') when he was not yet twenty, although only the second edition, published many years later in 1 CE, comes down to us. The title *Amores* undoubtedly alludes to the title previously used by Cornelius Gallus for his collection of love poetry and Roman readers would presumably have recognized the strong connections between the two works. Situating his own poetic voice, Ovid references some of his predecessors in the very opening lines of the work:

> Arms and violent wars I was preparing to produce
> > in a heavy metre, the subject matter matching verse form
> with the top and the bottom lines matching. But Cupid (they say)
> > has laughed and stole away one foot of my verse.   (*Amores* 1.1.1–4)

Carefully crafted, these lines teasingly inform Ovid's reader that his original intent was to write a true war epic. Indeed, any reader of Roman poetry would immediately recognize the first word of Ovid's poem, *arma*, as a direct allusion to Virgil, whose *Aeneid* opened with the very same word. Although Ovid may set out to follow in the footsteps of Virgil, however, he informs his audience that he has been ambushed by Cupid, who, stealing a 'foot', transforms Ovid's metre from the dactylic hexameter of epic to elegiac couplet.

In many ways, Ovid's opening follows Propertius' earlier use of *recusatio* in pointedly denying epic as a literary undertaking, yet a more overt playfulness permeates Ovid's choice of love poetry. So, too, Ovid picks up on Propertius' own encounter with Amor in his first poem, although in the earlier work the god does not seize a foot, but rather brings his own feet down forcibly on Propertius' head (1.1.4). The rest of Ovid's poem proceeds in the same self-deprecating tone as the mischievous god, in response to the poet's indignation, strikes him with one of his shafts, causing Ovid to bid farewell to both the metre and the theme of epic: 'Harsh wars, off you go, together with your metre' (28).

Other poems in the *Amores* likewise treat Ovid's specific choice of genre. In poem 2.1, the narrator claims that despite his best efforts, epic with its 'swift-footed Achilles' and 'mutilated Hector' does not amount to much when it comes to the locked doors of his ruthless mistress (2.1.30–33). Girls swoon over love songs and Ovid firmly asserts his adherence to that genre (37–38). In the same vein, Ovid displays his rejection of the tragic genre in *Amores* 2.18, a poem that seems to anticipate the previously discussed *Amores* 3.1 and is addressed to a poet named Macer.[58] Here Ovid confesses that he tried his hand at the tragic genre, but the demands of Amor and his disgruntled mistress interfered once again, 'and Love has triumphed over the tragic bard' (2.18.18).[59]

The initial sequence of poems in *Amores* 1 introduces the main themes that recur throughout Ovid's elegiac work and, in the second poem, the poet lies sleepless in his bed, aching from passion and deciding that it is futile to resist Cupid. He agrees to surrender and asks only that Cupid treat him as Cupid's 'cousin' Augustus treats those he has conquered (an artful poke at the Augustan promotion of the goddess Venus as a kind of ancestor[60]), that is, by taking them under his protection (1.2.51–52). While the *Amores* is generally an apolitical work, this poem employs the potent image of a triumph, an important Roman public spectacle (one whose appearance in love poetry we shall examine in the next chapter), in illustrating Cupid's power. In 24 BCE Augustus had pacified Spain and Gaul, and the 'mocking description of Cupid's triumph could, all too easily, be transferred to those real celebrations still fresh in everyone's memory'. Thus the poem can be read as 'a sharp piece of socio-political satire'.[61]

Throughout his work, as we have seen, Ovid continually responds to earlier elegists, whether expanding their ideas of *militia amoris*, reimagining lost tablets or drawing his own meaning from the exposure of the *puella*'s body.[62] Still, Ovid 'rewrites' these tropes with a jesting physicality and even salaciousness that continues to push their limits. Although Catullus was not an elegist *per se*, Ovid was undoubtedly aware of his 'indecent' poetic legacy and evokes it often, such as in *Amores* 2.6, a poem about the death of a parrot that clearly alludes to Catullus' earlier sparrow poems (2 and 3). Ovid also follows Catullus' lead in *Amores* 3.11 when he echoes Catullus' desperate appeal to himself to 'stop the insanity' and bid goodbye to his fickle mistress (Catullus 8). At line 34, Ovid explicitly references Catullus' famous mingling of love and hate (Catullus 85), ruminating 'on this side love, on this side hate'. As we saw in the previous chapter, both Ovid and Catullus likewise make boastful declarations about their sexual prowess, although Ovid's claim is perhaps offset by his own graphic admission of impotence (3.7.3–4). The same prurient approach is evident in *Amores* 2.15, where Ovid identifies himself with a ring he has given his mistress as a gift; fantasizing about the possibilities it gives for access to Corinna, the poem ends with an imagined erection from all the wishful thinking.

Throughout such passages, Ovid seems to revel in the artificiality of elegy as he tackles all the commonplaces of the genre. Such reiteration of elegy's major themes displays Ovid's awareness of the tradition, yet he seems to engage them with his 'tongue [...] firmly in his cheek'.[63] So is Ovid capable of pausing on a somber note and contemplating the alleged sufferings of his predecessors without any irony? *Amores* 3.9, a poem in which Ovid laments the death of Tibullus, who died around 19 BCE and whom Ovid calls 'the seer and glory' of elegy (5), is especially noteworthy in this regard. Poem 3.9 contains all the constituent parts of the formal funeral lament: an address to the mourners, praise for the deceased mingled with grief over his untimely demise, a ritual outburst against unjust fate, a deathbed scene followed by words of consolation, and a burial scene with accompanying prayer for the repose of the dead.[64] In the course of the poem, Ovid mentions both Delia and Nemesis, 'old love and new' (32), who gained immortality through the poet's work, and he envisions Tibullus being welcomed in Elysium by Catullus, Calvus and Gallus – the best of the early Roman love poets.

On the surface, this poem seems to be a serious expression of mourning, a melancholy and solemn contemplation of a young poet's untimely death with concomitant praise of his lasting legacy. Peter Green, however, points out that this poem contains many parallels to *Amores* 2.6, mentioned above, on the death of the parrot. Ovid's earlier poem is itself undoubtedly an allusion to Catullus' poem of double entendre and Green emphasizes that 'Ovid seldom produced effects by accident', so the correlation between the poem on the death of Tibullus and the death of the pet parrot is no 'random juxtaposition'.[65] Green proposes of Ovid that 'while his grief was genuine, one unregenerate corner of his mind may well have found the dead poet's private life mildly risible, and his verses not wholly free from excessive (i.e., parrot-like) *imitatio*'.[66] Even in his most somber thoughts, then, the narrator of the *Amores* remains potentially irreverent.

For some readers – especially those conditioned by the rhetoric of romantic love and their own pre-formed expectations of love poetry – Ovid's *Amores*, with its tone of amused detachment, may seem 'the work of an outrageous cad or else the pointless invention of an emotionally shallow mind'.[67] And in the final poem of *Amores* 3, Ovid gives the impression that he is bidding farewell to the entire genre: 'Mother of tender Loves, seek a new poet. My elegies are going around the final turning post' (3.15.1–2). Yet Ovid also lays claim in this poem to poetic fame by putting himself in the company of Virgil and Catullus (3.15.7). Several other poems in the *Amores*, like 3.15, point in the direction of the poet's claims to longevity, even immortality (e.g. *Amores* 1.15.8), engendering a subgenre of so-called *monumentum* poems familiar to modern readers mostly through Horace's famous ode (*Odes* 1.30).

Thus the choice of the elegiac genre does not ultimately entail a short-lived fame for Ovid, despite the limits he put on elegy in 3.15.

In weighing the status and prestige of the poet, the Augustan elegists on occasion make use of an important term for 'poet': *vates*, the poet as seer, a designation with religious connotations including an ability to predict the future.[68] Tibullus calls himself a *sacer vates* ('holy seer') in one of his poems (2.5.114), a poem we shall examine in the next chapter, while Propertius equates the calling of the poet with a prophet in 2.10 (19–20) – although, as we discussed earlier, he ultimately defers his own assumption of that grand position for a later time. Propertius labels himself a *sacerdos* or 'priest' in 3.1 (3), though, and he uses the term *vates* of a poet again in the first line of 4.6. Ovid subsequently shows his interest in the title beginning with the *Amores*, and he continually adjusts the idea to fit his poetic programme, seeking in part to redefine the role of poet as 'erotic *vates*', a term that may seem to many readers an oxymoron.[69]

Given the experimentation and innovation that defines the *Amores*, there is little doubt that Ovid's elegiac output must be treated as doing more than 'nailing down the lid of the coffin in which Roman elegy is to be interred'.[70] In order to understand fully what Ovid achieved with his love poetry, however, we need to look more closely at Ovid's other elegiac works to see how they continue to extend the boundaries of love poetry.

ELEGY AS EROTIC EDUCATION?

In 1 BCE–1 CE Ovid published the first two books of the *Ars Amatoria*, followed soon after by a third book. In the same period are also placed two other works: the *Remedia Amoris* and *Medicamina Faciei Femineae*, the latter a poetic celebration of refinement and sophistication in elegiac metre of which only a hundred verses survive. All three works follow a similar twist in the elegiac genre: they are all didactic. The *Ars Amatoria* provides advice for men on the seduction of women (Book 1), on how to retain their love (Book 2) and how women can, in turn, conquer and seduce men (Book 3).

Didactic poetry had serious predecessors; from Hesiod and Aratus in the Greek poetic canon to Lucretius' *De Rerum Natura* (*On the Nature of*

Things) and Virgil's *Georgics*, didactic poetry was generally not written in jest or for mere entertainment. By utilizing these models, Ovid therefore pushes the limits not only of the elegiac genre, but also of didactic poetry, combining the two in one sparkling and unbridled poetic tour de force. As we have seen, earlier love poets at times played with the idea of 'erotic education': Catullus and Propertius offer advice to their friends, Priapus advises Tibullus on how to pursue *pueri*, and the figure of the *lena* presents herself to the *puella* as an important mentor in the business of love. Rather than merely doling out 'ad hoc' advice, however, Ovid in the *Ars Amatoria* goes further in inventing a whole system of procedures and precepts.[71] Even more, Ovid's advice persistently calls attention to *cultus*, which acquires 'the power to convert wild and instinctual love (*amor/eros*) into an elaborate and dynamic cultural game played by both parties'.[72]

Ovid makes his task very clear from the beginning: 'Love must be ruled by skill' (*Ars* 1.4), making 'skill' supreme and refuting any traditional deference to Cupid as the setter of rules. For the first time we see love not as the emotion dominating *ego*, but rather the force to be dominated. Yet Ovid's attempt at bringing passion into a framework of rationality invariably threatens to trivialize the feeling of love and reduce it to the level of a strategy, one bolstered by a series of rote behaviours devoid of emotion.[73] Ovid's ideal lover is a far departure from the besotted and tormented lover of Catullus, Propertius and Tibullus. He (or she) is characterized by a complete lack of scruple and by a disregard for traditional morality and the much-praised *mos maiorum* ('the custom of the ancestors'). The absoluteness of a single beloved is completely forgotten as Ovid advises, 'Pick out any girl, and tell her: "You are the only one I fancy"' (*Ars* 1.42).

In later chapters we shall examine Ovid's use of urban topography in the *Ars Amatoria*, as well as some of the ways his playful account of love challenges contemporary Augustan morality and its expectations of respectability, leading to serious consequences for the poet. Here, however, we want to focus on the how the *Ars* provides Ovid with an opportunity to elaborate his evolving sensibility as poet. Emblematic of the new literary terrain he seeks to establish, Ovid mocks the previously revered sources of poetic inspiration in the opening book:

I will not lie, Apollo, that my skills have been given to me by you,
>   nor was I inspired by the voice of an aerial bird,
> nor did Clio or her sisters appear to me [...]
>   Experience sets this work in motion; obey an experienced poet.
>
>   (*Ars* 1.25–27, 29)

Instead of the divine inspiration claimed by former poets, Ovid emphatically asserts here that his poetry is based on the practice and experiences of the poet himself. Later the supreme confidence of Ovid's voice is further revealed as he aggressively places his poetry above epic: 'A happy lover awards with the green palm of victory my verses, more outstanding than Homer's or Hesiod's' (*Ars* 2.3–4). This same confident tone also characterizes Ovid's *Remedia Amoris* and *Medicamina Faciei Femineae*.

In the *Remedia*, which serves as a sequel to the *Ars* and an 'antidote' to any unhappy love gained by its methods,[74] Ovid demonstrates his awareness of the stern criticism levied against his poetry, but he does not feel any need to apologize or strike a defensive pose:

> Some recently have attacked my little books of poetry;
>   their criticism is that my Muse is scandalous.
> While I would please my readers in this way, while I am sung throughout the world,
>   whoever wishes, let him impugn my work.   (*Remedia* 361–365)

Later the instruction on love becomes fused with articulation of his poetic brilliance, as Ovid places himself on an equal footing with Virgil (*Remedia* 395–396) and writing about love turns out to be as much a path to immortality as epic.

This poem, however, is not without its paradoxes. In a sense, the *Remedia* becomes a renunciation of elegiac love and even a critique of the act of composing elegy itself.[75] For one, the advice given in the *Remedia* stands in direct opposition to that of the *Ars*, replacing the quest for love with more practical undertakings such as forensic work, warfare, travelling, hunting, fishing and farming. Near the end of the *Remedia*, Ovid even warns his readers away from two especially hazardous dangers, both leading back to the world of amatory pursuits: pantomime shows and love poetry. Both forms of expression, he claims, represent erotic passion so forcefully that they can easily cause anyone whose emotions are not stable to submit to the power of love (751–766). We have seen the same idea (namely that reading love poetry leads to loving) already exploited in earlier poets, but Ovid expands on the idea when he observes:

> Indeed Sappho once made me better for my mistress,
>> and Anacreon's Muse did not provide me with strict morals.
>
> Who can read the poems of Tibullus and remain untouched
>> or your poems, [Propertius,] whose main theme was Cynthia?
>
> Who can read Gallus and remain indifferent?
>> My poems also produce something of a similar effect. (*Remedia* 761–766)

Thus, Ovid once again establishes his place in a continuing line of love poets, although he remains evasive about the impact of his poetry on the reader in contrast to the others. Furthermore, Ovid places the *Remedia* in the same amatory tradition as his earlier work, provoking a contradictory conclusion: if Ovid wants his student to believe that all love poetry, and elegiac poetry in particular, is unsafe to read, then the *Remedia* itself, as an example of elegy, should fall into the category of harmful material.

The elegiac genre for Ovid, then, appears always to carry with it erotic connotations, causing the disease of love to recur if one is exposed to it in any form. But this premise directly contradicts the content of the *Remedia*, meaning that Ovid, in effect, creates a poem whose elegiac metre is diametrically opposed to its didactic intentions. Or, in Christopher Brunelle's apt phrasing, 'Ovid creates a previously unrecognized paradox between didactic content and elegiac style, and any student reading the *Remedia* to learn how to fall out of love should not be reading the *Remedia*.'[76] It is possible, therefore, to read these lines as Ovid's admission that both Greek and Roman love poetry hold enormous power, but that their time has come to an end and that Ovid himself is ready to turn the final page in the long and influential tradition, ultimately furnishing an antidote to the entire elegiac genre.[77]

In his later exilic poetry, Ovid radically reshapes the idea of the distressed lover, a figure now far removed from the slick world of earlier elegy, while also refocusing earlier claims about elegy's immortality to accommodate his own reduced circumstances. Despite occasionally doubting his poetic achievement in light of the fact that his poetry brought about his exile, Ovid nonetheless assertively states in the *Tristia* that his poetic talent will win him an everlasting fame, one that will range beyond Augustus' control of his destiny (*Tristia* 3.7.47–52). This bold declaration may be interpreted as a direct jab at Augustus' ruthless treatment of him or as Ovid's last attempt to appeal to Augustus' mercy, prospects we shall explore more fully in Chapter 6.

Ovid's nagging dissatisfaction with the association of elegy and love poetry manifests itself quite differently in his *Fasti*, a work composed between 2 and 8 CE. Left only half-finished, the *Fasti* consists of a poetic calendar in elegiac metre, focusing on the ancient myths and customs of Latium. The precise tone of the poem has been disputed by scholars, but given that Augustus served as the head of Rome's state religion, an elegiac poem focused on the Roman religious calendar might suggest a certain degree of conformism on Ovid's part.[78] The themes of the work underline Ovid's ascent from erotic to weightier themes while signalling, at the same time, the end of amatory elegy. Significantly, the programmatic opening of the *Fasti*, with its singling out of aetiology as its theme ('times [of festivals] with their causes'), closely echoes Propertius' attempts to become the 'Roman Callimachus' (Propertius 4.1a.64).[79]

We have already seen Propertius' multidimensional use of Callimachus in affirming his status as love poet, but we now want to turn more fully to another aspect of the Callimachean legacy: the interest in aetiology, a topic that invites broader examination of the Roman love poets' creative use of landscape, including their continuing fascination with the city of Rome itself.

V

COUNTRY
AND CITY

*But Rome will give you such beautiful women that you
will say, 'This city has everything in the world!'*

OVID, ARS 1.55–56

IN BOOK 12 OF HIS EPIGRAMS, Martial writes to a friend that 'Rome
gives you as many kisses on your return after fifteen years as Lesbia did not
give Catullus' (12.59.1–3). A sarcastic rejoinder to Catullus' exuberant kiss
poems, Martial's epigram crafts Rome as a more enthusiastic lover than Lesbia,
and so captures well the ways in which the city itself features as a dominant
presence throughout earlier Latin love poetry. The Augustan elegists in
particular respond in different ways to the *princeps'* ongoing attempts to
'rebuild' the city and establish Rome itself as a critical text of the new era.
As Catharine Edwards writes, 'topography, for Romans, perhaps played a
greater role than chronology in making sense of the past,'[1] and Augustus'
energetic urban programme, one that carefully juxtaposed the Roman past
and present, 'encouraged the community to engage in a dialogue on what it
meant to return to the values and virtues of early Rome.'[2] It was a conversation

the Augustan poets would enter with gusto, seeking in their own ways to interpret the meaning of the city and its remarkable transformations.

During the Augustan era, the world outside the city was also piquing the Roman imagination as expansion and military conquest brought more and more foreign spaces into Rome's horizon.[3] Closer to home, the ideals of rural life had long been promoted by the Roman upper class, many of whom owned estates outside the city to provide a retreat from their urban pursuits.[4] So it was not merely the city of Rome itself, but the intricate juxtaposition of worlds inside and outside the city, of city and country, imperial centre and its peripheries, that mattered in Augustan thought, and these oppositions were enthusiastically explored by the elegists in the course of defining the meaning of love, as well as the roles of its varied participants.

Since the elegiac poets were keenly aware of their forerunners, it is beneficial to look briefly at the meaning of landscape in both Catullus and Virgil before turning to the elegists themselves.

LANDSCAPE IN CATULLUS

Perhaps the most poignant evocation of the natural world in Catullus is poem 31, where the poet addresses Sirmio, an inlet near his hometown of Verona, rejoicing in his arrival home after a tour in Bithynia. In an earlier poem, Catullus punctures some of the pretentions of rural life, however, when he complains about the winds his 'little farm' is exposed to (poem 26). Humorously endorsing the pastoral setting as an alternative to – even a cure for – Roman public life, Catullus later addresses the farm itself in poem 44, noting wryly that he recovered there from a sickness he caught when reading one of Sestius' speeches (11–15).[5] Catullus imagines more determined activity outside the city in poem 11: announcing that he plans to embark on a trip with friends, he predicts an ambitious route that may include India or Parthian territory or even Gaul, where they can see 'the monuments of great Caesar' (10–11). Catullus concludes the poem with a poignant image from the pastoral world, professing that his love for Lesbia has been destroyed like a flower run over by a plough, an image we discussed in Chapter 2. In the course of the poem, then, Catullus begins by noting masculine achievement in the world outside the city, but he eventually turns to a feminine world of nature endangered by male intervention to illustrate his loss.

Catullus conveys a certain humour about the countryside, but Rome's urban setting remains more central to the overall feel of his poetry, supplying a notable frisson. Catullus' city is emphatically a living city, conjured almost entirely through people and their varied activities, both erotic and social. In poem 5, Catullus underlines the role of constant surveillance and gossip in the city (of which he is elsewhere an enthusiastic participant), urging Lesbia to ignore the 'talk of austere old men' (5). On the other hand, references to the actual topography and monuments of Rome are few. In a poem we have already looked at, Catullus pointedly leaves the forum to visit Varus' mistress (10.1), while she, in turn, wants to 'borrow' his non-existent slaves to go to the temple of Serapis (26). In poem 55, Catullus tries to chase down his friend Camerius, looking for him in places like the Circus Maximus, Jupiter's temple on the Capitoline and the portico of Pompey (1–8), the final space where, he says, he interrogated all the women until one, coarsely baring her breasts, jokingly told him to look for Camerius there (9–12). In an earlier poem (37), Catullus threatens to deface a lecherous bar near the temple of Castor and Pollux, where Lesbia has now allegedly taken up residence.

While Catullus utilizes both the city and the country in disparate ways, the opposition of *rus* and *urbs* becomes much more central to Augustan elegy and its contours derive in large part from the influence of a poet whose shadow, as we have seen, looms large on the Roman literary landscape: Virgil.

VIRGIL'S ARCADIA

At the centre of the Virgilian countryside – also known as Arcadia – is the farm, the plot of land cultivated and cared for by the individual farmer, a space at times idealized, albeit often entailing strenuous menial labour. Although Virgil is influenced by the pastoral *Idylls* of Theocritus, the Alexandrian poet's bucolic world remains blissfully unaware of the city as a competing site. In Virgil, on the other hand, the city of Rome is palpably present; there is a strong infusion of contemporary reality in Arcadia, including land confiscations, population displacement and even death as Virgil adapts the main features of earlier pastoral to his own more precarious Roman context.[6] Given the encroachment of traumatic events like war on Virgil's rural landscape, we can discern the presence of another meaning of the English word 'country' in Roman pastoral imagery: 'country' not as a rural space, but rather as political state or *patria* ('homeland'). Furthermore, Roman allusions to rural life allow not merely a contrast of place, but also one of time, for references to the more simple pastoral landscape of early Rome helped Augustan poets reconsider Rome's origins and, in so doing, 'express their questions, hopes, and fears for Rome's future'.[7]

In tracing the duelling meanings of country and city in Augustan elegy, we turn first to Tibullus, whose professed longing to lead the life of the trouble-free farmer distinguishes him from the rest of his Augustan cohort; yet his dream of rural bliss ultimately proves to compete precariously with his other desires.

Tibullus' Rural Dreams

Anyone who reads Tibullus for the first time would hardly identify erotic love as his primary theme, given that his passion for the countryside seems

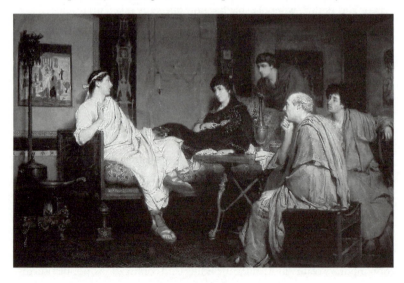

5.1　*Tibullus at Delia's* (1866) by Sir Laurence Alma-Tadema.

to dominate the work.[8] There are, however, a series of tensions that infuse his poetic landscape; as David Ross aptly observes,

> here is a poet of the city, urbane in every sense, who nonetheless finds in the country all that is ultimately of value – serenity, idealized sufficiency, the steadying values of the faith of our fathers, and productive peace [...] Yet, if these are Tibullus' ultimate values, why do we find them rather unsatisfying, as if something were missing?[9]

At times Tibullus crafts the Virgilian Arcadia as a bipolar world, one divided between unassuming felicity and powerful ambition – poles represented by *rus* and *urbs* respectively – a conceit that allows the desperate complexities of Virgil's Arcadia to become further crystallized and exposed.

DOMINA IN THE COUNTRY

As with Virgil's vision of the countryside, Tibullus' view of rural life involves a fair amount of manual toil. At the same time, Tibullus imagines his ideal landscape as a place suitable for love and song, and his enthusiasm for the countryside often seems eclipsed by his passion for Delia.[10] Tibullus' opening poem reiterates all the truisms of rustic simplicity and thriftiness: 'let my poverty lead me through a quiet life' (5) and 'if only, if only I could live content with little and no more be given to long journeys' (25–26).[11] Throughout, as Michael Putnam observes, 'the poet weighs two styles of living in the balance, the ambitious, practical, acquisitive political life of a Messalla and a poor, quiet, country existence towards which he aspires'.[12] Constant motion is juxtaposed with rest; action with idleness; ancestral wealth with humble existence. Such constant fluctuation also entails a movement between life and death. The happy sentiment that 'in the meantime, while fates allow, let us be in love' is thus immediately followed by the rather glum 'soon death will come with her head covered in darkness' (1.1.69–70).

Such mood swings highlight the paramount confusion of Tibullus' *ego* since they offer neither the elegiac surrender to the plight of love nor the relatively consistent pastoral serenity of the *Eclogues*. Although Tibullus frequently indulges in the fantasies of simple rustic charms, the reader nonetheless discerns 'him adding touches of sophistication or fastidiously criticizing it'.[13] In his deliberate treatment of the contrasting conventions of pastoral and elegiac poetry, Tibullus ultimately conveys to his readers that the only suitable landscape for love poetry is, in fact, the city and that the country can never fully accommodate its needs.[14]

Francis Cairns in his formative book on Tibullus describes him as a poet 'yearning for a past age', an 'idealized primitive Roman past'.[15] Yet, even as he may idealize the past, Tibullus rejects any possibility of turning back the clock or going back in time. Tibullus rejects the 'forefathers' riches or gains' (1.1.41) and he longs for the impossible reconciliation of his rural dream with the urban reality of his patron, Messalla Corvinus, and his mistress, Delia. In the second elegy of the first book, Tibullus hints that his rustic bliss is meaningless without Delia: 'If only with you, my Delia, I may yoke my oxen and pasture my flock on the familiar hill' (1.2.73–74).

In 1.5, Tibullus embarks on an idyllic portrayal of his life in the country, a scenario in which, having evoked the pastoral landscape as his setting, he labours in vain to incorporate both Delia and Messalla – refined urban dwellers 'whose life represents the opposite of Tibullus's pastoral imaginings'[16] – seamlessly into it, highlighting well the unfeasibility of his entire fantasy. Tibullus first inserts his *domina* Delia into his picture of rural bliss, and she initially seems transformed from an urban, capricious *puella* into a bustling farm girl: 'I will live in the country and my Delia will be there to guard the grain, while the threshing floor winnows the crops under the blazing sun' (1.5.21–22). Into this pipe dream, Messalla soon also makes his entrance: 'My Messalla will come here, for whom Delia will pluck down sweet fruit from the chosen trees' (31–32).

Despite Tibullus' efforts, Delia does not in the long run fit the part of the thrifty housekeeper buried in rural primitive simplicity;[17] Messalla's appearance in the countryside helps to underline the incompatibility of both with Tibullus' setup. For one, Delia's special preparations for Messalla demonstrate the incongruity of his presence: he is a special guest who requires suave, urbane treatment, marking him as someone who does not quite belong. As much as Delia is 'the practical flaw in the program'[18] of Tibullus' rural dream, then,

Messalla is even more so.[19] So that the idyllic scene ends with the poet's own admission that he dreamed the whole thing up (1.5.35).

Such sentiment is reinforced in the second book of the corpus when Tibullus' *domina* Nemesis momentarily enters the countryside only to demonstrate that it is irreconcilable with her urban demands for an ostentatious lifestyle. Tibullus in his disappointment subsequently sums up his attitude towards the countryside:

> Farewell to the crops, if only there be no girls in the country,
>> let acorns be our fare and let us drink water according to ancient custom.
> Acorns fed the ancients and they always had love.
>> What harm was there if they had no furrows sown with the seed? (2.3.71–74)

In effect, Tibullus proposes that the ancestors were not familiar with elaborate agriculture or the accumulation of wealth, and because of that their love was gentle and open. But the countryside of contemporary times has become destructive to his relationship with the *domina*, whose demands of luxury prove that, in modern times, only wealth can foster love. There are no girls to pursue in the country, at least not the kind that the poet envisions as desirable.

DREAMING OF ROME

Like all of the Augustan poets, Tibullus is attuned to the sharp contrast between the rural Rome of the past and the marvellous city taking shape around him. The juxtaposition of Rome's early modesty and the splendour of the present city was a favourite trope of Augustan writers.[20] Virgil's influential pairing of Rome's past and present occurs in the *Aeneid* as Evander takes Aeneas on a tour of the site that will become Rome, instructing the young man about the modest origins of settlements in Latium while alluding to Rome's future greatness there (8.306–365).[21] Significantly, Evander recounts the earlier 'Golden Age' under Saturn and then hints at the return of such an age under Augustus (8.347–348; see also *Aeneid* 6.791–795).[22]

Literary depictions of Rome could present all phases of the city positively: past, present and future. But in their individual treatments, poets might choose to impose an unbridgeable gap between past and present or, conversely, emphasize continuity between the two, perhaps even causality, in the last case implying that Rome is great in the present precisely because of its more modest past. So, too, while the trope might call attention to the superiority of the present, it could also be used to highlight the flaws of modern-day Rome, casting its strivings for grandiosity in a distinctly negative light.[23] Rather than any simple or clear-cut literary device, we therefore need to interpret appropriations of Rome's past landscape within an ongoing and wider cultural conversation about Augustan Rome, one that continually 'navigated the area between praise and polemic'.[24]

Tibullus' most openly 'Roman' poem, 2.5, moves 'with subtlety between past and present, city and country, war and peace'.[25] Set initially at the new temple of Apollo on the Palatine, the poem presents a hymn to Apollo in honour of the induction of Marcus Valerius Messalla Messalinus, Messalla's eldest son, into the college in charge of the Sibylline books – books traditionally thought to predict Rome's future. As Tibullus reflects on the role of the Sibylline prophecies, he starts with the famous encounter of Aeneas and the Cumaean Sibyl, one most famously related by Virgil in Book 6 of the *Aeneid*. At that point, Rome resides only in prophecy:

> Romulus had not yet marked the walls of the eternal
> city not to be dwelled in by his brother Remus.
> Back then cows grazed on the grassy Palatine
> and humble huts stood upon Jupiter's citadel.   (2.5.23–26)

Tibullus purposely references both the Palatine and Capitoline hills in this passage, both of which were essential to the construction of collective memory about the Roman past. Broadly speaking, the Palatine was associated with Romulus' initial founding of the city and the Capitoline was renowned for housing the first temple to Jupiter.[26] As Tibullus reminds his audience, the Palatine Hill, where the luxurious residences of the Roman aristocracy were then located, was once a pasture for cattle, while the Capitoline Hill, where the splendid temple of Jupiter Optimus Maximus was built, was once covered by the lowly huts of Rome's unpresumptuous ancestors.[27]

Tibullus' explicit mention of the city walls traced by Romulus and his even more poignant allusion to Remus in this passage are also noteworthy, as is the poet's fairly neutral phrasing, which obscures Remus' violent demise.[28]

Tibullus' Sibyl then delivers her prophecy to Aeneas amid the humble rural surroundings, addressing the city of Rome directly to add more poignancy to her words and closing with her expansive prediction of the city's future glory:

> Now, bulls, crop the grass of Seven Hills
>> while you may: before long this will be the site of a great city.
> Rome, your name is destined to rule the world
>> wherever Ceres looks down from heaven on tilled land,
> from the place where the sun rises and where
>> the Ocean bathes Sun's panting horses in its flowing streams.   (2.5.55–60)

While such visions may seem mystifying to Aeneas, the Sibyl's prediction reinforces for the Augustan audience outside the poem a bright account of its own future: the city on Seven Hills, which looked so unassuming in Aeneas' times, is destined to rule the entire extent of the sun's course. In light of Tibullus' overall tone in the poem, it is worth noting that 2.5 is the earliest surviving Latin reference to Rome as the *urbs aeterna*, the 'eternal city' (23).[29]

This juxtaposition of Rome's once-modest pastoralism with its present opulence becomes even more pronounced in the poetry of Propertius and Ovid, with Ovid firmly resolving the Tibullan vacillation between rural dream and contemporary Roman reality in favour of the latter. Propertius, for his part, experiments at times with the isolation of the countryside, but he increasingly fastens his eye on the city, using it as a dynamic setting for his pursuit of Cynthia as well as a means for weighing the Augustan era's evolving discursive and political manoeuvres.

Propertius: The Lover and the Augustan City

As we discussed in Chapter 4, Propertius uses Milanion's taming of Atalanta in his opening poem to illustrate what he perceives to be the proper course of love. While we considered his use of the *exemplum* in relation to the other love poets, noteworthy here is the way Propertius' account plays on the frequent association of women with the world of nature, a conceit that suggests that the 'wild' *puella* (Atalanta and, by extension, Cynthia) inherently requires 'domestication' at the hands of men.[30] A related trope widely used in ancient myth and literature often draws on this elision of women and nature: love

5.2 *Propertius and Cynthia at Tivoli* by Auguste Jean Baptiste Vinchon.

as a kind of hunt. In poem 2.19, Propertius exploits this idea more openly, writing first of Cynthia's intention to leave the city, then his own decision to pursue her in her rural isolation.

While he adopts Milanion as a kind of roadmap for masculine penetration of the countryside, Propertius importantly offers another motive for leaving the city in 1.1, begging to be conveyed to the ends of the earth where no woman will know how to find him (29–30). This delineation of two very different uses of space outside the city (the acquisition of love versus the escape from love) suggests some of the density of meaning Propertius invests in these spaces, and he continues to experiment with a range of threatened departures from Rome throughout Book 1.

LEAVING THE CITY

The departure of a friend or lover is a standard theme in ancient poetry (often called a *propemptikon*; see *Amores* 2.11), and Propertius plays it to the hilt. In poem 1.6, Propertius presents separation from the city as fitting for those men, such as his friend Tullus, who serve Rome.[31] While he lavishly praises Tullus' deep concern for his country, Propertius ultimately protests that he himself is unable to join Tullus, held back by Cynthia's ardent pleas. We can witness a similar contrast of masculine pursuits in Tibullus 1.1 and 1.5, poems in which Tibullus urges his patron Messalla to pursue ambitious undertakings without him. Propertius later shows Tullus conversely enjoying greater leisure as he drinks the finest wines, reclining alongside the Tiber; yet even these activities, Propertius avows, cannot compete with the pleasures of love (1.14).

While she seems to force Propertius to stay in the city, Cynthia herself is depicted on the verge of leaving Rome, or having left, in a number of poems in Book 1. In 1.8, Cynthia threatens to take a voyage to distant Illyria, but, in a surprising turnabout, Propertius soon reveals that she has changed her mind. He happily exclaims: 'I am dear to her, and because of me, Rome is called dearest' (1.8b.31) – a line whose very construction emphatically places Propertius between the city and his beloved, serving as a crucial mediator between the two. His own intimacy with the city, and Cynthia's complementary distance from it, is reiterated in 1.12 when Propertius asks Rome why it is accusing him of idleness due to Cynthia when Cynthia has, in fact, gone away (1–4). In the preceding poem, Propertius with great consternation places Cynthia outside Rome at Baiae, an ancient resort whose reputation might be something akin to Las Vegas today.[32] Unlike Tibullus, Propertius does not conjure idealized visions of his own life on the farm, but he does experiment in two poems near the end of Book 1 with what it might mean to locate himself in more rural settings (1.17 and 1.18). Using such remote locales ostensibly to escape Cynthia's grasp,[33] Propertius soon finds that such flight proves unsuccessful since Cynthia pervades even these wildernesses.

Towards the end of Book 3, Propertius revisits some of his travel scenarios; in 3.21, for example, he diagnoses a trip to 'learned Athens' as a cure for his love (25–30). In the next poem, Propertius once again addresses Tullus, urging him to return to Italy. Painting a glowing homage that 'may profitably be compared with Virgil's famous hymn to the beauties of Italy in *Georgics* 2.136–176',[34] Propertius announces that 'all marvels yield to Roman land. Nature placed here whatever it has anywhere' (3.22.17–18). Yet Propertius also uses the city of Rome itself in Books 2 and 3 as a means for staging the roles of male lover and female beloved, one that covertly fashions the city as a site of masculine privilege.

ROMANCING THE CITY

Beginning with Book 2, Propertius intensifies the role of Rome as it becomes both the setting for and witness to his romantic (mis)adventures. Like Catullus and his nosy old men, Propertius portrays the city constantly scrutinizing his affair, asserting in one poem that no street corner is silent when it comes to the two lovers (2.20.22; see *Amores* 3.1.21). Using a strategy we discussed in Chapter 4, Propertius deftly conflates those watching the lovers with those reading his poetry, asking: 'Is it true, Cynthia, that you are being conveyed all over Rome and openly conducting yourself with shame?' (2.5.1–2). Later, Propertius imagines an interlocutor openly challenging him: 'You can talk, when you are already a subject of gossip with your infamous book and your Cynthia is read around the whole forum!' (2.24.1–2).

Rome also supplies the specific sites that help define the lovers and their conduct. Near the end of Book 3, Propertius specifies that his house is located on the Esquiline (3.23.23–24; see also 4.8.1–2), a neighbourhood that might help advertise the poet's distance from the corridors of Augustan power.[35] He cites the Campus Martius and the theatre as places that hold no interest for him without Cynthia (2.16b.33–34),[36] although he subsequently names the theatre as a place ripe with the possibility of new seductions (2.22a.3–10). Accusing Cynthia in one poem of not appreciating the portico of Pompey, Propertius proceeds to describe it in loving detail (2.32.11–16), a passage that might have additional resonance if the portico was associated with prostitution, as some scholars have argued – a connotation that would also add texture to Catullus' search there for his friend.[37] When Cynthia, in turn, seeks to deprive Propertius of the temptations of the city in dictating the terms of his punishment in 4.8, she forbids him from going to Pompey's portico while also warning him about the forum during holidays; she likewise cautions him not to look around in the theatre or gaze too closely at a passing litter (75–78).

While Rome provides the backdrop for male seduction (a function of the city we shall also witness in Ovid's poetry), the city is also the primary site where Roman conquest acquires its substance and meaning for Propertius, even as he insists on his own inability to take part. Such a strategy is captured well by poem 3.4, which presents Propertius' ostensible excitement at Augustus' pending campaign against Parthia. For even as he enthuses about the prospect of foreign conquest, Propertius continually emphasizes the exhibition of such feats in Rome itself. 'Far away lands,' he proclaims, 'are preparing triumph' for us (3). Later, Propertius describes the spectacle of the triumph that he will witness, but specifies that he will watch it while leaning on the bosom of his *puella*, underlining his preference for the *puella* over *bellum* (15–16). After urging long life for Augustus – the progeny, he claims, of both Venus and Aeneas (19–20) – Propertius concludes once again with a reminder of his own more passive preferences when it comes to imperial efforts: 'May the plunder be for those whose labours merit it; it will be enough for me to cheer along the Sacred Way' (21–22).[38]

The Roman triumph, an important public celebration of Rome's military achievement, held enormous significance for the Romans,[39] and it became a symbol the love poets could use to carve out their own perspectives on Rome and its values. Propertius' ambivalent participation in Augustus' triumph had an important precedent in elegy, for in the one surviving fragment by Cornelius Gallus, the poet likewise depicts himself as a humble spectator of Julius Caesar's achievements: 'My fates will be sweet for me then, Caesar, when you will be the most important part of Roman history. After your return I will survey temples of many gods made richer by your spoils.'[40] Like Propertius, Gallus distances himself from the world of military conquest by proclaiming: 'The Muses produced poems that I would be able to declare worthy of my mistress.'[41] Extending even further the idea of the triumph, we have seen that Ovid imagines displaying the brutalized Corinna in triumph, and he conversely places himself in Cupid's triumph in 1.2 (23–50). Moreover, while in exile Ovid indulges in 'anticipatory wishful thinking'[42] about what Augustus' triumph over the Germans might look like, a way of both placating the *princeps* and stressing his own absence from the city, where he would have been able to witness such an event in person (*Tristia* 4.2).[43]

Like Tibullus, Propertius incorporates the temple of Apollo on the Palatine into his love poetry in dramatic fashion. As we shall see, Propertius probes more critically the temple's connections to the events at Actium in Book 4; here he focuses primarily on the physical appearance of the temple and its environs. Propertius begins the poem by explaining that he is running late because 'the golden portico of Apollo was opened by great Caesar [Augustus]' (2.31.1–2).[44] The poem then gives a detailed account of the whole complex, taking the reader by stages into the temple's interior, that is, through the colonnade decorated with the Danaids,[45] past the statue of Apollo in the courtyard and the altar, through the doors of the temple, and finally to the cult statues themselves (3–16). Throughout Propertius' account, a number of themes stand out: the associations of Apollo with poetry, the geographic mastery of Rome under Augustus (portrayed in the specification of various building materials brought from every corner of the Roman world) and the domination of art over nature.[46] In all, the superiority of the Augustan structure can be summed up by Propertius' claim that the god actually prefers the Roman temple to his own homeland (10).

In the next section, which modern editors have often treated as a separate poem, Propertius calls attention to Cynthia's conspicuous absence (2.32.1–10). Chiding her with the accusation that her reputation is in danger throughout the whole city (23–24), Propertius once again highlights Cynthia's incessant departure from Rome, proposing that 'it is not the city, mad one, but my eyes that you are running from!' (18). Propertius soon turns to another recurring theme involving the city: the scandalous behaviours taking place there. Rome is fortunate, Propertius asserts, if one woman acts contrary to the day's fashion (43–44). In an earlier poem, Propertius goes even further in blaming Romulus himself for the current state of morals: 'You, nurtured by the harsh milk of the she-wolf, were the author of such crime, Romulus, you taught how to rape the virginal Sabines with impunity; because of you, Love dares whatever it wants at Rome' (2.6.19–22). Such attitudes anticipate Propertius' turn to another claim involving the city: the necessity of defending it vigorously, especially from women, a group whose desires make them increasingly foreign, a threat to both Rome and its male citizens.

DEFENDING THE CITY

As we discussed in Chapter 3, Propertius rejoices at a night of love with Cynthia in poem 2.15; in explaining his good fortune, Propertius soon makes an abrupt turn to quite a serious topic, professing:

> But if everyone wished to live such a life
>   and rest their limbs weighed down by wine,
> there would not be cruel iron or a warlike fleet,
>   nor would the Actian sea toss our bones,
> nor, continually besieged by her own triumphs,
>   would exhausted Rome let down her hair in mourning.
> This, at least, they will rightly be able to praise:
>   my cups have injured no gods.   (41–48)

In these lines, Propertius explicitly sets his self-proclaimed lifestyle as a lover against the militaristic activities and ambitions that produced the civil wars, presenting Actium as a national tragedy, an affront to the gods, while personifying Rome itself as a woman given over to grief. Propertius' critique is complex, including where exactly his indictment falls. On the one hand, he seems to be condemning Augustus' victory, even refuting the idea of a golden age with his subtle reference to 'cruel iron'.[47] But, on the other hand, does Propertius specify 'my' cups precisely to draw a distinction between himself and Antony, given the latter's highly publicized predilection for wine and women? Regardless of whether he means to take sides, the passage powerfully insinuates that Rome needs to be protected from the 'wrong' kind of men, a forceful rebuttal to any assumption that the love poets' refusal of public life involves a lack of concern for the state's welfare.

Throughout his work, Propertius also steadfastly places his *puella* in opposition to the city, either because she is not where she should be (perhaps aligned with the world of nature) or because she is causing dismay to its residents, including himself. But Cynthia also remains eminently urbane – both a product of the city and an ardent consumer of its many delights, and that quality is equally disconcerting to Propertius. Unlike Ovid, as we have seen, Propertius professes a preference for Cynthia in her 'natural' state, one unmarred by cosmetics or elaborate adornment (e.g. 1.2). While such a conceit serves a range of purposes, for Propertius it also hints at a topic that will grow in importance: Roman women's dangerous susceptibility to luxury and foreign merchandise, making the city with its prosperous economy a site of their potential undoing.

Propertius begins to map the spatial dimensions of Cynthia's alleged avarice in 2.16. Accusing Cynthia of being interested in a rival (a *praetor* returning from Illyria),[48] Propertius chortles that she cares not about a lover's position, but only about the size of his wallet (2.16b.11–12). Lamenting to Jupiter that his *puella* 'is ruining herself for an unworthy price' (16), Propertius further charges that she 'always sends me to the ocean to seek jewels and orders me to bring gifts from Tyre' (17–18), a new and more insidious reason for masculine departure from the city, one driven by female greed.[49] Playfully evoking the image of Rome's simpler past, Propertius wishes that no one at Rome was rich and that the Roman leader lived only in a hut, an allusion to the alleged remains of Romulus' hut still visible on the Palatine (19–20).[50]

The potential dangers of female insatiability and 'shameful love' become even more apparent in the next part of the poem when Propertius raises the spectre of Antony, 'the leader who filled the waters of Actium with the empty shouting of his doomed soldiers' (37–38). More damningly, as Propertius intimates, while 'scandalous' love forced Antony to seek the ends of the earth, it was in retreat from battle, not in pursuit of lavish presents (39–40). Propertius then closes his comparison with overt praise for Augustus, who, Propertius claims, by the same hand both conquered and set aside weapons (41–42). This final endorsement of Augustus is jarring, especially given the previous poem, but, as we shall see, it contributes to an emerging image of Augustus as the purveyor of a very particular mode of order.

In the remainder of the poem, Propertius warns Cynthia that Jupiter may yet rain down (literally) on her expensive clothing and, shortly after, Propertius' anxieties over the dynamics of female consumption become even more apparent when he accuses Cynthia of 'madness' in using foreign dyes and cosmetics (2.18.23–24). Reiterating that nature's way is best, Propertius calls a 'Belgian rouge disgraceful to a Roman face' (25–26), a claim that reveals a kind of nationalistic fervour or perhaps panic: can Cynthia's foreign accoutrements mask or even erode her Roman identity? Later, in response to Propertius, Ovid appears more sanguine about female boundaries and cosmetics (not least because, as we shall see, he so heartily endorses the latter) and he carefully closes off any possibility of permanent damage from Corinna's misguided toilet, proposing that she can make do with a wig from the hair of German slaves until the 'native' hair that she has scorched grows back (1.14.45–56). Ovid's callous prescription is obviously made possible by the 'goods' (including slaves) emanating from Roman imperial expansion, and the path of such 'products' into Rome is directly named in Propertius. For even as the Sacred Way connotes the route of triumph, a homage to masculine enterprise, Propertius also identifies it as the place both to purchase luxury goods (2.24.13–14) and to participate in a related form of commercial traffic, one in women, meaning prostitutes brought from the east (2.23.15–22).

Propertius further intimates the association of Roman women with foreign commodities when he complains about Cynthia's worship of the Egyptian goddess Isis in poem 2.33,[51] a poem replete with geographic symbolism.[52]

Insisting that the Roman city remains at odds with such female outsiders, Propertius warns Isis that 'the Nile does not find favour with the Tiber' (2.33a.20). In the line preceding, Propertius even threatens that he will expel her from 'our city' altogether – a claim that allows the poet, even if only in his fantasy, to assume the role of *princeps* since Augustus in 28 BCE 'debarred the practice of the Isis cult from within the boundaries of the *pomerium* and, in 21 BC, from within the first milestone of the city'.[53] Cleopatra was perhaps Isis' most notorious worshipper, and Propertius uses the Egyptian queen to drive his most forceful illustration of women's perilous incompatibility with the city in poem 3.11.

Propertius begins 3.11 by asking why anyone should be amazed that a woman has taken him under her control, an opening that leans heavily on the trope of *servitium amoris*; he then offers a series of historical and mythological *exempla* to illustrate his dilemma, concluding with 'the one who lately fastened disgrace on our weapons' (29). While avoiding direct mention of Antony, Propertius graphically associates Cleopatra with various vices, including drunkenness and promiscuity, in the lines that follow.[54] Still, it is Propertius' focus on her threat to Rome that predominates, proclaiming at one point that Cleopatra demanded Rome's walls as her dowry (31–32). The drama is heightened even further when Cleopatra suddenly seems to penetrate the city itself, daring to stretch mosquito nets across the Tarpeian rock and to give verdicts among the statues and weapons of Marius (45–46).[55] What does it matter to have shaken off the rule of Tarquin the Proud – an event that led to the start of the Republic – Propertius mutters, 'if a woman is to be endured' (49)?

Propertius next addresses Rome directly, calling on the city to take triumph and grant long life to Augustus (49–50). Turning to Cleopatra, the poet reminds her of her own flight to the Nile and that she 'accepted the shackles of Romulus' (51–52). Reiterating the value placed on the Roman triumph, Propertius describes seeing Cleopatra's body displayed on the streets of the city (although sources attest an effigy was actually put on show).[56] Yet, in her dying moment, Cleopatra finds her own voice and speaks directly to Rome, affirming its absolute victory over her because of its leader: 'You had no need to fear me, Rome, with such a citizen!' (55). As we have seen, the female voice is noteworthy in Propertius, and here it is used to record Cleopatra's complete capitulation. A couplet plagued by uncertain reading follows, which may emphasize again the threat of a woman to the city that presides over the entire world (57).[57]

Modern scholars have long weighed Propertius' seeming identification with Antony in this poem and elsewhere in trying to assess the poet's 'politics'.[58] But, as this poem suggests, Propertius' antagonistic pairing of Cleopatra and Augustus may in fact be more salient than any affiliation with Antony. For Propertius progressively appropriates Augustus' defeat of Cleopatra as a model in shaping the aspirations of his own *ego*, a gesture that claims the authority of the *princeps* in managing his own romantic affairs while also simultaneously eroticizing the very encounter that initiated Augustus' rise to power. Whether Propertius can ultimately 'be' Augustus in relation to Cynthia's Cleopatra is, of course, doubtful (so, too, whether we can take his valourization of the *princeps* in this context as any straightforward political statement), but the strategy nonetheless makes provocative use not of classical myth, but rather an event central to Augustan self-narrative in providing a powerful *exemplum* of the inexorable male conquest of woman's threatening difference.

In the two poems following, Propertius elaborates not only the dangers faced by women in the imperial city, but also the danger they present to it. In poem 3.12, he exhorts the soldier Postumus not to abandon his wife Galla, dreading what may happen to her once she is left alone (17–18), while in 3.13 the temptations of the city's economy have a more personal consequence: they make Roman woman greedy, and women, in turn, drive up their own prices for a night of love.[59] In poem 3.16, Propertius renders the city in more everyday terms, expressing his nervousness at being called out at night, but hoping that, as a lover, he will be kept safe on the city's dark streets. Soon after, the book comes to a close, and with it Propertius' primary focus on his *ego*'s romantic adventures. It remains now only to look at the role of the city in Book 4, where, as part of his turn to Roman aetiology, Propertius uses the topography of Rome to pore over the meaning of Rome's past and the Augustan present.

WRITING THE CITY

Book 4 presents a palpable change for Propertius in terms of his overall project. Jeri DeBrohun argues that 'Propertius knew that his decision to increase the thematic range of his elegy with Roman *aetia* would create a conflict with his own earlier definition of elegy as exclusively amatory'; she adds, 'Propertius planned from the outset of Book 4 to make this conflict an integral part of his new elegiac program.'[60] Although 'greatest Rome' (*maxima Roma*) might seem to displace Cynthia as the poet's main theme in 4.1, DeBrohun sees throughout Book 4 a persistent tension between private love (*amor*) and public patriotism (*Roma*).[61] In literary terms – taking each term as representative of elegy and epic respectively – there is a kind of 'bipolar poetics' in Book 4, a push-and-pull already contained in the alternating lines of the elegiac couplet itself.[62]

The overall flow of Book 4 is puzzling, and just as scholars have difficulty in pinning down Propertius' intentions in Book 4 – the shape-shifting Vertumnus of 4.2 serving as a nice symbol of the book's many twists and turns[63] – many have argued that his representations of Roman aetiology and landscape communicate a similar ambiguity. Tara Welch has gone further in arguing that Propertius sees the Augustan city as coercive, its monuments shaping 'morality, identity, and behaviour into forms more in tune with the state.'[64] She later expands: 'The elegies in Book 4 make audible the process of self-expression, individuation, and even defection all but drowned out by the overwhelming – and persuasively symphonic – legacy of Augustus' city of marble.'[65] To put it another way, living among the Augustan monuments is perhaps not as easy as admiring them. In assessing the specific contribution Propertius makes to contemporary conversations about the city, we want to focus on three themes that emerge from poems not yet considered: the residual tensions Propertius perceives in Roman identity as witnessed in the landscape (4.1); the promotion of a violent view of Rome's past rather than a nostalgic one (4.10); and the ultimate role of poetry, rather than Augustan monuments, in defining Rome (4.6).

As we saw in Chapter 4, poem 4.1 opens with Propertius' announcement that he plans to change his style of poetry (4.1a.1–70) and now write in service to Rome (60). In the second half of the poem, however, his proposed plans are immediately rebuffed by the astrologer Horos, who orders Propertius to continue writing erotic elegy (4.1b.71–150). Significantly, Propertius opens the poem with an explicit contrast of the Roman past and present: 'All you see here, stranger, where greatest Rome is, was hill and grass before Phrygian Aeneas' (1a.1–2); he continues that the cattle of Evander once rested where the temple of Apollo on the Palatine stands (3–4), a clear allusion to the passage in *Aeneid* 8. Propertius then proceeds to scan other sites and note their relation to the past, including Remus' house, where the two brothers once shared a single hearth (10).[66] He calls attention to the simple warfare of olden times and the various groups making up Rome's early population, observing provocatively that 'the Roman foster child has nothing except the name from his ancestry: he would not believe that a she-wolf was the nurse of his bloodline' (37–38).

The general terms of Propertius' vision have been much debated, not least which version of Rome he holds in higher regard, if either.[67] Hans-Peter Stahl argues that the panorama of Rome relies on the speaker's standing on the Palatine, which for Stahl suggests a perspective in accordance with that of the *princeps*.[68] Yet Welch proposes that Propertius' striking assertion about contemporary Romans' attitudes to the she-wolf (who was credited in Roman myth with nurturing Romulus and Remus as infants) suggests, 'in temporal terms, the Roman foster child is alienated from his own past'.[69] Moreover, Propertius' own latent alienation is expressed in other parts of the poem as a disjunction between Rome and Umbria. Crediting the she-wolf with having walls grow from her milk and proclaiming that he in turn will attempt to 'lay down walls with pious verse' (55–57), Propertius pointedly defines the rewards of his poetry in terms of his homeland: 'Bacchus, give me leaves of your ivy so that proud Umbria might swell with my books: Umbria, home of the Roman Callimachus!' (62–64). Perhaps trying to reconcile the two opposing geographic sites, he later exhorts, 'Rome, smile, this work rises for you' (67).

In his response, Horos again calls attention to Umbria as a competing source of Propertius' identifications, reminding the poet that Umbria bore him and also reminding him of the suffering he endured there, including gathering his father's bones long before the appropriate time (1b.121–130). Such images allude to the brutal conflicts waged on Italian soil and 'open the possibility for variations across Italy in ways of viewing Rome'.[70] More fundamentally, 'these recollections of the elegist's early life serve as further reminders to the poet that his own sorrowful personal circumstances have rendered him ill-equipped for the kind of large-scale, patriotic Roman undertaking he has proposed'.[71] Thus, while Rome may have relied on the assimilation of outside groups from its earliest times – yielding a population of 'foster children' in Propertius' phrasing – it does not mean that the violence in such encounters was easily forgotten. Propertius' unsettling poems at the end of Book 1 attest to the persistent scars of the Perusine War, and Propertius makes his interlocutor in 4.1 a *hospes* – a 'stranger' or 'visitor' – to Rome, while other figures in Book 4, such as Vertumnus with his Etruscan origins, are also distinguished by their outsider status.[72]

Rome's early military battles are the central theme of 4.10, which recounts the origins of the temple of Jupiter Feretrius on the Capitoline. Romulus had allegedly first founded the temple in honour of his defeat of Acron, King of Caenina and 'thereafter any Roman commander who defeated the enemy commander in single combat was awarded the right to dedicate the spoils as *spolia opima*'.[73] Augustus restored the temple prior to Actium; its potential dialogue with the larger temple of Jupiter Optimus Maximus, also on the Capitoline, is disputed.[74] In recounting the stories in which *spolia opima* had been earned by three earlier Roman leaders, Propertius seems to be 'venturing onto swampy ground',[75] since Augustus had recently contrived to deny Crassus rights to the *spolia* in 29 BCE and, from then on, it would become the sole privilege of the *princeps*.[76] In his look back at these figures from Rome's early history, Propertius conspicuously focuses on their violence; while Romulus is praised for his prowess, a residual brutality is nonetheless attached to his image as Rome's founder. The very first word of the Romulus section is the jarring *imbuis*, a verb meaning 'to dampen' or 'to stain', one often used of weapons and blood, suggesting that Romulus 'dips in blood' the example of first conquest (5).[77] In the case of Cossus, Propertius expressly sympathizes with defeated Veii, contrasting its glorious past with its humble present, where now men 'harvest fields on your bones' (27–30). Far from treating the Roman past as a carefree Golden Age, then, poem 4.10 seems to stress 'the violence that is at the heart of Rome's identity'.[78]

Notably, in the opening lines of 4.10, Propertius claims that he ascends a great height, but that the prospect of glory gives him strength, since a crown (*corona*) taken from an easy peak does not yield pleasure (3–4); Welch and others have argued that the reference to a crown here, rather than the garland he requests elsewhere, is significant. When we extend the idea of climbing to mean the Capitoline itself, where the Roman triumphal procession ended, such symbols allow Propertius, in essence, to stage his own triumph as poet, appropriating an event whose symbolic importance for the Roman state we have previously considered.[79] In an earlier poem, poem 4.6, Propertius explains the origins of the temple of Apollo on the Palatine, likewise placing poetic composition in competition with both Rome's military achievements and their commemoration in the Augustan urban landscape.

The temple of Apollo on the Palatine, as we have seen, was closely connected to Augustus' victory at Actium; its intricate decorative programme could 'be used to evoke simultaneously the naval battle at Actium, Augustus himself as victor in that battle, and also the vital aid rendered by the god Apollo himself'.[80] In 4.6, Propertius gives a vivid account of the supposed battle, giving special focus to Apollo's imposing participation on Augustus' side. Calling it 'one of the strangest and most contested poems in his poetic corpus', Welch notes that critical response to this poem has varied greatly, including debate over the degree to which it praises or criticizes Augustus in its depiction of the precise event on which the *princeps'* rise to power had been predicated.[81] Its relation to earlier appearances of Actium in Books 1–3 (e.g. 2.16 and 3.11) at times seems awkward,[82] although it takes a familiar sideswipe at Cleopatra when comparing the two sides (4.6.21–22). In the course of the poem, Apollo delivers a lengthy pep talk to Augustus, whom he calls 'saviour of the world' (37), and Julius Caesar, looking down from the heavens, proclaims provocatively: 'I am a god', and that this is proof Augustus is of his blood (60).

In portraying the actual battle, which, after the grand build-up of speeches, devolves almost immediately to Cleopatra's flight (63 ff.), Welch argues that the poem 'exposes the fiction of the temple, namely, the discrepancy between what happened at Actium and how it was represented in the city'.[83] Even more, Propertius' claims about the role of poetry itself are central to the poem's interpretation, for Propertius begins 4.6 by setting the stage for his role as *vates* and he later opens the final part of the poem by proclaiming that Apollo – who was earlier described as appearing at Actium in the guise of the god who rained arrows down on the Greeks in the Trojan War (31–34) – wants his lyre back now that he has been victorious (69).[84] While this preference for his poetic role gives Apollo the appearance of the cult statue described in 2.31, unlike in the earlier poem, Propertius ultimately says very little about the actual temple, so that, by the end, the poet's role in constructing the memory of the battle seems to outweigh Augustus' own monument.

Indeed, the centrality of poetic creation to any understanding of the Roman past and its shaping by the Augustan city seems to echo throughout Book 4. Propertius appropriates the vocabulary of Roman city-building, a prominent theme in Virgil's *Aeneid* as well, when he claims in 4.1 to 'lay down walls' with his own poetry (1a.57); his boast in the same poem that the work 'rises' for Rome also suggests a kind of construction.[85] Viewing Propertius as a kind of architect in language, Welch argues that the poet adopts an adamantly dynamic role in his depiction of Rome, serving not as a passive reporter of contemporary Rome's urban renewal, but rather 'a rival to Augustus in the creation of Rome's urban identity'.[86] Taking Propertius' poetry as a whole, we can witness across his four books, then, the role of the city (as well as the shadow of the world outside) in Propertius' rambunctious, if tortured, pursuit of love and also in his attempt to come to terms with the darker meanings of a world increasingly inscribed by Roman power.

Less than a generation later, Ovid would find his own pleasures in the Augustan city, as well as develop his own, often derisive, treatment of rural landscapes and Rome's legendary past. For Ovid, the dream of the countryside and nostalgic reminiscences about the past Golden Age would become fused into one and treated as the antithesis of both Rome and of his own era.

Ovid: Cultus *and the Augustan City*

Throughout his elegiac poetry, Ovid remains a loyal devotee of the city of Rome and of what Cicero terms in his *De Oratore* 'the scent of urbanity' (3.40.161). In his treatment of pastoral themes, Ovid accordingly adheres to a straightforward premise: the pastoral countryside equals primitivism; thus, time and again Ovid rejects the prevailing attempts to sentimentalize Rome's rural origins. Only once in the *Amores* does Ovid turn to the country-side with any degree of reverence, when he describes a journey together with his wife to Falerii for the festival of Juno (3.13), but this poem is set awkwardly apart from the rest of the work. For one, mention of the poet's own wife (as opposed to someone else's) is rather strange in the context of love poetry. Secondly, this is not an amatory poem, but a poem about sacred Roman festivals, anticipating the future author of the *Fasti* more than the self-proclaimed 'adviser on love'. Indeed, the whole poem projects a sense of the elegiac *ego* gravely misplaced as Ovid dutifully observes the rites and solemnly prays, but seemingly cannot wait to get away. In the following poem, he returns to the urban landscape and his elegiac mistress with great relief, or so it seems.

LEAVING THE PAST BEHIND

Shortly before, in 3.8, Ovid presents his most detailed commentary on the Golden Age in the *Amores*, a discussion closely related to Ovid's general views of the countryside. In this poem Ovid laments that his poetic genius, which used to be valued more than gold, is no longer considered precious (3–4). Later in the poem we find out that Ovid's disappointment has a personal source: his mistress has dumped him for a wealthier man who is also, to add to the offence, a newcomer without any pedigree. The argument of the poem focuses, as Green notes, 'on the charge of feminine gold-digging' and 'bitter reproach for the girls who – whether through avarice or sexual incli-nation – found soldiers attractive as lovers'.[87] In lines 35–44 Ovid launches into somewhat vague praise of Saturn's reign, which he paints as oblivious to precious metals and wealth, giving 'crops without husbandry' (39). But in this evocation of the lost Golden Age, 'Ovid does no more than pay traditional lip-service to a kind of dim mesolithic paradise, the nomadic hunter's world, minus all the back-breaking business associated with farming.'[88]

While contemplating the changed mores of his day, Ovid cannot help but make a dig at Augustus for having his own temple and divine cult

(3.8.52–53) – a far cry from the simplicity of the ancestors. In a society where the ruler verges on treating himself as a god, Ovid seems to ask why his subjects should reject newly found refinement and luxuries in preference of Rome's once humble beginnings. After hinting at the hypocrisy of the *princeps*' public nostalgia for the past (the kind of 'jest' that may have elicited, as we shall see in the next chapter, a belated response from Augustus), Ovid then casts passionate reproaches at the degeneration of human nature: navigation, trade and urban civilization destroy the innocence of the old days as the Romans 'break into the ground for gold instead of crops, the soldiers possess wealth acquired by blood' (53–54).[89] The stern philosophical nature of these reproaches and complaints seems at odds with the framing of the poem, however: namely, the jealousy Ovid's *ego* feels towards his more successful rival. Hence Ovid's longing for the Golden Age or the undisturbed countryside only matters in so far as he 'translates' it into romantic terms, using it in a fairly limited, and so intentionally banal, way. For Ovid, the reign of Saturn and the pre-urban community associated with it represent the time when a cruel object of elegiac passion was not greedy and the poor poet's song sufficed as a gift of love.[90]

The Golden Age and images of rural life are both strongly opposed to Rome in Ovid's work. While Ovid conveys his awareness of the preceding tradition as a way of displaying his impressive erudition, he continually ensures that the reader also understands his complete indifference to, and even rejection of, the Augustan reverence for past values.[91] In the *Ars Amatoria*, such ideas come into even greater focus as Ovid frankly voices his rejection of the rustic past in favour of his own refined age, announcing in Book 3:

> Let the old times delight others. I am thankful that I was born
>> now: this very age suits my tastes
> not because now delicate gold is dug out from the ground,
>> not because chosen shells come to us from different shores,
> not because mountains crumble from all the marble quarried,
>> not because the sky-blue waters are pushed back by large palaces,
> but because now we have refinement and in our lifetime
>> that tasteless crudity of our ancestors is no more.   (*Ars* 3.121–128)

This passage, which emphasizes Ovid's partiality to his own time, demonstrates well his rhetorical artistry, with the last causal explanation ('but because') underscoring all the preceding causal clauses since it cannot occur without those activities, including the mining of gold,[92] a feat also mentioned in *Amores* 3.8. The ethical complications that are the price one pays for *cultus* cause Ovid little concern.

Without the luxury and greed that violate the pristine state of nature there is no *cultus*, a quality that for Ovid represents the most attractive feature of his times, since 'it is both the agent and the outcome of empire',[93] as the lines just before acknowledge:

> Crude simplicity belongs to the past. Rome is golden now
> and possesses the vast riches of the tamed world.
> Look what the Capitol is now and what it used to be.
> You would say that today's sight belonged to a different god.
>
> (*Ars* 3.113–116)

Here, Ovid's elegiac protagonist revels in his civilized age. His ardent preference for the 'golden' Rome of his era clearly showing, the 'different god' referred to in the final line is *cultus* itself, whom 'Ovid here sets up as his own prime divinity'.[94] In this way, Ovid openly takes pride in the imperial economy, the 'vast riches' that caused Propertius such anxiety. Indeed, as the epigraph to our chapter suggests, Ovid earlier implies that the sheer availability of desirable women in Rome evidences the Empire's great bounty.[95]

In the *Medicamina Faciei Femineae*, a poem about 'looking good', Ovid similarly explores female adornment in connection with the wealth of the Empire. Openly mocking the laudation of olden days, Ovid portrays the women of the past as happy with menial tasks and household chores (11–17), underlining their difference from the young girls today, who are delicate and pampered, their clothes refined, their hair perfumed and ears weighed down by exotic gems (17–22). Unlike Propertius, Ovid does not begrudge women their extravagant taste; in fact, he thinks of himself and the men of his circle as equally prone to self-indulgence (24–25). For Ovid, then, the terms *rusticitas* ('country life') and *rusticus* ('country dweller') bear entirely the pejorative connotation of 'unsophisticated'.[96] The *mores maiorum* ('customs of the ancestors') are as anachronistic for Ovid as drinking cheap wine from clay goblets amid pasturing sheep. One might call Ovid's elegy 'sober'[97] or even 'shallow',[98] but his disparagement of rural life must be understood in partnership with the prodigious power he accords Rome throughout his poetry.

ENJOYING ROME

Ovid's *Amores* generally avoids precision in time and space and it has only one poem with a recognizably Roman setting: the circus (*Amores* 3.2). In this poem Ovid describes an outing with his 'new mistress' (57) at the circus during the chariot races. The whole event is treated as foreplay, leading to the winning-over of his new object of affection. While his *puella* cannot take her eyes off the racing chariots, Ovid is equally busy gazing at her, imagining what hidden treasures her summer dress conceals and comparing the challenges of chariot racing with his own amatory task (5 ff.). In all, Ovid's poem celebrates the dynamic competition at the heart of the city, both athletic and erotic. As Ovid's elegy matures from the *Amores* to the *Ars Amatoria*, his landscape becomes unequivocally focused on Rome. In the *Ars*, Ovid explicitly 'advocate[s] the use of Augustan monuments for transgressive sexual practices'.[99]

Ovid's portrayal of the city as a hotbed of erotic pleasure is impressive in its detail and his pride in being able to reimagine Rome in such lascivious terms is obvious, such as when he advises his reader to visit sites like Pompey's shady colonnade, or the colonnade that Octavia built for her dead son Marcellus, or Livia's portico full of old paintings (*Ars* 1.67–74). As we have seen, Pompey's colonnade featured in both Catullus and Propertius, and P.J. Davis suggests that each place listed by Ovid in this passage 'has dynastic associations'.[100] Octavia's portico, for example, was associated with Claudius Marcellus (42–23 BCE), Augustus' heir, who died at the age of nineteen before he could fulfil all the promise invested in him (see also Propertius 3.18). The portico of Livia, Augustus' wife, is also mentioned as a fitting place to pick up girls, a joke perhaps especially piercing given Livia's prominent association with the Augustan moral programme.[101] While each of these landmarks was undoubtedly very familiar to Roman readers, Ovid uses them expressly to shock his public by suggesting they are places for an easy pick-up instead of quiet contemplation and reverence.[102] The list of the sites given here, mostly of recent construction, is repeated at *Ars* 3.389–396 (with the addition of Agrippa's portico of the Argonauts and the theatre of Marcellus), a complementary passage addressed to women who want to hunt for an easy acquaintance in the city.[103]

When advising men on the best places to seduce women, Ovid also makes use of Roman history, interpreting it perversely for his own benefit. Thus, in the first book of his *Ars*, Ovid flippantly recalls the rape of the Sabine women, a story that held great import for the Romans, especially in its links to the Roman institution of marriage.[104] According to the legend, when the first Romans found themselves in need of wives they forcibly took the daughters of their neighbours, the Sabines, after inviting them to attend a theatre performance in Rome. The episode is depicted on the frieze of the Basilica Aemilia, dating to the Augustan era, where Tarpeia's punishment is also portrayed.[105] Augustan writers were quite sensitive to the myriad connotations of the Sabine story. Virgil, for one, dealt with this episode by

5.3 *The Rape of the Sabine Women* (1627–1629) by Pietro da Cortona.

placing more emphasis on the subsequent reconciliation of the Romans and Sabines rather than on the act of rape (*Aeneid* 8.635–641) and Livy, while treating the event in more detail, expressly justified the Romans' actions by placing blame on the girls' parents and their refusal to cooperate with the Romans (1.9).

Ovid, on the other hand, uses the story in a completely inverted way, namely to illustrate the erotic possibilities of the theatre, eagerly exclaiming: 'Romulus, you were the only one who knew how to provide bounty for your soldiers: if you give me these benefits, I will become a soldier' (*Ars* 1.131–132). There is invariably a paradox in Ovid's use of one of 'the most venerable national legends as the origin and authority for the practices of elegant and sophisticated Rome';[106] such grating appropriation perhaps allowed Ovid to disorient the reader or even aggressively parody the Augustan narrative of a more virtuous Roman past by suggesting that the sexual freedom of the present had its origins in the actions of the city's very founder. Ovid might also be drawing a sharp distinction between Rome's uncouth ancestors and their descendants, to whom the refined and elegant poet is trying to teach better manners.[107]

Ovid's mythologizing of Rome, and corresponding de-mythologizing of the rural landscape, brings adamant closure to elegy's multivalent exploration of the *rus/urbs* opposition. Significantly, the ultimate rejection of the *rusticitas* that we see in Ovid is conditioned in part by his predecessors, for already in Virgil's *Eclogues* the idea of the *rus* as an uncomplicated refuge is beginning to fray. Following Virgil's lead, Tibullus and Propertius in their turn re-evaluate the ideals of pastoralism as well as the image of Rome's past, and so enter into complex dialogue with the Augustan era and the *princeps'* attempts to rewrite Rome in both historical and topographic terms.

Ovid would ultimately suffer the most serious consequences for his conversations with Augustan Rome, leading to his forced departure from the city. Despite the drastic changes in his own personal fortunes, Ovid's preference for *cultus* remains nevertheless unaltered in his exilic poetry, as we shall see. Moreover, Rome itself will become Ovid's elusive beloved, the cruel mistress unresponsive to all his pleas to open the locked door – and not, as Martial would have it, a lover ready to give the returning exile thousands of kisses.

VI

LOVE AND EXILE

Finally, I am not the only one to have written about tender love:
but I alone am punished for writing about love.

OVID, *TRISTIA* 2.361–362

IN THE LINES ABOVE, Ovid expresses bitterness that he was seemingly the
first Roman poet punished for writing love poetry. The plight of the exile is,
to say the least, not foreign to contemporary artistic sensibility. If anything,
it strikes a chord with modern readers; especially those of us who have been
displaced or misplaced recognize in Ovid's unceasing pleas the anguished
state of nostalgia that manifests itself in the recurring obsessions, tricks of
memory and physical ailments so vividly and accurately described by him.
In this chapter, we want to trace the development of Latin love poetry to a
perhaps surprising destination: Ovid's writings from exile. These writings
are crucial for any understanding of love poetry, in part because Ovid uses
his exilic work to reflect back on his earlier erotic writing. Even more, Ovid's
exile poetry sheds light on the variability and adaptability of love poetry,
given that it adapts many of love poetry's conventions, including its overall
mood, as an anguished Ovid seeks reconciliation with a city and society
from whose company he has been so dramatically banished.

In the following pages we pursue several goals. While acknowledging a certain degree of futility in determining the precise reasons for Ovid's exile, we would nonetheless like to address this 'non-question that has led to much ingenious but fruitless surmise',[1] especially since love poetry, and more specifically the *Ars Amatoria*, is at the core of most speculations about Ovid's heartbreaking banishment. We therefore offer a reading of the *Ars Amatoria* focusing on what in the entertaining and risqué work might have enraged the man responsible for Ovid's banishment: Augustus. More importantly, we want to explore the continuity between Ovid's love poetry and his exilic work, for even if Ovid's amatory elegiacs were the reason for his exile, he conspicuously adopts the elegiac metre in the *Tristia* and *Epistulae ex Ponto*, and not a more 'serious' metre like hexameter, presumably encouraging his readers to draw connections with his earlier amatory writing. Still, as we shall see, despite their many links, what ultimately emerges from the juxtaposition of Ovid's poems in Tomi and his earlier works is a 'contrast between the artificiality of the world of the *amator* [lover] and too real world of the *exul*'.[2] Finally, we shall discuss the ways in which Ovid takes the opportunity to revisit his own evolving ideas about what it means to be a love poet.

A Poem and a Mistake?

Ovid's exile to Tomi, the modern Romanian city of Constanţa, remains one of the great mysteries of Latin literature. While Ovid tells us that the circumstances of his exile were generally known in Rome (*Tristia* 4.10.99), we have no mention of it in contemporary Roman sources; nor is it mentioned for centuries following his death. The fact that Ovid is the only source for the event has led to considerable difficulty in determining what actually happened (if anything) and why.[3] Since the *ego* of Latin poetry is a sophisticated and often manipulative construct, how reliable can we take Ovid to be in recounting the traumatic events of his own life? We can begin to gauge Ovid's credibility by examining the descriptions he gives of his place of banishment.

In the first book of the *Tristia*, Ovid poignantly recalls the last night he spent in Rome. While recalling tearful goodbyes to his friends and his loyal wife, Ovid reaches the highest pitch in his lament when he exclaims: 'It's Scythia where I'm being sent, it's Rome that must be left behind: each one an excuse for delay' (*Tristia* 1.3.61–62). As this stark contrast indicates, Ovid's repeated longing for his beloved Rome is intertwined in his exilic poetry with frequent characterizations of Tomi as an inhospitable and barbaric landscape, a portrayal most likely influenced by Virgil's description of Scythia in the third *Georgic* (339–383).

Yet Tomi was not some remote savage colony lacking in culture. Located at the tip of a small peninsula seventy miles south of the main Danube delta, in 8 CE it formed part of the still unsettled Roman province of Moesia. Originally a colony of the Greek city Miletus, Tomi was a trading centre, a teeming harbour and a fishery.[4] As various inscriptions demonstrate, it still used Greek at the time of Ovid's exile, and the level of education and literacy in the province, especially among the elite, was much higher than Ovid repeatedly suggests. Even Ovid is forced to admit in one passage that the citizens of Tomi honoured him as a poet and that the Greek-educated provincials were not indifferent to his literary merit (*Ex Ponto* 4.14.55–56). Set against our knowledge of what Tomi was actually like, Ovid's colourful description of its inhabitants as unkempt barbarians wielding poisoned arrows and riding horse carts in unceasing winter terrain seems more a well-worn stereotype than an accurate ethnographic observation.[5]

Such a biased account of Tomi alerts readers to the fact that they should treat with equal scepticism Ovid's identification of the actual reasons for his banishment, especially since he remains rather vague about them. He tells us in the second book of the *Tristia* only that two 'crimes' caused his exile from the city: *carmen et error*, a poem and a mistake (2.207–208). Many generations of scholars have been puzzled by this combination; were both the poem and the mistake equally to blame? Or was one the cause and the other merely a pretext?

What Ovid means by 'mistake', we can only speculate since we know only that he was a witness or enabler of some kind of forbidden activity.[6]

6.1   Created in 1887 by the Italian sculptor Ettore Ferrari
(1845–1929), the statue of the Roman poet Ovidius Publius
Naso is located in the centre of Constanţa, Romania.

Some theories propose a delicate situation in which Augustus or a member
of his family was involved[7] or Ovid's participation in some kind of political
treason[8] or violation of sacred religious rites. One widely accepted view is
that Ovid was somehow involved in the scandalous and illicit affair of Julia
Minor, Augustus' granddaughter, and Decimus Junius Silanus.[9] The extent
of Ovid's participation in the affair is not clear, though. There was no public
prosecution launched against him, and Ovid makes it clear that he was
not condemned by the senate in its judicial capacity but that his fate was

decided unofficially, without a public trial or appearance in court (*Tristia* 2.131–132).[10] While Ovid did not suffer loss of citizenship or property (relegation in Roman law only required exclusion from certain places – in Ovid's case, Rome – and Augustus left his property alone), the fact that the main malefactor in the supposed affair, Silanus, did not suffer any significant punishment beyond Augustus' withdrawal of his friendship seems rather odd. Only a mere witness or marginal participant in any presumed offence, Ovid apparently bore the full brunt of Augustus' anger and was dispatched to the remote part of the Empire.[11]

Still, to take only a 'mistake' as the cause of exile is to imagine Ovid somehow acting against Augustus' interests, a stance that 'would have been pitifully one-sided and perhaps historically inconceivable'.[12] As a young man, Ovid had refused to embark on the *cursus honorum*, the traditional ladder of political offices for members of the aristocracy (*Tristia* 4.10.33–38), and the whole direction of his life clearly shows that he was a man far removed from politics and any tendency towards organized conspiracy.[13] As we mentioned in Chapter 4, the *Ars Amatoria* is the poem Ovid seems to be alluding to as the *carmen* behind his exile.[14] Yet, it is equally hard to discern whether the frivolous *Ars Amatoria* was the main reason for Ovid's downfall.

Thibault asserts that 'Augustus punished Ovid far too severely and much too late, if the *Ars Amatoria* was the real cause of this punishment',[15] but Ovid accuses his enemies in Rome of bringing the unsavoury passages from his poetry to the attention of the enraged *princeps* (*Tristia* 2.77–80). It is also possible that Augustus punished the poet so many years after the poem was written because the so-called mistake 'triggered a long restrained eruption of the emperor's feelings',[16] although Green suggests that the poem may 'have been dragged in (almost ten years after its publication!) to camouflage the real, politically sensitive charge'.[17] In his formative study, Ronald Syme offers perhaps the best solution: the poem and the mistake are 'in a tight nexus. Neither charge was good enough without the other'.[18]

As we discussed in Chapter 1, several moral laws were passed in 18 BCE and the years following; the *Ars Amatoria* could have been seen as an embarrassment for the *princeps* and his attempt at moral reform in light of such legislation. Making matters worse, the *Ars* was published between 1 BCE and 1 CE, right after a scandal that involved Augustus' very own daughter, Julia, who was relegated to the island of Pandataria on charges of adultery involving not one but several aristocratic lovers in 2 BCE.[19] The timing of publication might seem, then, in extremely bad taste.

Debates over Ovid's potential textual transgressions have frequently involved attempts to assess the degree of his so-called 'anti-Augustanism'.[20] As we argued in Chapter 1, however, labels like 'pro-' or 'anti-Augusan' generally do not allow for the range of feeling or nuance that the Augustan era surely evoked from its participants and observers; moreover, as Alessandro Barchiesi points out, we do not really even know 'what it meant to be "against"' in this context.'[21] In Ovid's case, in particular, such an approach defies recognition of the complexity of his poetry at different stages of his career. In assessing Ovid's prospective response to Augustan moral reform, it is also important to remember that Ovid had not lived through the turbulent contexts that produced Augustus' policies and so may have underestimated their importance to the *princeps*. Born in 43 BCE, Ovid was only twelve at the time of the battle of Actium and he never experienced the devastating civil unrest and agonizing fall of the Republic witnessed by the older Augustan poets. He was truly the son of the *pax Augusta* ('Augustan peace') and enjoyed every benefit brought by Rome's growing empire. Generally speaking, 'Ovid represents not so much the opposite of Augustan culture as its fullest flowering.'[22]

In 8 CE, furthermore, the year of his relegation, Ovid was Rome's most distinguished poet, one who had produced several books of erotic elegy, a tragedy, an epic and an unfinished poem on the Roman calendar. Virgil and Horace were dead and Ovid's poetic achievement stood out as extensive and impressive. As Thomas Habinek aptly observes, 'the political commitments of Ovid's poetry differ from those of his predecessors (and successors), but they are no less complex and consequential.'[23] In many ways, Ovid seems to serve as the voice of his generation, of the sophisticated and fashionable Roman upper-class youth, both men and women, and his unabashed endorsement of an upper class engaging, on the face of it, in free-wheeling extra-marital affairs seems to reflect well the image of the times.[24]

Moreover, in playfully advocating a life far removed from Augustan moral standards, it could not have escaped Ovid's attention that Augustus himself was not exactly adhering to his precepts in his own private life. Augustus, after all, had divorced his first wife, Scribonia, and forced Tiberius Claudius Nero to yield to him his then six-months-pregnant wife, Livia. In Book 2 of his *Tristia*, Ovid even hints at those embarrassing circumstances when trying to justify his own indiscretions (2.161–165). Augustus' affair with Terentia, the wife of his close friend and adviser, Maecenas, was also no secret.[25] How sanguine Augustus would have been about criticism of his policies or allusions to his own hypocrisy, even if done in jest, is a crucial question. It is true that early in his career Augustus had enthusiastically participated in the ribald arena of political discourse we saw presented in Catullus' poetry. But, over time, the *princeps* increasingly 'withdrew from the sort of competitive accusations of immorality which had characterized political disputes under the republic'.[26] By setting himself apart, Augustus seemingly drew a line between himself and other public figures in Rome, one bolstered by his relentless consolidation of power; it is that line Ovid may very well have crossed.[27]

Ovid's Roman audience – Augustus among them – would surely have been familiar with the love poets' longstanding indifference to the institution of marriage and growing demands for procreation. That attitude might have frustrated Augustus, but he had been familiar with the genre since Cornelius Gallus and did not seem to have had any difficulty with Propertius or Tibullus, or even with Ovid's *Amores*, in which the poet had notably 'presented himself as a flagrant adulterer [...] and in terms which explicitly recalled provisions of the *Julian Law on Suppressions of Adultery*' (e.g. 2.19 and 3.4).[28] In that respect, the *Ars Amatoria* added nothing new to the *Amores*.[29] In all, Ovid's own poetry is our only evidence for how Augustus read the *Ars Amatoria* and why it became 'the art of making oneself hated'.[30]

A careful reading of Ovid's exilic poetry supports the general view that Ovid's feelings towards Augustus involve 'a severe internal conflict that could not help manifesting itself in his poetry'.[31] But before we turn more fully to these later writings from Tomi, we want to take a closer look at the actual text of the *Ars Amatoria* to figure out what sorts of attacks Augustus might have perceived in the work.[32]

The Art of Provocation?

Looking at the poem's form, Miller argues that the *Ars Amatoria* 'must have been particularly galling to Augustus since it adopted the pose of didactic poetry. Certainly, the position of *praeceptor amoris* ['adviser on love'] was a common trope in elegy, but it had never been developed in this kind of systematic fashion.'[33] In the work, the persona of the 'adviser' replaces the traditional *ego* of love poetry as Ovid makes his agenda clear from the outset: 'If anyone among the Roman people lack knowledge in matters of love, let him read this and let him love after he is educated reading my verse' (*Ars* 1.1–3). Ovid remains true to this initial promise throughout, and his advice on how to seduce appears in considerable detail, ranging from specific locations to matters of sexual technique.

One of the ideal circumstances for seduction, according to Ovid, is the military triumph, which we discussed in Chapter 5. Here Ovid's account starts with an inspired panegyric to Roman conquest in all parts of the world, as well as to Caesar Augustus himself (*Ars* 1.177–214); eventually, the scenario dissolves into advice on how to become acquainted with a girl who also happens to be present (1.215–228): 'Answer all her questions [...] pretend you know even when you don't' (1.221–222). Any initial pride in the display of Roman military prowess thus turns into a dismissive gaze at the passing spectacle, the whole purpose of which becomes the seduction of a fellow spectator. In a similar way, Ovid appropriates the popular trope of *militia amoris*, comparing the self-indulgent pursuit of erotic pleasure to service in the Roman military. He names the hardships in both pursuits: inclement weather, endless journeys, painful wounds and the requisite sleeping in the open air (2.233–238).

In prescribing methods of seduction, Ovid promotes several questionable techniques: the use of excessive drinking to boost self-confidence (1.237–240); the befriending of the girl's maid (1.351–354); the employment of excessive flattery and promises (1.619–620 and 1.631); even the use of excessive force (1.673–680). The final example is one of many that have led Lowell Bowditch to conclude that 'for all its urbane wit, there is something chilling, even monstrous about the *Ars*.[34] Ovid's mocking rendition of Romulus' arrangement of the first Roman marriages through the kidnapping and rape of the Sabine women also renders the pursuit of love in a way that is unsettling for a modern reader. As far as Ovid's contemporaries were concerned, such irreverent treatment of sensitive issues could have been read as critique of Augustan attempts to control marriage.[35]

Advice, however questionable, on the seduction of girls in Book 1 evolves in Book 2 into advice on how to keep that captured prey. What emerges clearly from this book is that Ovid is not talking about courtship that leads to marriage. In fact, throughout the poem he makes several references to Augustan marriage laws, showing his keen awareness of the ongoing legislative efforts, at times apparently mocking them. Already at the start of Book 1, Ovid makes it a point to clarify that he sings of 'safe Venus' and that 'there will be no cause for indictment in my poem' (33–34). The Latin word he uses in these lines for 'indictment' is *crimen* (literally 'crime'), an important detail given later events. These cautionary lines display Ovid's knowledge of the laws' provisions and we find the same disclaimer in Book 2, where the 'adviser on love' reminds his readers again about his moral infallibility: 'there is no play going on here except what is allowed by the law' (599–600). Ovid's 'adviser' clearly understands the difference between the relationship of a husband and wife and the love that he urges his 'pupils' to pursue. In the same book, the 'adviser' draws a sharp distinction between the legal joining of a man and a woman (which obliges people to 'come to a single bed') and love that is 'substituted in place of the law' (which presumes the free choice of a partner, unrestrained by any legal or social constraints) (153–158).

These sorts of disclaimers intensify in Book 3, which is addressed to women. Ovid's 'adviser' writes at the end of the proem to this book that 'nothing except wanton love is learned from me' (27); he then returns to the issue again thirty lines later: 'girls, whom modesty and the laws and their own rights allow, seek advice here' (57–58). In this way, Ovid goes to considerable length to make sure that he does not promote adultery and that his advice is not directed at respectable Roman matrons (3.483–484 and 3.611–616). Previously, in Book 1 of the *Ars*, Ovid makes the same distinction, urging married women 'who wear hairbands and those whose hem covers their ankles' to stay away (31–34), a sentiment he desperately repeats in *Tristia* 2.247–250.

The obvious question, then, is what kind of women were excluded from Augustus' legislation and thus considered fair game for Ovid's advice? It is again among Ovid's disclaimers in Book 3 that we learn more precisely about this presumed class of women:[36]

> Let the bride be afraid of her husband: let the guarding of the bride be planned;
>> this is appropriate, the laws and the ruler and modesty command.
> But that you should be watched, whom ceremony just released,
>> who could handle that? (*Ars* 3.613–616)

The language of these lines is a bit opaque, but it suggests that while married women must obey the laws, freedwomen, that is, ex-slaves freed by the ceremony of manumission, are exempt from it.[37] These, then, are presumably the kinds of women who are able to follow Ovid's advice for illicit affairs. But is Ovid really being as careful as he seems?

Several scholars have argued that Ovid constructs a consciously mixed female addressee: someone between a proper Roman *matrona*, accepted and respected by society, and a frivolous, venal good time girl or *meretrix*, a type of a girl perpetuated and enshrined in Roman elegiac discourse.[38] Moreover, despite Ovid's claims to stick to the letter of the law, the laws themselves failed to specify which types of woman were subject to their provisions and which were exempt.[39] Nor is Ovid consistent in avoiding the promotion of adultery. Time and again he slips; in one passage he advises his reader to pursue 'secret Venus' (*Ars* 1.275) and in another to seek out a 'secret affair' (2.730), *furtivus* or 'secret' in both passages carrying connotations of adultery rather than free love. Elsewhere, in Book 1, he advises an eager lover to befriend his mistress's husband (1.579); on another occasion he proposes that the lover should stealthily approach his girlfriend's litter and speak in riddles to avoid any detection of the affair (1.488–490).

Book 3 is perhaps the most explicit of all three in its decisive rejection of traditional values, as Ovid reminds his readers that they must play around and enjoy their youth while it lasts (*Ars* 3.61), that frequent childbirth damages their looks and ages their body (3.81–82), and that there is nothing wrong with artificial adornment and finery when one tries the art of seduction (3.13 ff., and *passim*). Extending this idea of 'finery', Ovid is once again most impassioned when singing the praises of contemporary Rome and its *cultus*, proclaiming 'crude simplicity' a thing of the past and refinement the rule of the day (3.121–128).[40] He teaches Roman ladies how to dress and walk and which positions to assume during sex, likewise how to educate themselves, refining both their conversation and their minds.

The *Ars Amatoria* is unique in its structure, addressing both men and women in turn, thus seemingly involving both parties equally in the pursuit of love. However, some scholars have argued that Ovid draws the traditional cultural distinction between 'active' male and 'passive' female roles in his didactic poem. While Ovid demonstrates the progress of men's sexual journey from the public sphere at the beginning of Book 1 to the privacy of the girl's bedroom at the end of Book 2, Book 3 starts and ends its instruction in the girl's bedroom, thus relegating the women completely to the private sphere.[41] The attention that Ovid pays in Book 3 to women's appearance and comportment is also striking when compared to the emphasis he places on shaping men's more active modes of behaviour, only perfunctorily urging that men stay clean and shaved.

More fundamentally, it has been argued that the self-proclaimed 'adviser on love' is 'essentially hostile towards real women, whom he regards as savage, offensive and physically flawed', and that he aims 'to make [them] more amenable to the male audience by replacing the natural with the artificial'.[42] As Eric Downing phrases it, 'women are shaped to the literary parts needed by men to play at and succeed at their literary game'.[43] It also appears that the intended audience of Ovid's advice in Book 3 is not always exclusively female. Occasionally Ovid distances himself from his female readership and delivers his teachings from the male perspective, suggesting that there is an implied male audience for whom the advice he gives to women may be useful as well.[44]

Taken together, the three books of the *Ars Amatoria* show us an Ovid who light-heartedly mocks the moral aspirations of Augustus, takes militarism as a metaphor for sexual pursuit and conquest, treats Roman spectacles and Roman law as sources of amusement and opportunities for seduction, and brands the Augustan emphasis on marriage and family values boring and unworthy of the lifestyle to which his generation has grown accustomed. Earlier classical scholarship saw Ovid's *Ars Amatoria* as a prolonged elaboration on the sentiment expressed at *Ars* 3.121–128, a passage discussed in the last chapter: Rome is indeed 'golden' now and 'Ovid is delighted to be a citizen of modern Rome because it offers the proper sort of refined *cultus*. Immorality is irrelevant compared to inelegance.'[45] But a number of more recent studies 'have refashioned Ovid into a poet whose humour, instead of glorifying the erotic world of Rome, condemns it'.[46] Even if Ovid's work fits better into this latter reading, it is hard to believe he stood alone in his refusal to return to the crude habits and primitive outlook of the Republican forefathers. Rather it seems more likely that he expressed sentiments common to his generation, yet perhaps underestimated the seriousness of Augustus' attempts to turn back the clock and so change the habits of the young Roman *beau monde*.

In his exilic poetry, Ovid repeatedly reflects on the nature of his sins and singles out the *Ars Amatoria* as his unintentional literary trespass, expressing regret that he ever wrote such a poem and confessing that he both condemns and hates it (*Tristia* 3.1.8). In exile, Ovid's elegiac voice thus changes, becomes somber. However, as Miller points out, 'the exilic poetry does not abandon the subject position of amatory elegy but recasts it.'[47]

Exile Poetry as Love Poetry

Ovid's exile poetry is seen by most of its readers as tedious and monotonous, 'a dreary epilogue to a brilliant career'.[48] The first work composed in exile, the *Tristia*, consists of five books of poems united by a single theme: lament over the exiled poet's desperate condition. These poems were primarily intended as an apology to the angry *princeps*, an attempt on Ovid's part to soften Augustus' alleged anger. Across the five books of the *Tristia*, we see the evolution of the poet as he adapts to his new status as exile and, as the years pass by, increasingly recognizes the impossibility of his return. Book 1, ostensibly written onboard ship,[49] was sent to Rome as early as the autumn of 9 CE – right after Ovid arrived at Tomi – and it depicts Ovid as a man completely shaken by his fate but still confident that the situation can be rectified. After a heartbreaking account of Ovid's last night in Rome (1.3), we are invited to share with the poet the vicissitudes of his journey into exile and his supposedly private appeals to both his loyal friends (1.8) and his faithful and much-suffering wife (1.6).

While the first book of the *Tristia* is unquestionably bitter, it still contains traces of Ovid's former acerbic wit and irony. Book 2 of the *Tristia*, however, changes tone to a certain degree and is addressed to Augustus as a single book-length poem combining self-justification with an appeal for mercy. Ovid's frustration pokes through in many allusions to Augustus, such as when he compares Augustus to a 'vengeful and arbitrary avatar of Jupiter', one who randomly hurls thunderbolts against his enemies.[50] But praise for Augustus is also present; he is called 'merciful Caesar' (2.27), and his anger is even called 'just' as Ovid thanks Augustus for sparing his life and his property (2.129–130).

Book 3, in turn, chronicles Ovid's first year in Tomi with an emphasis on his sickness at heart, a condition that manifests itself in his declining physical health (3.1.1, 8.23–34), which would from then on become the main rationale in arguing for commuting his place of exile (8.37–42). It is also in Book 3 that we first encounter numerous descriptions of Ovid's place of exile as a joyless, cold, barbaric terrain. As Ovid's hopes of return were increasingly abandoned, especially by Book 5 (5.2.77–78, 10.49–50), they were notably replaced by an insistence on maintaining continuous and prolific correspondence with those left in Rome through the verse-letters of *Epistulae ex Ponto*, a work started by Ovid in 12 CE that was carefully planned and designed for public consumption.

The addressees of *Epistulae ex Ponto* were carefully chosen, ranging from Brutus (Ovid's literary representative in Rome), Fabius Maximus and Cotta Maximus (the patrons with whom the poet connected his hopes of return) to Ovid's wife and various other men of letters.[51] The poems in this collection repeat the worn-out themes of the *Tristia*: bitterness, complaints about

Ovid's deteriorating health, frustration at the persistent silence from Rome and pleas for transfer combined with flattery of the *princeps*. While the subjects of these poems are not particularly new there is nonetheless a new sense of distance from the trauma of exile, with Ovid at times even engaging in a kind of self-parody. He muses at one point, for example: 'If anyone had told me: "You'll end up by the Euxine [Black Sea] scared of being hit by an arrow from some native's bow," my reply would have been, "Have a purge, your brain needs cleansing"' (*Ex Ponto* 4.3.51–53). Even if Ovid remained hopeful about his return to Rome until his death, *Epistulae ex Ponto* projects an acceptance of grim finality, a feeling especially evident in 3.7, when the poet addresses his remaining friends. As if fully acknowledging for the first time that his death will occur far away from his beloved city, Ovid writes: 'I have come to the Getic land: then let me die here, let my misfortunes end their course as they began!' (19–20).

Ovid's exilic poetry was a radical new departure from the elegiac tradition and it 'stands alone in classical Roman literature as an unprecedented meditation on the state of exile itself, on the psychological pressures bearing upon an individual isolated from the native land, the family, friends and the literary culture which define his entire being'.[52] At the same time, it is deeply connected to earlier Latin love poetry; in many ways, 'the exile poetry is the final and most spectacular twist to elegiac love'.[53] Indeed, it is remarkable how skilfully Ovid adapted the elegiac conventions to his new circumstances. The autobiographical mode of the *Amores* combined with the epistolary techniques created in the *Heroides* helped give the exilic poetry a new direction and voice.[54]

Patrcia Rosenmeyer proposes that Ovid's choice of the letter form for his exile poetry must be interpreted as 'an authorial statement of identification – on some level – with his earlier epistolary work, the *Heroides*', and that he sees himself as an 'abandoned hero of sorts'.[55] The *Heroides* and exilic poems share the themes of abandonment and loneliness; several of Ovid's former heroines re-emerge in his exilic poetry, including Medea, who is also the heroine of Ovid's lost tragedy (*Tristia* 3.9.15).[56] The epistolary format is itself key in situating both texts as conversations with absent friends and lovers and such dialogue 'is perhaps the single most important exilic form' in which the 'personality or reaction of the addressee, whether "real" or "imagined", is almost as important as that of the exile'.[57]

Interestingly enough, in Ovid's exilic poetry it is not his wife – whom he mentions often and with gratitude (*Tristia* 1.2.37, 1.3.16–17, 1.6.3) – who becomes 'his desperate, unrequited, and ultimate love'.[58] Rather, as Lyne phrases it, 'Ovid revives the techniques of the amatory mode when framing his suit to Augustus and his longing for Rome.'[59] In portraying himself as a kind of forlorn lover, then, Ovid transfers *ego*'s longing for the resistant *puella* to Augustus or, more often, to Rome itself in a cruel re-enactment of the stock *paraclausithyron* of earlier love poetry. In the very first poem of the *Tristia*, acknowledging the differences between his poetry's potential entry to Rome and his own exclusion, Ovid ruefully laments: 'Little book – I do not begrudge it to you – you are off to the city without me, going where your only creator is banned!' (*Tristia* 1.1.1–2). Rome anchors Ovid's elegiac poetry, but this time it functions as a site of melancholy rather than possibility since it necessarily reiterates Ovid's loss; in one passage, the poet agonizes: 'Rome and home haunt me. All the places I know and long for. Whatever of me is left in the city, I have lost' (*Tristia* 3.2.21–22).

In *Epistulae ex Ponto*, Ovid even returns in his imagination to specific Roman sites; we see once again his attachment to – and knowledge of – various Roman monuments, although such structures now testify to the poet's palpable longing for Rome rather than the 'urban erotics'[60] of his *Ars Amatoria*:

> I return to the sites of the beautiful city
> > and my mind sees all of them with its eyes.
> Now the forums, the temples, the theatres clad in marble,
> > now the paved porticoes float over me.   (*Ex Ponto* 1.8.33–36)

A.J. Boyle explains: 'As the lover defined himself by his relationship to his inaccessible mistress, so the poet defines himself by his relationship to the inaccessible monuments of Rome.'[61] Eventually, as if an elegiac lover giving up on his fickle *domina*, Ovid gives up on Rome, proclaiming that he is ready to 'face death here, by the shores of the Black Sea' (*Ex Ponto* 1.7.40).

Tomi accomplished Augustus' goal of cutting Ovid off from Rome and the wider landscape of Greco-Roman culture, not to mention from the free-spirited ultra-sophisticated aristocracy whose mouthpiece the poet had become. Exile deprived Ovid of his former audience, one that was both appreciative and highly attuned to poetry, not to mention literate in Latin. Indeed, Ovid bitterly claims that the barbaric language is invading his mind and preventing him from writing, forcing him to communicate only by gestures.[62] He laments that 'I'm the barbarian here, understood by nobody' (*Tristia* 5.10.37) and later that 'writing a poem you can read to no one is like dancing in the dark' (*Ex Ponto* 4.2.33–34). Rome's greatest living poet has seemingly lost his most sympathetic audience and so also his very identity.

Ovid returns elegy to its long forgotten origins in lamentation, noting that 'a dirge best fits a living death' (*Tristia* 5.1.47–48). In a letter addressed to his wife, Ovid even anticipates his imminent demise (*Tristia* 3.3.29–32) and writes his own epitaph:

> I who lie here, sweet Ovid, poet of tender passions,
>> became a victim of my own sharp wit.
> Passer-by, if you have ever been in love, do not begrudge me
>> the traditional prayer: 'May Ovid's bones lie soft!'   (*Tristia* 3.3.73–76)

It is significant that even in the lines Ovid envisions written on his tombstone, he wants to be remembered as a love poet. Ovid even uses a very specific word for 'soft' in the last line – the adverb *molliter* derived from the adjective *mollis*, a term associated with both writing about love and a 'failure' of masculinity. The audience that Ovid intends to capture with this epitaph, moreover, is not just any passer-by but a lover, someone who would have undoubtedly been familiar with Ovid's erotic outpourings and advice. The irony of this epitaph is nicely reminiscent of the pre-exile Ovid: the poet admits that his poetic talent has caused his downfall but nonetheless he does not shy away from linking his literary identity directly to the genre that caused his downfall.

The Poet in Exile

The first two books of the *Tristia* ultimately fell on deaf ears and Ovid's hopes of reprieve faded as the years went by. In Book 3, Ovid visibly shifts his focus from the misery of exile to the immortality of his poetic achievement, a sentiment provocatively expressed in poem 3.7 when he proclaims: 'there is nothing we own that isn't mortal save talent, the spark in the mind [...] my talent remains my joy, my constant companion: over *this*, Caesar could have no powers' (43–44, 47–48). Perhaps consciously echoing Propertius' pronouncement that while Augustus has greatness in war, he does not control love (2.7.5–6), Ovid's claim to immortality here becomes an important declaration of the limits of the regime that so recklessly did away with its greatest living poet.

The exile poems vacillate between Ovid's defence of poetry as a worthy occupation and his insecurity about the relevance of his Muse. As Ovid begins to aspire 'to new, more rueful, forms of canonicity',[63] he simultaneously begins to negate his poetic talent. In one poem, he declares that his misfortunes can fill the whole *Iliad* (*Ex Ponto* 2.7.34), but in another claims that his talent is wasted because of disuse (*Tristia* 5.12.21–22), that his sorrows weigh him down so much that he no longer seeks poetic glory (37–44), and that his devotion to the Muses caused his unfortunate exile (45–50). Yet Ovid also expresses fondness and gratitude to his Muse:

> Muse, thank you: for you offer solace,
>> you come as rest from my sorrow and as medicine.
> You are my leader and companion; you take me away from Ister
>> and give me a place in the middle of Mount Helicon.
>
> (*Tristia* 4.10.117–120)

While these lines offer some closure perhaps to Ovid's doubts about his worthiness as a poet, it is also important to note that he praises his Muse for being able to transport him to a site of supreme poetic inspiration, one linked to the Greek epic poet Hesiod and also claimed by Propertius in 3.3.

Heartbroken over his banishment from Rome, Ovid still uses his unfortunate situation to crystallize his position in the Greek and Roman literary canon. As a result, the exilic poetry contains Ovid's most extensive survey of Greek and Latin poetry (*Tristia* 2), a poetic autobiography (*Tristia* 4.10) and a catalogue of contemporary poets (*Ex Ponto* 4.16), the two former of which we examined in Chapter 4. Especially notable for the current discussion is the fact that, as Ovid positions himself among the Roman elegists specifically, he reminds his audience that Gallus also suffered a precipitous downfall, but he is hasty to point out that Gallus was not punished for writing poetry but rather for his 'indiscreet talk' (2.445–446).

Ovid's overall point in composing these elaborate lists is to show 'that his oeuvre lies entirely within the boundaries set by seven centuries of tradition'[64] and that Augustus chose to read and censure the *Ars Amatoria* in a way not intended by the author. The crucial discussion of literary genealogy in *Tristia* 2 – one that casts previous literary classics in a consistently erotic light – culminates when Ovid finally reaches the *Aeneid*, a work endorsed and admired by the *princeps* himself. However, Ovid takes a very distinct approach in his characterization of the Roman epic, highlighting the popularity of Aeneas' sojourn with the Carthaginian queen, Dido:

> Even the lucky author of your *Aeneid* has brought
> arms and the man onto Carthaginian couches –
> no other part of the whole work is more widely read
> than a story of forbidden love...   (*Tristia* 2.533–536)

Barchiesi observes that the reference to the *Aeneid* in this passage 'is an implicit statement that Ovid has prostituted and abused his talent in the useless and wanton erotic lesson of *Ars Amatoria* – unless the comparison between the two poems shows itself capable of reversal'.[65] And the 'reversal' of both Augustus' perception of the *Ars Amatoria* and, consequently, his own fortune is exactly what Ovid aims for in these lines.

Despite Ovid's frequent assertions that his poetry is deteriorating, then, 'the fact remains that [Ovid's] writing shows no real signs of deterioration from its pre-exilic standard.'[66] By making such claims Ovid clearly seeks to elicit sympathy from his readers, especially those in Rome. Yet an interesting claim about the continuing vitality of Ovid's Muse is made in *Epistulae ex Ponto* when Ovid announces that he has recited a poem on the apotheosis of Augustus, in the Getic language using Latin metre, to an eager and apparently now-civilized local audience (*Ex Ponto* 4.13.17 ff.). There is no other evidence for the existence of such a poem and elsewhere Ovid repeatedly expresses contempt for the Getic language, especially as far as his Roman audience was concerned (*Tristia* 5.2.67, 5.7.17, 5.12.55). What should we make then of these contradictory statements?

Ovid's claim about composing poetry in Getic and fully mastering that language along with 'Sarmatian' (*Tristia* 5.7.56, 5.12.58; *Ex Ponto* 3.2.40), even if only mere fantasy, opens several new avenues in the genre of love poetry: first, elegy becomes radically 'cross-cultural' because such a claim reaffirms Ovid's standing as a poet in any land and in any language; secondly it celebrates something completely different from love, the longevity and sturdiness of poetic talent; and, thirdly, it marks a Latin poet's discovery of potential audiences other than a Roman one.[67] The last factor is perhaps especially important: previously Rome-focused – even Rome-obsessed – Ovid seems to be developing broader horizons over which no single ruler or regime can claim control.

The closing poem of *Epistulae ex Ponto* (4.16), an autobiographical epitaph of sorts, presents the summit of Ovid's claim to literary immortality. 'No talent is hurt by death' (2–3), Ovid pronounces at the beginning of the poem; he then delivers a catalogue of contemporary Roman poets, poets with whom Ovid compares himself (5–46). Among them are some, such as Varius Rufus, who were indeed rated highly by their contemporaries. But Ovid concludes triumphantly: 'If it is seemly to say so, my talent was distinguished, and among all that competition, I was fit to be read' (45–46). Even in this last stroke of his poetic pen, then, Ovid unintentionally delivers 'a really lethal literary joke, one that only time could – and did – validate'.[68] For none of the literary competition so meticulously and earnestly alluded to by Ovid in this poem survived the ruthless selection of time.

Ovid, on the other hand, achieved posthumous fame and an influence on later writers comparable only to that of the great Virgil himself. In peculiar fashion, the posthumous fame of these two great Roman poets seems to alternate. Robert Graves observes that 'whenever a golden age of stable government, full churches, and expanding wealth dawns among the Western nations, Virgil always returns to supreme favor'.[69] Conversely, as Theodore Ziolkowski points out, the popularity of Ovid re-emerges 'in times of cultural and political upheaval' because Ovid became largely recognized as the 'ur-exile' and his works 'exemplify change and metamorphosis'.[70] Indeed, as we shall now see in turning to our final chapter, Ovid would come to have a special place in the imagination of poets of later eras; his lament would spread and be emulated from England to Italy, from France to Russia, and his presence evoked in modern Romania with a tenderness and sensitivity Ovid refused to grant to the inhabitants of that region when he lived there.

VII

DEATH AND AFTERLIFE

Death does not end everything.

PROPERTIUS 4.7.1

WITH OVID, the brilliant and exuberant genre of Roman amatory elegy came to an end, although elegy would resurface as a major literary form in many national contexts over the centuries,[1] often returning to its original roots in mourning, a function preserved in poems like Catullus' address to his deceased brother (poem 101) and Ovid's account of Tibullus' death (*Amores* 3.9). In this chapter, we would like to survey the 'afterlife' of Latin love poetry; more strictly defined, our approach shall consider two related aspects: first, how people in later centuries came to know the Latin love poets and, second, how later authors entered into conversation with these authors in terms shaped by their own literary and historical contexts.

Examination of the transmission and dissemination of classical culture belonged for many years to the field of scholarship known as 'the classical tradition' and scholars employed terms such as 'legacy', 'influence' and 'literary canon' in documenting antiquity's continuing reach.[2] In recent years, though, the notion of a static 'classical tradition' has been supplanted by the concept of 'reception', which better conveys the dynamics involved in the appropriation of, and often resistance to, this tradition.[3] Reception thus denotes not rigid imitation of classical culture, but rather vigorous conversations that entail conflict with, and even transformation of, classical texts and ideas. We shall explore a number of sites of reception in the second part of our chapter, but first we begin with narrower concern: how the work of the Latin love poets survived into modern times.

Outlasting the Ravages of Time

Any tracing of the transmission of the love poets begins with a simple question: how did ancient audiences themselves gain access to such poetry? Generally speaking, scholars believe that earlier Greek lyric poetry was performed orally and often in relation to specific occasions or settings.[4] With the rise of written culture across the Greek period, scholars and writers of the later Hellenistic era, especially in Alexandria, became much more visibly engaged with written texts.[5] Later, the Romans relied on the Greek texts transmitted by the Alexandrians, as well as Alexandrian literature itself, as we saw in Chapter 1. Although Latin literature could be performed orally,[6] Roman audiences presumably also involved readers,[7] but it is difficult to determine whether certain types of poetry were passed among limited social or literary communities (e.g. Catullus and his friends) or were made more widely available; perhaps both.[8] Rates of literacy, of course, help determine potential audience size, and, by one estimate, less than fifteen per cent of the population in Italy was literate around the first century BCE, although there was, as in most historical periods, a distinct bias towards literacy among the upper classes.[9]

We can witness the continuing resonance of Latin love poetry in the works of later Roman writers. Martial, active towards the end of the first century CE, as we have seen, credits Cynthia and Corinna with giving their respective authors their poetic abilities (see Chapter 4),[10] and he would enter into even more enthusiastic dialogue with Catullus, emulating the style of Catullus' shorter epigrams and also playfully adapting Catullan obscenity. Already in Martial, we see the treatment of Catullus' infamous sparrow as a phallic symbol.[11] Writers such as Quintilian and Apuleius were also central in transmitting certain ideas about love poetry – providing, for example, the alleged 'real' names of the *puellae* – and we can similarly discern the abiding popularity of certain authors from references to their work in graffiti at Pompeii.[12] Later, Propertius' influence in particular extended to poets of late antiquity such as Ausonius (*c.*310–*c.*394 CE) and Claudian (*c.*370–*c.*404 CE).[13]

We can also examine the legacy of ancient writers through their extant manuscripts, that is, through the copies of their work that have survived over the centuries. Ancient 'books' were initially made of rolls of papyrus, although, by the fourth century, scrolls had given way to the 'codex', which consisted of sheets of parchment bound together at the left side like a modern book. Like scrolls, codices relied on the skill of their copyists and at times contained only rudimentary punctuation or barely legible handwriting, serious limitations that lasted up until the invention of the printing press in 1440. A countless number of scrolls and codices has been lost over time. The texts that do survive are thus in many ways exceptional and have depended for their survival on both luck and human selection – in the latter case, choices circumscribed by the interests and needs of various communities, not least, in early periods, those of monasteries.[14] Modern scholars have aimed at a more detailed study of the manuscript tradition than was possible in earlier periods, seeking to ascertain, for example, the relationship between the surviving manuscripts of an individual author, including which manuscripts derive from which, while also ideally establishing the oldest possible version of an author's text (a version that may itself no longer exist) called an 'archetype'.[15]

There is evidence that many classical authors were still in circulation in the early sixth century CE. During the so-called 'Dark Ages' (*c.*550–*c.*750 CE), however, the copying of classical texts was severely limited and 'the continuity of pagan culture came close to being severed'.[16] It would take the Renaissance, lasting approximately from the fourteenth to the seventeenth century, to initiate a major renewal of interest in classical antiquity.[17] Renaissance engagement with classical texts involved not only the enthusiastic promotion of classical learning, but also greater circulation and study of the surviving manuscripts themselves, as scholars sought to correct the significant errors that had already crept into the manuscript tradition. While some corruptions were fairly easy to rectify (e.g. spelling mistakes), other problems are, and continue to be, more difficult to identify and resolve (such as the omission of a word or line), requiring conjecture about the original text. Notably, some ancient authors suffer from a more corrupt manuscript tradition than others, leading to varying disputes over the best way to restore an author's original text.[18]

In the following pages, we want to trace in brief the manuscript tradition of each of our poets: that is, how each survived into the modern era.

CATULLUS

Perhaps the most dramatic part of Catullus' transmission is how close it came to not happening: his work survives through the Middle Ages by only a single manuscript. Julia Haig Gaisser suggests that Catullus' popularity had already declined precipitously by the start of the third century CE due in part to the image of his work promoted by writers like Martial, a style that soon fell out of fashion.[19] Even at Catullus' re-emergence in the Renaissance, Martial, whose work was then more widely known, continued to serve as an important aide in interpreting Catullus.[20] For over a thousand years, Catullus' poetry was seemingly lost with the exception of one poem (62), which was included in a ninth-century anthology from Tours, France. The dramatic rediscovery of Catullus' entire work (such as survives) is attested in an epigram written in the early fourteenth century, an epigram whose precise meaning is difficult to interpret, although it apparently celebrates the return of a manuscript of Catullus to his home city of Verona.[21] Although it has itself since been lost, this manuscript, called 'V' for Verona, was subsequently copied, and it provides the foundation for all extant copies of Catullus' work.

As we mentioned in Chapter 1, it is unlikely that Catullus' manuscript tradition preserves the collection as he intended or even organized it. Already in the second century CE, Aulus Gellius was weighing variant versions of Catullus' text,[22] and the descendants of V suggest that Catullus' work continued to acquire serious corruptions across the centuries.[23] The first print edition of Catullus was produced in Verona in 1472, an edition that also featured Tibullus, Propertius and Statius' *Silvae*.[24] While this edition would help increase Catullus' popularity, it did not resolve the myriad textual problems now associated with his work. In the modern era, textual critics have generally disparaged earlier attempts beginning with the Italians to 'correct' Catullus' text. Still, despite their own attempts to remedy the situation, 'the text of Catullus remains a work in progress, 700 years after its resurrection and repatriation.'[25]

TIBULLUS

We touched on the manuscript tradition of Tibullus in earlier chapters, especially with regard to the controversy surrounding the authenticity of the Sulpicia poems. Since Tibullus' surviving manuscripts are so limited in number, scholars have sought other sources in which poetry attributed to Tibullus appears. One of these sources is the so-called medieval *florilegia* (literally 'collection of flowers'), or poetic anthologies, which provide some aid in establishing the original texts of many ancient authors. In the case of Tibullus, these anthologies are especially helpful since they antedate both of our existing manuscripts by one to three centuries. The first of the two extant anthologies belongs to an early eleventh-century manuscript from Freising and 'gives the impression of being a school reader'.[26] In his comprehensive analysis of both *florilegia*, Francis Newton concludes that the selections contained in the first collection 'so far as we can determine, represent faithfully the text and orthography of the complete Tibullus from which they are ultimately derived'.[27] The second anthology containing excerpts of Tibullus is found in Venice also in a manuscript of the eleventh century. These fragmentary excerpts offer some help in reconstructing Tibullus' text, but they are never longer than a single line.

PROPERTIUS

The manuscripts of Propertius are notoriously problematic; like Catullus, Propertius survived the Middle Ages by only a single copy. Although he disappears from view for centuries, Propertius was clearly known to intellectuals in the Loire Valley in the twelfth century.[28] His oldest surviving manuscript, N, was produced sometime around 1200 CE in northern France, and around fifty years later another (seemingly less accurate) copy, A, was made for the library of Richard de Fournival.[29] Francesco Petrarca (1304–1374), known to English readers as Petrarch, later encountered A in the Sorbonne and brought his own copy of it back to Italy, providing the basis for the flourishing study of Propertius' work in Italy during the fifteenth century.[30] The text of Propertius was given even wider circulation following its publication in 1472, producing a 'vulgate' (or most commonly accepted) version that derived primarily from Petrarch's copy.[31]

As we inherit his text, Propertius seems a unique and provocative poet, one whose word choice, for example, is often jarring and whose transitions between ideas are often unexpected. Such an aesthetic makes Propertius seem appealingly 'modern' to many readers,[32] but is this style actually 'Propertian' or is it rather the consequence of a haphazard and clumsy history of copying?[33] Given the challenging nature of his manuscript tradition, Propertius' editors thus remain at the forefront of his reception and interpretation.[34] Furthermore, editors over the centuries have differed widely in their assessment of exactly how corrupt Propertius' manuscripts are and have adopted techniques that range from the 'conservative' (adhering as much as possible to the actual manuscripts) to the 'sceptical' (intervening more aggressively in the received text).

Seeking a control for their conjectures, some editors have tried to derive a sense of Propertius' style from the comments of other ancient writers, yet such characterizations of his work are sparse and generally inconclusive.[35] Arguments for emending (or not) Propertius' text thus invariably derive from an editor's cumulative sense of Propertius' style based on the surviving text, making textual arguments at times both circular and subjective.[36] In the preface to his 1901 edition, J.S. Phillimore remarked dryly: '*quot editores, tot Propertii*,' roughly translated as, 'there are as many Propertiuses as there are editors' – a useful warning to anyone working closely with Propertius' poetry. For our purposes, it is perhaps enough to acknowledge that although Propertian editing in the twentieth century began in a more conservative fashion, recent editors have adopted a more sceptical approach.[37]

One recent editor, Stephen Heyworth, pointedly returns on a number of occasions to emendations suggested by one of Propertius' most famous critics: the English poet A.E. Housman (1859–1936).[38] Housman's engagement with Propertius was complex and lifelong; the fact that he failed his final exams at Oxford is credited by some to his all-encompassing dedication to the poet. Although he worked in the Patent Office in London between 1882 and 1892, Housman re-entered the academy when he was appointed Chair of Latin at University College London in 1892 and, in 1911, he was named Professor of Latin at Cambridge. During his career, Housman produced texts of Latin authors such as Juvenal (1905) and Manilius (1903 and 1912), but his edition of Propertius was never published and was evidently destroyed after his death.[39]

Attempts to link Housman's enduring interest in Propertius to his own poetry, especially *A Shropshire Lad* (1896), have been discouraging,[40] but the British playwright Tom Stoppard, in his critically acclaimed play *The Invention of Love* (1997), presents Housman as a man whose textual obsessions and homosexual longings are deeply and inextricably woven together. Explaining his fascination with Propertius specifically, Stoppard's Housman reflects that: 'Propertius looked to me like a garden gone to wilderness, and not a very interesting garden either, but what an opportunity! – it was begging to be put back in order. Better still, various nincompoops thought they had already done it [...] hacking about, to make room for their dandelions.'[41] Earlier, Stoppard's Housman articulates the central romance of texual criticism: that is, the possibility that every conjecture allows the one making it 'to be the first person for thousands of years to read the verse as it was written'.[42]

OVID

John Richmond is sobering in his statement that 'all study of Ovid ultimately is based on our imperfect knowledge of what he actually wrote.'[43] The extant Ovidian manuscripts, which contain large portions of his poetry, do not date earlier than the ninth century CE.[44] For most of Ovid's work, we therefore depend on what survives from the Carolingian Renaissance of the ninth and tenth centuries or later. Moreover, since Ovid was such a prolific author, we do not possess a single manuscript that contains all of his works.[45] The *Amores* comes to us in two ninth-century French codices, which provide almost the entire work, and in one eleventh-century Italian manuscript, which preserves the whole work; the *Ars Amatoria* is transmitted in a French codex of the ninth century as a whole poem and in two codices of the eleventh century, one Italian, one (fragmentary) German or Swiss. The text of the *Remedia Amoris* depends on three manuscripts: one ninth-century French and two eleventh-century Italian codices.

The *Heroides* come down to us in substantial fragments from one ninth-century French manuscript, which seems to have been copied from a poor 'archetype'; the rest of the tradition of the *Heroides* is in even worse condition. The *Epistulae ex Ponto* is contained in one ninth-century French codex, which stops in the middle of the second poem of Book 3; two German manuscripts of the twelfth century are our only source for the whole poem. The *Tristia*, like the *Heroides*, also fell victim to a poor tradition and the earliest version of the poem is present in two almost illegible leaves of a codex, probably German, from the tenth century. In producing an edition of the *Tristia*, scholars thus are forced to use one fragmentary manuscript and another Italian codex, both belonging to the eleventh century. The best manuscript of the *Medicamina Faciei Femineae* also dates to the eleventh century.

It was obviously a significant challenge for the earliest scholars of Ovid to produce a reliable text of his elegiac poetry. Further complicating matters was Ovid's growing popularity beginning in the eleventh century. From that point on, there were continuing attempts to produce a single volume of all Ovidian works – a task that might seem admirable, but that often led to the inclusion of spurious works by those editors who tried to be comprehensive, thus inadvertently contributing to the confusion of transmission. Hence a large number of codices from the twelfth and thirteenth centuries that survive today contain texts markedly different from the earlier manuscripts listed above, making it virtually impossible to reconstruct which manuscripts are derivative and which can be traced to a more ancient original or archetype.[46]

Even the first print edition of Ovid in 1471 did not offer a fully reliable text and was emended numerous times.[47]

While the restoration of ancient texts was a major focus of Renaissance intellectuals, writers and artists also derived patent inspiration from an ancient world that was now breathing new life. Beginning with the Renaissance, we can witness centuries of lively engagement with Latin love poetry, both in successive attempts at translation – which would help widen awareness of the love poets' original work – and in more open-ended and creative expressions.

EARLY LITERARY RECEPTIONS

As we have seen, Petrarch played a key role in Propertius' textual transmission; he may also have been instrumental in bringing Tibullus back to Italy from France.[48] Even more, Petrarch's own love poetry about the unattainable Laura fundamentally shaped later receptions of Latin elegy. In the next century, Giovanni Pontano (1429–1503), an important Italian poet of the fifteenth century, 'produced two remarkable collections of poetry in the style of Catullus, and within a few years Catullan poetry was established as a recognizable and popular genre'.[49] As with poets of later generations, many Renaissance writers focused their response to Catullus on two specific themes: 'kisses and sparrows'.[50] During this era, there was already growing concern about whether the Latin love poets, given their frequent lasciviousness, belonged in educational settings, with many arguing that they should only be available to more mature readers.[51]

Significantly, from 1472 on, Propertius, Tibullus and Catullus were often printed together, comprising, as one scholar phrases it, 'the triumvirs of love'.[52] The influence of these poets is clearly visible in the work of the so-called 'neo-Latin' poets of the fifteenth and sixteenth centuries, especially that of the Dutch poet Janus or Johannes Secundus (1511–1536).[53] Propertius also inspired Renaissance poets such as Ludovico Ariosto (1473–1533) and Torquato Tasso (1544–1595). In France, Pierre de Ronsard (1524–1585) published numerous poetic works influenced by both Propertius and Ovid. Tibullus, on the other hand, became renowned as 'a sentimental, melancholy poet of love and the countryside' and his popularity, albeit modest, lasted well into the nineteenth century. Pietro Bembo (1470–1547), an Italian poet and cardinal, was clearly inspired by Tibullus, while Chateaubriand (1768–1848), a French writer, diplomat and historian recalls in his *Mémoirs* how he fell under Tibullus' spell as an adolescent.[54]

Still, the popularity of the other love poets was in many ways completely overshadowed by Ovid, who held considerable sway in the courtly poetry of the medieval period;[55] in particular, his *Amores* informed 'the secular erotics of the troubadours'.[56] Although Dante (*c*.1265–1321) lists Ovid 'among the great ancient poets in Limbo, third after Homer and Horace',[57] Ovid's pagan legacy was viewed in the Middle Ages with some discomfort. While Chaucer (*c*.1343–1400) puts him second on the list of great classical epic poets between Virgil and Homer,[58] Petrarch accuses Ovid of having a 'lascivious and lubricious and altogether womanish mind'.[59] The *Metamorphoses* is generally considered the chief Ovidian work from which later ages drew inspiration, and it was only during the Renaissance that the discomfort associated with Ovid's amatory works began to dissipate.[60] The range of Ovid's literary output continued to make his reception diverse as he alternately presented himself in the 'roles of dangerous immoralist, tragic exile, natural or ethical philosopher, medical doctor [...] and magician'.[61]

From the eleventh century on, the *Heroides* in particular was treated as a didactic work 'providing models of faithful love to be imitated'.[62] The genre of amatory verse-epistle, however, did not fully impact French literature until the fifteenth century, when the form started to be cultivated by writers like Christine de Pizan (1363–1430) and Georges Chastellain (*c*.1415–1475). By this time, the moral message of the *Heroides* had completely overshadowed their entertainment value and the poems erroneously began to be seen by some as redemptive poetry written in exile in an attempt to regain the favour of Augustus.[63] In the sixteenth century, the genre of poetic love letters became popular with several writers like André de la Vigne (*fl*. 1485–1515), Guillaume Crétin (*c*.1460–1525) and Fausto Andrelini (*c*.1462–1518). In particular, Andrelini placed the genre in the service of the state, and especially noteworthy are his verse-epistles, which illustrate the 'imaginative reworking of Ovid' as Andrelini transports 'Ovid's elegiac laments into the political realm of pre-Renaissance France'.[64] Written in Latin in the name of Queen

Anne de Bretagne, these letters aim to celebrate Louis XII's victorious Italian campaign and address the events at the French king's court through mythical allegories. Drawing on the example of that most chaste of ancient wives, Penelope, Anne emerges as the ruler of state and even toys with the idea of entering military combat at the side of her husband. Guillaume Crétin, a popular French poet and courtier, translated the first of Andrelini's epistles into French and later composed his own Heroidean-style letter in which the women of Paris write in encomiastic style to their absent king Charles.[65]

Ancient Love in Modern Times

Inspired by his travel to Italy in 1786–1788, Johann Wolfgang von Goethe (1749–1832) composed his *Römische Elegien* (*Roman Elegies*), a work in elegiac metre that shows the clear influence of the earlier Latin love poets.[66] As with the Roman poets, Goethe finds 'material' in his beloved Faustine (18.9), although Faustine is an emphatically loyal mistress, one whose stable love for the poet epitomizes a larger 'ideal of harmony between art and nature, present and past'.[67] Throughout, Goethe's vision of antiquity underscores the relevance of the past, casting the ancient world as neither a 'closed period nor a boring topic at school, but an engaging present'.[68] Having provided a general survey of the love poets' transmission and early reception, we would like in the remainder of the chapter to focus more closely on a number of nineteenth- and twentieth-century receptions, all of which attest to the depth and geographic breadth of the love poets' modern influence. We begin with a closer look at Catullus' arrival in England and Propertius' unique place in the work of Ezra Pound.

CATULLUS IN ENGLISH

In Renaissance England, as elsewhere, Ovid gained considerable popularity, although the dynamics of his reception varied. Christopher Marlowe (1564–1593) and Benjamin 'Ben' Jonson (1572–1637), for example, focused on different aspects of Ovid's 'pagan Muse'. While Marlowe revelled in Ovid's libertine twists and offered an eager public the first complete uncensored translation of the *Amores*, Ben Jonson, a contemporary of Shakespeare's, was uncomfortable with Ovid's sexual license and avoided the *Amores*, embracing instead Ovid's exilic elegy in his work *The Forest*.[69] Among his other works that show classical influence, John Donne (1572–1631) composed a series of love poems, the most infamous of which was an expansion of Ovid's account of his mid-afternoon encounter with Corinna in *Amores* 1.5.[70] Despite social and educational barriers, many women in Renaissance England also wrote poetry responding to Ovid's work. Both Isabella Whitney (active in the second half of the sixteenth century) and Anne Wharton (1659–1685) adapted Ovid's *Heroides*, while Christabella Rogers (active in the seventeenth century) wrote a poem in imitation of Ovid's programmatic first poem of the *Amores*, this time defying Cupid in preference of moral philosophy.[71]

It is generally agreed that Catullus reached England later than other classical writers, although the early Tudor poet John Skelton (active in the late fifteenth and early sixteen centuries) called himself 'the British Catullus', suggesting that at least a general sense of Catullus' work had arrived by then.[72] John Bernard Emperor traces Catullus' influence on English lyric poetry in the first half of the seventeenth century, placing special emphasis on the work of Thomas Campion (1567–1620) – who, like many poets, authored his own take on Catullus' poem urging Lesbia to live and love (poem 5) – and Robert Herrick (1591–1674).[73] Catullus' work nonetheless received an enormous boost in England with the first printed edition there in 1684.[74] As in other periods, the Lesbia and sparrow poems continued to dominate as points of artistic reference;[75] in 1798, for example, Samuel Taylor Coleridge (1772–1834) produced his own version of Catullus 5.[76]

In the nineteenth century, Catullus' poem about Sirmio (31) and his lament for his dead brother (101), poems previously overlooked in his reception, became popular.[77] Alfred Tennyson (1809–1892) relied on both 31 and 101 in composing a poem to his own deceased brother, 'Frater Ave atque Vale'.[78] Poem 31 appealed especially to the Romantic sensibility and was admired, for one, by Savage Landor (1775–1864).[79] Poem 101, on the other hand, was referenced by the Victorian poet 'most obviously devoted to Catullus', Algernon Swinburne (1837–1909), in his moving tribute to Baudelaire entitled 'Ave atque Vale'.[80] Later, the American lyric poet Sara Teasdale (1884–1933) commemorated Swinburne's own death with a poem proclaiming of the much-admired Swinburne that 'Catullus waits to welcome him'.[81] Catullus was also taken up by other women writers during this era, including the American poet Edna St. Vincent Millay (1892–1950), who united both Lesbia and the sparrow via the necessity of death in the poem 'Passer Mortuus Est'.[82] The American author Dorothy Parker (1893–1967), with her characteristic dry humour, portrayed Lesbia mocking Catullus' role as poet, writing, 'He's always hymning that or wailing this', having Lesbia conclude: 'That stupid fool! I've always hated birds...'[83]

From the earliest spread of his work, Catullus' reputation for obscenity coloured his reception, at times dampening his appeal, while at others presumably fostering it.[84] Indeed, although many of the love poets were targets of censure at different historical moments, Catullus' work, more than any other, has been subject to harsh critique and often ruthless censorship: in his *Don Juan*, the English poet Lord Byron (1788–1824) remarks that 'Catullus scarcely has a decent poem' (I.xlii.3), and a commentary on Catullus written as recently as 1961 simply omitted thirty-two of his poems.[85] Well into the twentieth century, many classical scholars continued to obfuscate Catullus' desires for Juventius. As Gaisser phrases it, 'they could render the homosexual invective Catullus hurled against his enemies, but they could not allow a homosexual romance to the poet himself.'[86]

In his poem, 'The Scholars', the Irish author W.B. Yeats (1865–1939) uses Catullus to illustrate the great divide between 'elderly, tepid, bourgeois scholars' and 'young, warm-hearted, bohemian love poets who write about the pain of love'.[87] The British poet Sidney Keyes (1922–1943) seems to capture well the resonance of Catullus in giving voice not only to longing, but also to the disenchantment felt by the young generation as they approached the mid-twentieth century at a time of devastating war. In his translation of Catullus 11 from May 1942, Keyes thus conveys the Sapphic image of the butchered flower by lamenting, 'And never look to me for love again – / My love's like any flower of the fallow / Cut down and wasted by the passing plow.'[88] The poignancy of Keyes' translation would prove to have unbearable echo in the fact that just under a year later he was killed in action in Tunisia at the age of twenty-one.[89]

Some thirty years before, the American poet Ezra Pound (1885–1972), another poet deeply marked by war, first travelled to Sirmione in Italy, the area so beloved by Catullus, which became an important location for Pound also throughout his life.[90] Pound was influenced by a number of Latin authors over the course of his career. In a letter, he stated directly that 'Catullus, Propertius, Horace and Ovid are the people who matter. Catullus most.'[91] As such valuation intimates, Pound's engagement with Catullus was extensive.[92] Openly scornful of Virgil, he would later turn to Ovid's *Metamorphoses* as an epic intertext for the major work of his later years, the *Cantos*.[93] But it is Pound's dialogue with Propertius that perhaps best reveals his modernist reimagining of Latin poetry.

POUND'S *HOMAGE TO SEXTUS PROPERTIUS*

Without question, the events of Pound's later life have played a profound role in his troubled reputation today. Perhaps most dramatically, following a series of essays and radio broadcasts in ardent support of Italian Fascism, Pound was indicted for treason in 1943 by the United States and eventually surrendered to American troops in 1945. Following his brief imprisonment in Italy, he was flown to the United States, where he was judged mentally unfit and committed to St. Elizabeths Hospital for the Criminally Insane. Pound remained there until 1958, returning to Italy after his release for the remainder of his life.

Pound's *Homage to Sextus Propertius* comes at a much earlier point in his career, in the shadow, in fact, of the First World War.[94] Pound finished the *Homage* in 1917 and published it in parts, beginning in 1919.[95] Since 'not until the twentieth century do we find anything like a nonscholarly interest taken in Propertius,'[96] Pound was in many ways 'a pioneer in championing the poetry of Propertius'.[97] In July of 1916, Pound had written to Iris Barry that 'if you CAN'T find *any* decent translations of Catullus and Propertius, I suppose I shall have to rig up something',[98] and the first wave of criticism narrowly assessed the work as a translation of Propertius, leading one reviewer (a professional classicist) to remark notoriously that 'if Mr. Pound were a professor of Latin, there would be nothing left for him but suicide'.[99] Pound himself fired back by noting that 'the philologists have so succeeded in stripping the classics of interest that I have already had more than one reader who has asked me, "Who was Propertius?"'[100]

Rather than providing a straightforward translation of the earlier poet, Pound sought to use Propertius' *persona* as a kind of 'mask through which Pound registered his protest at what he thought was the monstrous state of society and culture in which he found himself living'.[101] Later, in 1931, Pound wrote that his identification with Propertius was due to a profound sense that they both stood opposed to overreaching state power, suggesting that the poem 'presents certain emotions as vital to me in 1917, faced with the infinite and ineffable imbecility of the British Empire, as they were to Propertius some centuries earlier, when faced with the infinite and ineffable imbecility of the Roman Empire'.[102] In calling attention to Propertius' use of irony, moreover, Pound set himself strongly against the more sentimental readings of the Latin poet that had tended to dominate his reception, as limited as it was.[103] Throughout the work, Pound engages in extensive word-play and jarring juxtaposition, features reminiscent of Propertius' surviving text. Key to Pound's overall sense of Propertius' aesthetic was a quality he later called *logopoeia*, which Pound described loosely as 'the dance of the intellect among words', an intensity of thought expressed in language.[104]

The *Homage* itself consists of twelve sections, involving (with the exception of three lines from Book 1 and poems 2.1 and 3.16) a reworking of three clusters of poems from Propertius' second and third books: specifically, poems 10–15 and 28–34 from Book 2 and the first six poems from Book 3.[105] Pound's work treats a number of themes and poems that we have looked at previously, including Propertius' joyful recounting of night-time struggles with his lover (VII; cf. 2.15) and one of the poems where Cynthia is allowed to rebuke the poet for his spying (X; cf. 2.29b). Even more, his only inclusion of lines from Book 1 allows him to charge his lover with 'levity', that fundamental trait of the *puella*, culminating in a startling modern image encapsulating what it means for the *ego* to be an example to other lovers: 'The harsh acts of your levity! / Many and many. / I am hung here, a scare-crow for lovers' (XI).[106] Yet, for as much as he weighs Propertius' notions of love, Pound continually highlights the theme in Propertius that was for him most pressing: that is, the nature of poetic production itself, including 'the relation of the artist to society'.[107]

Pound's vibrant response to Propertius illustrates the ways in which writers of later eras used ancient poetry as a means for deliberating some of the most pressing issues of their day, as well as their own, at times tormented, place within it. With these themes in mind, we want to turn in our final section to Ovid's modern legacy in a part of the world where his influence is perhaps less well known, but no less profound.[108]

Ovid in Modern Exile

Since the early Renaissance, artists and scholars have been fascinated by Ovid's fate. In eras of political upheaval, massive displacement and banishment, Ovid has become, as we noted previously, an 'ur-exile', the archetypal banished poet who embodies the ideals of free-thinking and artistic individualism in the face of absolutism.[109] Since 'banishment, displacement, and the return of the exiled constitute a consistent world-wide modern phenomenon',[110] Ovid provides in the words of one critic a 'typology of exile literature'.[111] From Dante and John Milton to John Masefield and Joseph Brodsky, poets thus 'have focused on their own sense of identification with a predecessor's paradigmatic exile'.[112] In the twentieth century, when exile became also a political act, the identification with Ovid became even more prominent among those who, for one reason or another, were forced to flee their homeland or suffer major changes while still living in it. So, too, for many eastern European writers Ovid's example required the balancing of 'two key personae, the lover and the exile'.[113]

RETURNING TO TOMI: OVID IN ROMANIA

As we saw in the previous chapter, Ovid expresses unrestrained contempt for Tomi, finding it increasingly difficult to adjust to its culture, language and customs. During the centuries after Ovid's death, the memory of the exiled poet was forgotten in the actual territory of his exile as it changed rulers and endured various invasions. Indeed, the cultural rehabilitation of Ovid's legacy in the region did not occur until 'the humanistic Renaissance of the seventeenth century';[114] from then on, Ovid's poetry has produced continuous (albeit at times sporadic) responses from modern Romanian authors, who invest Ovid's exile with meanings ranging from national unity to artistic freedom.[115]

Published in 1885 by Vasile Alecsandri, a prominent Romantic poet and playwright, the drama *Ovidiu* expands creatively on the main facts we know about Ovid's life. In the solid tradition of our ancient poets, the play revolves around love and hate: Ovid is caught up in a complicated romantic situation with Corina and her former lover Ibis, while pursuing a secret love affair with Augustus' granddaughter Iulia (i.e., Julia), an affair that causes his exile. While in exile, the poet longs for his native land as he reminisces about his past life in Rome, juxtaposing it with his joyless present existence. However, upon his deathbed Ovid has a prophetic vision about the fall of the Roman Empire and the rebirth of a new Rome in Dacia. It is in this last vision that Alecsandri's national concerns become evident: the author emphasizes Romania's Latin origin and, in so doing, asserts his country's legitimate claim to the values of the West, as well as a return to the common cultural source of Western civilization.

Born in 1944, Marin Mincu penned a fictional 'journal' by Ovid in Italian: *Il diario di Ovidio* (1997), published later in a Romanian version. The journal's fictional entries present Ovid's meditation on life, art, love and, once again, spiritual discovery. What is especially surprising in Mincu's rendition is that Ovid's exile is presented as voluntary: Rome was too corrupt, Augustus was a tyrant and the poet never could find true love until he came to Dacia and discovered the pure love of a local woman, Aia. Andrei Codrescu's 1990 essay 'Exile: a Place' – a work written in English – takes Ovid's exile as a model for his own departure from his homeland.[116] For Codrescu, who escaped from Soviet Romania, Ovid's Tomi is no longer a miserable place of confinement, but a place of freedom and exploration, one that offers the opportunity of writing in another language and winning over a new audience for his poetry. This new paradigm for thinking about poetic exile as freedom from the confinement of one's homeland is also especially prominent in another tradition of Ovidian reception, this time in Russia.

OVID IN A 'COLD CLIMATE'[117]

Ovid's exilic plight resonated with Russian poets almost from the inception of Russian national poetry. Unlike their Romanian counterparts, Russian poets were not particularly interested in reimagining Ovid's discourse of love; rather the dilemma of his exile fascinated and drew them in infinitely more. In the Russian reception of Ovid, we clearly see a tendency also explored in Ovid: the homeland as an unattainable and unresponsive beloved, the source of every hope and every sorrow. Russian poets – 'homesick and sick of home'[118] – developed and honed this theme of their love-hate relationship with their motherland, whose allure and emotional distance fuelled their poetic inspiration.

Alexander Pushkin (1799–1837), the first Russian poet *par excellence*, mentions Ovid several times, dedicating a whole poem to him ('To Ovid') while in exile himself. In that poem Pushkin, who was exiled by tsar Alexander to Bessarabia (today's Moldova), a site geographically very close to Tomi, identifies with the Roman poet, but views his exile as a liberation of sorts. At the beginning of the twentieth century, the theme of Ovidian exile was taken up once again by Osip Mandelshtam (1891–1938), who perished in Stalin's Gulag. In several of his poems Mandelshtam returns to Ovid and, following Pushkin's example, also offers the view of exile as liberation.[119] However, the most compelling and modern treatment of Ovid occurs in the poetry of Joseph Brodsky, Russia's own 'ur-exile'.

Ovid occupies an important place in Brodsky's poetry throughout its whole evolution. Following in the footsteps of Pushkin and Mandelshtam, Brodsky – a pariah of the Soviet state – found in Ovid his ancient double, not only in biographical terms but also in terms of poetics. In 1964–1965, during the time of his exile in the north of Russia, Brodsky wrote two poems connected with Ovidian themes, 'A Fragment' and 'Ex Ponto', the latter with a subtitle 'The Last Letter of Ovid to Rome'. The former contains traces of

Ovid's own melancholy and equates exile with death through the refrain 'Naso is not ready to die' and other persistent references to dying. The poem ends with the rather depressing stanza:

> Naso, don't disturb Rome.
> You yourself forgot
> to whom you're sending letters.
> Maybe to the dead.
> Just a habit. Check again
> (don't take it as offence)
> the address and then
> cross out Rome please
> and insert: Hades.[120]

For Brodsky the portrayal of Rome is inextricably connected with that of his own unattainable beloved, the city of St Petersburg. 'Ex Ponto' continues the Ovidian theme in Russian poetry promulgated earlier by Pushkin and Mandelshtam. However, while both Pushkin and Mandelshtam 'edit' Ovid's sadness and nostalgia and cast it in a more optimistic light, Brodsky stays remarkably close to the plight of the original *Ex Ponto*:

> To you, whose pretty features
> perhaps do not fear fading
> into my Rome, which, like you, has not changed,
> since our last meeting,
> I am writing from sea. From sea. The ships
> strive to these shores after a storm
> in order to prove that this is the edge of the Earth
> and in their holds there is no freedom.[121]

In this short poem Brodsky concisely establishes what he has in common with the ancient poet: his abandoned beloved whose features haunt him, the city as a stand-in for that beloved, the proximity of the sea, and his feelings about being on 'the edge of the Earth'. However, the journey back is seen as a futile endeavour, a thought that permeates several of Brodsky's early poems.

The theme of exile from Rome reappears several times in his poetry of this period, but especially in the 'Letters to a Roman Friend' with the subtitle 'From Martial' (1972). In this poem, written on the eve of Brodsky's permanent departure for the West, the theme of exile is intertwined with the theme of empire also prominent in Brodsky's poetics. The poem belongs to the 'genre' of letters to Rome, which immediately identifies it as an Ovidian allusion. The subtitle, however, 'From Martial' introduces the context of invective poetry, irony and satire in relation to empire:

> Perhaps, indeed, Postumus, chickens are not really birds,
> but there is misery in having chicken brains.
> If one's fated to be born in an empire,
> let him live in a remote province, by the seashore.
>
> It is far from the Caesar and the blizzard;
> one does not need to fawn, be cowardly or hurry.
> There, you say, the governors are thieves?
> But thieves are dearer to me than the bloodsuckers.[122]

In this poem, the 'joy' of exile characteristic of Pushkin's and Mandelshtam's response to Ovid reappears. The distance from Rome is seen as a liberating experience, an opportunity for creative contemplation and heroic endeavour. In that respect Brodsky's approach to the fate of exile differs drastically from Ovid's. Although, for Ovid, Rome represents the Golden Age of civilization – the exile from which equals cultural death and the return to which is the ultimate goal – for Brodsky, exile is yet another moment replete with irony and the conviction that return is not an option. Brodsky indeed never returned to his beloved city.

CONCLUSION

Indeed, it is harder to see how a picture is painted than it is to see what it claims to represent, which is the first thing that leaps to the eye.

PAUL VEYNE

IN THIS STUDY, we have aimed to enrich the experience of reading Latin love poetry, poetry that has held its various audiences enthralled for two thousand years. While love poetry may appeal to today's readers in large part because of its emotional immediacy, at the core of our work is recognition that the distance of several thousand years creates a divide between us and the poets, a gap that can only be bridged by unravelling layer upon layer of these sophisticated works. Clearer understanding of the relationship between the ancient love poets and their poetic personae (love poetry's *ego*), the historical surroundings that conditioned their sensibilities, the intended audiences of their texts and the gender dynamics of Roman society contributes enormously to our enjoyment and appreciation of Latin love poetry's canvas.

Taken together, the love poets remind us that while love is a feeling we may share across the centuries, it is also one patterned uniquely by who we are, where we are, and when we are. So, if the love poets convey different modes for loving in the time of Roman civil war and during the age of Augustus, what does love look like today, in the twenty-first century, with the social structures we have woven, the cities and countrysides (not to mention countries) we inhabit, and the political and economic realities in which we live? It is perhaps because they help open such purposeful examination of life and love that the Latin love poets remain so relevant today.

NOTES

INTRODUCTION

1   The following Latin texts are used in this study: Kenneth Quinn (ed.), *Catullus: The Poems*, (2nd edn., London, 1973); Michael C.J. Putnam (ed.), *Tibullus: A Commentary* (Oklahoma, 1973); S.J. Heyworth (ed.), *Sexti Properti Elegos* (Oxford, 2007); J. Henderson (ed.), *Ovid. Heroides. Amores* (Cambridge, 1977); E.J. Kenney (ed.), *P. Ovidi Nasonis Amores, Medicamina Faciei Femineae, Ars Amatoria, Remedia Amoris* (Oxford, 1961; repr. 1995); G.P. Goold (ed.), *Ovid. Tristia. Ex Ponto* (Cambridge, 1988). For the 'Sulpicia' poems, G.P. Goold (ed.), *Catullus, Tibullus and Pervigilium Veneris* (Cambridge and London, 1913). Unless otherwise specified all translations are our own.

2   While some scholars date the start of the Augustan era to Augustus' victory at Actium (31 BCE), the formal settlement of power and titles that would define his long reign took place in 27 BCE.

3   Tara S. Welch, *The Elegiac Cityscape: Propertius and the Meaning of Roman Monuments* (Columbus, 2005), p. 153. See also Christopher Nappa, *Reading after Actium: Vergil's* Georgics, *Octavian, and Rome* (Ann Arbor, 2005).

4   Cicero once asserted that every Roman had two homelands, their birthplace and Rome, their 'shared homeland' (*communis patria*) (*De Legibus* 2.5).

5   See, for example, Brigette F. Russell, 'The emasculation of Antony: the construction of gender in Plutarch's *Life of Antony*', *Helios*, 25/2 (1998), pp. 121–137.

6   Reinhold Meyer, 'The declaration of war against Cleopatra', *Classical Journal*, 77/2 (1981–1982), pp. 97–103.

7   For more background, see Robert A. Gurval, *Actium and Augustus: The Politics and Emotions of Civil War* (Ann Arbor, 1995).

8   See Brian W. Breed, '*Tua, Caesar, Aetas*: Horace *Ode* 4.15 and the Augustan Age', *The American Journal of Philology*, 125/2 (2004), pp. 245–253.

9 See, for example, Andrew Wallace-Hadrill, 'The Golden Age and sin in Augustan ideology', *Past & Present*, 95 (1982), pp. 20–22.

10 Karl Galinsky, *Augustan Culture: An Interpretive Introduction* (Princeton, 1996), p. 91; also Christine Perkell, 'The Golden Age and its contradictions in the poetry of Vergil', *Vergilius*, 48 (2002), pp. 3–39. Predicting the advent of a miraculous child who would change the world, Virgil's poem was later interpreted in a Christian key by Christian apologists.

11 Paul Zanker, *The Power of Images in the Age of Augustus*, tr. A. Shapiro (Ann Arbor, 1990), pp. 167–172. The event was commemorated in Horace's *Carmen Saeculare*; see Duncan Barker, '"The Golden Age is proclaimed?": the *Carmen Saeculare* and the renascence of the golden race', *The Classical Quarterly*, N S 46/2 (1996), pp. 434–446.

12 Jennifer A. Rea, *Legendary Rome: Myth, Monuments, and Memory on the Palatine and Capitoline* (London, 2007), p. 131.

13 Zanker, *Power of Images*, pp. 201–210. On Romulus, Rea: *Legendary Rome*, pp. 38–42.

14 See Beth Severy, *Augustus and the Family at the Birth of the Roman Empire* (New York and London, 2003) and Kristina Milnor, *Gender, Domesticity, and the Age of Augustus: Inventing Private Life* (Oxford, 2005); for the connections to love poetry, see Hunter H. Gardner, 'The elegiac *domus* in the early Augustan principate', *American Journal of Philology*, 131/3 (2010), pp. 453–493.

15 For possible economic motives behind the laws, see Andrew Wallace-Hadrill, 'Family and inheritance in the Augustan marriage laws', *Proceedings of the Cambridge Philological Society*, N S 27 (1981), pp. 58–80.

16 For a full discussion of each law, see Catharine Edwards, *The Politics of Immorality in Ancient Rome* (Cambridge and New York, 1993), pp. 37–41; also Kristina Milnor, 'Augustus, history, and the landscape of law', *Arethusa*, 40 (2007), pp. 7–23.

17 A.J. Boyle, *Ovid and the Monuments* (Bendigo, 2003), p. 2.

18 Scholars have difficulty fitting this poem into the actual timeline of when individual laws were introduced, however; see Paul Allen Miller, *Subjecting Verses: Latin Love Elegy and the Emergence of the Real* (Princeton, 2004), p. 143.

19 Cf. Cicero's account of Rome's impressive transformations at *Laws* 2.35.95–96.

20 Boyle, *Ovid and the Monuments*, p. 35.

21 On Augustus' extensive urban programme, begin with Diane Favro, 'Making Rome a world city', in K. Galinsky (ed.), *The Cambridge Companion to the Age of Augustus* (Cambridge and New York, 2005), pp. 234–263 and Susan Walker, 'The moral museum: Augustus and the city of Rome', in J. Coulson and H. Dodge (eds), *Ancient Rome: The Archaeology of the Eternal City* (Oxford, 2000), pp. 61–75. For contemporary accounts of Augustus' aims, see Suetonius, *Augustus*, 29–31 and Augustus' so-called '*Res Gestae*' in Alison E. Cooley (ed.), *Res gestae divi Augusti: Text, Translation, and Commentary* (Cambridge and New York, 2009).

22 Zanker, *Power of Images*, p. 51; see also Rea, *Legendary Rome*, pp. 29–38.

23 Barbara Kellum, 'Sculptural programs and propaganda in Augustan Rome: the temple of Apollo on the Palatine', in E. D'Ambra (ed.), *Roman Art in Context: An Anthology* (Edgewood Cliffs, 1993), p. 83.

24 Zanker, *Power of Images*, p. 195.
25 Ibid., p. 201. For the 'Hall of Fame', see T.J. Luce, 'Livy, Augustus, and the Forum Augustum', in K.A. Raaflaub and M. Toher (eds), *Between Republic and Empire: Interpretations of Augustus and His Principate* (Berkeley, Los Angeles and London, 1990), pp. 123–138.
26 Ibid., p. 194. Augustus regained the standards through diplomacy. See Charles B. Rose, 'The Parthians in Augustan Rome', *American Journal of Archaeology*, 109 (2005), pp. 21–75.
27 See Peter White, 'Poets in the new milieu: realigning', in Galinsky, *The Cambridge Companion to the Age of Augustus*, pp. 321–339.
28 Alessandro Barchiesi, 'Learned eyes: poets, viewers, image makers', in K. Galinsky (ed.), *Age of Augustus* (Cambridge, 2005), p. 281.
29 J.P. Sullivan, *Propertius: A Critical Introduction* (Cambridge, 1976), pp. 10–11.
30 On Rome's perceptions of its early history, see Matthew Fox, *Roman Historical Myths: The Regal Period in Augustan Literature* (Oxford and New York, 1996).
31 For one view of Virgil's 'patriotism', see Walter R. Johnson, 'Imaginary Romans: Vergil and the illusion of national identity', in S. Spence (ed.), *Poets and Critics Read Vergil* (New Haven and London, 2001), pp. 3–16.
32 Bruno Snell, 'Arcadia: the discovery of a spiritual landscape', in *The Discovery of the Mind*, tr. T.G. Rosenmeyer (Oxford, 1953), pp. 281–310.
33 For a detailed interpretation of *Eclogue* 10, see Gian Biagio Conte, *The Rhetoric of Imitation: Genre and Poetic Memory in Virgil and Other Latin Poets*, tr. C. Segal (Ithaca, 1986), pp. 100–129.
34 See Paul Veyne, *Roman Erotic Elegy: Love, Poetry, and the West*, tr. D. Pellauer (Chicago and London, 1988), pp. 102–104.
35 See, for example, Richard P. Saller, *Personal Patronage under the Early Empire* (Cambridge, 1982).
36 For a general introduction to patronage, see Barbara K. Gold, *Literary Patronage in Greece and Rome* (Chapel Hill and London, 1987).
37 On Maecenas, see G. Williams, 'Did Maecenas "fall from favor"? Augustan literary patronage', in Raaflaub and Toher (eds), *Between Republic and Empire*, pp. 258–275.
38 Gold, *Literary Patronage*, p. 126.
39 White, 'Poets in the new milieu', p. 328.
40 Ibid., p. 331.
41 On Augustus' relationships with the poets, see White, 'Poets in the new milieu', pp. 332–337. For Horace's complex treatment of Augustus, see Michael C.J. Putnam, 'Horace *Carm.* 2.9: Augustus and the ambiguities of encomium', in Raaflaub and Toher (eds), *Between Republic and Empire*, pp. 212–238.
42 Begin with Jasper Griffin, 'Augustus and the poets: "*Caesar qui cogere posset*"', in F. Millar and E. Segal (eds), *Caesar Augustus: Seven Aspects* (Oxford and New York, 1984), pp. 189–218. Also D.C. Feeney, '*Si licet et fas est*: Ovid's *Fasti* and the problem of free speech under the Principate', in Anton Powell (ed.), *Roman Poetry and Propaganda in the Age of Augustus* (London, 1992), pp. 1–25. Self-censorship is even more difficult to trace; early in his career, Augustus (then Octavian) made

obscene allegations against Asinius Pollio. Pollio, in refusing to respond, explained: 'It is not a trivial thing to write poems against one who can proscribe you,' (discussed in Edwards, *Politics of Immorality*, p. 62).

I. BEGINNINGS AND BACKGROUNDS

1   For more on Roman poetry's audience, see Tony Woodman and Jonathan Powell, *Author and Audience in Latin Literature* (Cambridge, 1992); also Kenneth Quinn, 'The poet and his audience in the Augustan Age', in Hildegard Temporini and Wolfgang Haase (eds), *Aufstieg und Niedergang der römischen Welt: Geschichte und Kultur Roms im Spiegel der neueren Forschung*, 2.30.1 (1982), pp. 75–180.

2   For a brief history of the debate over the origins of Roman elegy, see Gian Biagio Conte, *Latin Literature: A History*, tr. J.B. Solodow, rev. Don Fowler and Glen W. Most (Baltimore and London, 1994). See also the classic works of Archibald Day, *The Origins of Latin Love Elegy* (Oxford, 1938; repr. New York, 1972); Georg Luck, *The Latin Love Elegy* (New York, 1959); and R.O.A.M. Lyne, *The Latin Love Poets from Catullus to Horace* (Oxford, 1980).

3   For a general introduction to lyric poetry, see Walter R. Johnson, *The Idea of Lyric: Lyric Modes in Ancient and Modern Poetry* (Berkeley, Los Angeles and London, 1982) and Paul Allen Miller, *Lyric Texts and Lyric Consciousness: The Birth of a Genre from Archaic Greece to Augustan Rome* (London and New York, 1994).

4   Miller comes to a different conclusion about Sappho 16 in relation to Homer in *Lyric Texts*, pp. 92–96, namely that Sappho is ultimately 'reinscribed in that same tradition' from which she seems to want to distance herself (p. 96).

5   Miller reads this poem as actually affirming Homeric values in *Lyric Texts*, pp. 19–20, 35.

6   Luck, *Latin Love Elegy*, pp. 17–18.

7   Day, *Origins*, pp. 102–110; cf. Luck, *Latin Love Elegy*, pp. 22–25.

8   For a more detailed account of the erotic themes in Alexandrian epigram, see Auguste Couat, *Alexandrian Poetry under the First Three Ptolemies*, tr. J. Loeb (Chicago, 1991), pp. 181–188.

9   Callimachus' corpus, still limited, was nonetheless expanded by important discoveries in the twentieth century; see Frank Nisetich (tr.), *The Poems of Callimachus* (Oxford, 2001), pp. xxiv–xxxi.

10   Kathryn J. Gutzwiller, *Poetic Garlands: Hellenistic Epigrams in Context* (Berkeley, Los Angeles and London, 1998), p. 183; for Gutzwiller's discussion of the *Epigrammata* at length, see pp. 183–226.

11   Although the *Aetia* survives only in fragments, we retain a sense of the overall structure given the summaries of the poem that exist; we also have an especially good understanding of the 'Lock of Berenice' since Catullus offers his own version of it in poem 66 (see also Catullus 65.16).

12   Nisetich, *Poems of Callimachus*, p. 27.

13   Kathleen McNamee, 'Propertius, poetry, and love', in Mary DeForest (ed.), *Woman's*

Power, Man's Game: Essays on Classical Antiquity in Honor of Joy K. King (Wauconda, IL, 1993), p. 218.

14 Nisetich, *Poems of Callimachus*, pp. 62–63.

15 Ibid., p. 63.

16 Ibid.

17 J.P. Sullivan, *Propertius: A Critical Introduction* (Cambridge, 1976), p. 68. See also Peter E. Knox, 'Catullus and Callimachus', in Marilyn B. Skinner (ed.), *A Companion to Catullus* (Malden, 2007), pp. 152–171.

18 Richard Hunter, however, cautions that our understanding of Callimachus' original poetics is distorted since the Roman poets took only the features of his style that suited their purpose. See Richard Hunter, *The Shadow of Callimachus: Studies in the Reception of Hellenistic Poetry at Rome* (Cambridge, 2006), p. 2; also James Zetzel, 'Recreating the canon: Augustan poetry and the Alexandrian past', *Critical Inquiry*, 10 (1983), pp. 83–105.

19 John F. Miller, 'Callimachus and the Augustan aetiological elegy', in Temporini and Haase (eds), *Aufstieg und Niedergang*, pp. 371–417.

20 On love poetry's links to comedy, see Sharon L. James, 'Introduction: constructions of gender and genre in Roman comedy and elegy', *Helios*, 25/1 (1998), p. 5.

21 Suggesting he died young, Ovid imagines Catullus in Elysium with ivy on his 'youthful temples' in the *Amores* (3.9.61–62). Jerome records Catullus' death in the year 58 BCE at the age of thirty (a date that contradicts the presumed date of individual poems), while Cornelius Nepos only affirms that he was dead by 32 BCE (*Atticus* 12.4). See Marilyn B. Skinner, *Catullus in Verona: A Reading of the Elegiac Libellus, Poems 65–116* (Columbus, 2003), p. xx.

22 Ibid., p. xxi.

23 The label 'Lesbian' did not have connotations of female homosexuality in this era, although ancient writers clearly recognized Sappho's love for other women.

24 Modern perceptions of Clodia have invariably been shaped by Cicero's attacks and Catullus' corresponding laments about her alleged fickleness, but Skinner has provided a more nuanced account of her life in Marilyn B. Skinner, *Clodia Metelli: The Tribune's Sister* (Oxford and New York, 2011).

25 See Cicero, *Epistulae ad Atticum* (*Letters to Atticus*) 7.2.1, *De Oratore* (*On the Orator*) 161 and *Tusculanae Quaestiones* (*Tusculan Disputations*) 3.45; cf. Horace's attack at *Satires* 1.10.18–19. Perhaps in response to such scorn, Catullus twice sarcastically calls himself 'the worst of all poets' in sending his thanks to Cicero for an unspecified favour in poem 49.

26 For the controversy over the ordering of Catullus' surviving poems, as well as their potential division into separate works, see Marilyn B. Skinner, 'Authorial arrangement of the collection: debate past and present', in Skinner (ed.), *Companion to Catullus*, pp. 35–53.

27 Luck, *Latin Love Elegy*, pp. 48–50. See also Paul Allen Miller, 'Catullus and Roman love elegy', in Skinner (ed.), *Companion to Catullus*, pp. 410–413.

28 Conte, *Latin Literature*, p. 258.

29 The very subject of the line is suggestive, evidently alluding to the river Hypanis,

which separates Asia from Europe; see David Ross, *Backgrounds to Augustan Poetry: Gallus, Elegy and Rome* (Cambridge, 1975), p. 39. Other positive assessments of Gallus include: Michael Putnam, *Vergil's Pastoral Art: Studies in the* Eclogues (Princeton, 1970), p. 354 and Friedrich Solmsen, 'Tibullus as an Augustan poet', *Hermes*, 90 (1962), pp. 295–325.

30 The prominent British classicist Ronald Syme, for example, once dismissively observed that 'C. Cornelius Gallus requires brief introduction or none at all' in Syme, 'The origin of Cornelius Gallus', *Classical Quarterly*, 32 (1938), p. 39.

31 Florence Verducci, 'On the sequence of Gallus' epigrams: *molles elegi, vasta triumphi pondera*', *Quaderni Urbinati di Cultura Classica*, 45 (1984), p. 119–120.

32 The inscription is dated to 15 April 29 BCE, *Corpus Inscriptionum Latinarum*, vol. III, 14147, 5. For more information on inscriptions concerning Gallus, see Victor Ehrenberg and A.H.M. Jones (eds), *Documents Illustrating the Reigns of Augustus and Tiberius* (2nd edn., Oxford, 1955; repr. 1963).

33 For different views of Gallus' trespasses, see Richard A. Bauman, *The* Crimen Maiestatis *in the Roman Republic and Augustan Principate* (Johannesburg, 1967); Richard A. Bauman, Impietas in Principem: *A Study of Treason against the Roman Emperor with Special Reference to the First Century A.D.* (Munich, 1974); and G. Barra, 'Il crimen di Cornelio Gallo', *Vichiana*, 5 (1968), pp. 49–58.

34 Franz Skutsch, *Gallus und Vergil* (Leipzig and Berlin, 1906), pp. 127 ff.

35 See Archibald W. Allen, '*Sunt qui Propertium malint*', in J.P. Sullivan (ed.), *Critical Essays on Roman Literature: Elegy and Lyric* (Cambridge, MA, 1962), pp. 107–148.

36 See J.P. Elder, 'Tibullus: *Tersus atque elegans*', in Sullivan (ed.), *Critical Essays*, pp. 65–105.

37 Conte, *Latin Literature*, p. 326.

38 Ibid.

39 Some scholars today continue to speak of Tibullus' four books, but others adhere to the original three-book division; we shall follow the latter convention throughout this study.

40 Conte, *Latin Literature*, pp. 326–327.

41 Lawrence Richardson, jr, *Propertius: Elegies I–IV* (Norman, 1977), p. 6.

42 Ibid.

43 For estimates of the dates for individual books, see ibid., pp. 8–11.

44 Propertius' use of this event to close Book 1 has often puzzled scholars; see, for example, Paul Allen Miller, *Subjecting Verses: Latin Love Elegy and the Emergence of the Real* (Princeton, 2004), pp. 70–73; and Nigel Nicholson, 'Bodies without names, names without bodies: Propertius 1.21–22', *Classical Journal*, 94/2 (1998–1999), pp. 143–161.

45 See R.O.A.M. Lyne, 'Propertius 2.10 and 11 and the structure of books "2A" and "2B"', *Journal of Roman Studies*, 88 (1998), pp. 21–36. Lyne reviews previous editorial policies and agrees with some scholars that it was originally two books, focusing attention on possible closure after 2.10 and 2.11.

46 Some scholars argued that the second edition never actually existed but was Ovid's witty fiction 'designed to act out an unexpectedly literal form of adherence to the

Callimachean poetic principle of "less is more'". See Joan Booth, 'The *Amores*: Ovid making love', in Peter E. Knox (ed.), *A Companion to Ovid* (Malden and Oxford, 2009), p. 73; Alessandro Barchiesi, *Speaking Volumes: Narrative and Intertext in Ovid and Other Latin Poets* (London, 2001), pp. 159–166. A detailed interpretation of the cohesion of the *Amores* as a whole is offered by Niklas Holzberg, *Ovid: The Poet and His Work* (Ithaca, 2002), pp. 46–53.

47 For the historical background, see Francis Cairns, 'Catullus in and about Bithynia: poems 68, 10, 28 and 47', in D. Braund and C. Gill (eds), *Myth, History and Culture in Republican Rome: Studies in Honor of T.P. Wiseman* (Exeter, 2003), pp. 165–190.

48 See Ronald Syme, 'Piso and Veranius in Catullus', *Classica et Mediaevalia*, 17 (1956), 129–134.

49 Catharine Edwards, *The Politics of Immorality in Ancient Rome* (Cambridge and New York, 1993), p. 27.

50 See William C. Scott, 'Catullus and Caesar', *Classical Philology*, 66/1 (1971), pp. 17–25.

51 See the excellent discussion at Duncan F. Kennedy, '"Augustan" and "anti-Augustan": reflections on terms of reference', in Anton Powell (ed.), *Roman Poetry and Propaganda in the Age of Augustus* (London, 1992), pp. 26–58.

52 Sullivan, *Propertius*, p. 58.

53 Miller, *Subjecting Verses*, p. 130. Later, Miller writes of Propertius' second book: 'What we see in book 2 is neither a rebel in Augustus' camp, nor a collaborator, nor an abstracted aesthete, but the vision of an erotic subject who is placed under more and more tension as he is brought into closer and closer contact with the discourse of the Augustan regime' (p. 133).

54 Kennedy, '"Augustan" and "anti-Augustan"', p. 26.

55 R.O.A.M. Lyne, 'The life of love', in Paul Allen Miller (ed.), *Latin Erotic Elegy* (London and New York, 2002), p. 348.

56 Ellen Greene, *The Erotics of Domination: Male Desire and the Mistress in Latin Love Poetry* (Baltimore and London, 1998), p. xiii.

57 Edwards, *Politics of Immorality*, p. 20.

58 Ibid.

59 Ibid., p. 25.

60 Ibid., pp. 63–97.

61 Ibid., p. 65.

62 For Antony's alleged response, begin with Eleanor Huzar, 'The literary efforts of Mark Antony', in Temporini and Haase (eds), *Aufstieg und Niedergang*, pp. 639–657. Allusions to Mark Antony, Augustus' most intimate rival, are significant in Augustan poetry, and Propertius especially seems to identify with Antony on a number of occasions. We shall consider this dynamic in Chapter 5.

63 Fulvia, who helped lead troops against Octavian in Perugia, is a fascinating figure in her own right: see Charles L. Babcock, 'The early career of Fulvia', *The American Journal of Philology*, 86/1 (1965), pp. 1–32; and Diana Delia, 'Fulvia reconsidered', in S.B. Pomeroy (ed.), *Women's History and Ancient History* (Chapel Hill and London, 1991), pp. 197–217.

64 Craig A. Williams, *Roman Homosexuality: Ideologies of Masculinity in Classical Antiquity* (New York and Oxford, 1999), pp. 147–148.

65 Greene, *Erotics of Domination*, p. xiii.

66 David Wray, *Catullus and the Poetics of Roman Manhood* (Cambridge and New York, 2001), p. 58.

67 Monica R. Gale, 'Propertius 2.7: *Militia Amoris* and the ironies of elegy', *Journal of Roman Studies*, 87 (1997), p. 85.

68 Marilyn B. Skinner, '*Ego mulier*: the construction of male sexuality in Catullus', in J.P. Hallett and Marilyn B. Skinner (eds), *Roman Sexualities* (Princeton, 1997), p. 143.

69 Skinner, '*Ego mulier*', p. 143; cf. Lyne, 'The life of love', p. 359. Hunter H. Gardner, 'Ariadne's lament: the semiotic impulse of Catullus 64', *Transactions of the American Philological Association*, 137/1 (2007), p. 158, also reviews the critical discussion.

70 For a lengthier discussion of the trope in Propertius, see Gale, 'Propertius 2.7', pp. 77–91.

71 See Leslie Cahoon, 'The bed as battlefield: erotic conquest and military metaphor in Ovid's *Amores*', *Transactions of the American Philological Association*, 118 (1988), pp. 293–307.

72 Gian Biagio Conte, *Genres and Readers*, tr. G.W. Most (Baltimore, 1994), p. 37.

73 Frank O. Copley, '*Servitium amoris* in the Roman elegists', *Transactions of the American Philological Association*, 78 (1947), p. 290.

74 R.O.A.M. Lyne, '*Servitium amoris*', *The Classical Quarterly*, 29/1 (1979), p. 117. See also Paul Murgatroyd, '*Servitium amoris* and the Roman Elegists', *Latomus*, 40/3 (1981), pp. 589–606.

75 As Jonathan Walters explains, slaves were in very real terms 'under the control of their owner, under orders, most specifically that their bodies belonged to their owner, to do with as he or she wished'; see Jonathan Walters, 'Invading the Roman body: manliness and impenetrability in Roman thought', in Hallett and Skinner (eds), *Roman Sexualities*, p. 39.

76 See Murgatroyd, '*Servitium amoris*', pp. 595–596.

77 Murgatroyd, '*Servitium amoris*', p. 596. Copley likewise argues that Roman elegy places particular emphasis on physical punishment; see Copley, '*Servitium amoris*', p. 299.

78 See K.R. Bradley, *Slaves and Masters in the Roman Empire: A Study in Social Control* (New York and Oxford, 1987), pp. 113–137.

79 In contrast to Propertius' fairly light punishment, Cynthia demands that Lygdamus be shackled and sold (79–80). In 4.7, Cynthia likewise requests the torture of Lygdamus and Nomas (35–38).

80 William Fitzgerald, *Slavery and the Roman Literary Imagination* (Cambridge and New York, 2000), p. 31.

81 Earlier, he callously compares two quite different meanings of 'freedom', equating Corinna's freedom in being able to meet her lover with the slave's potential manumission (2.2.15–16).

82 Slaves often serve as mediators between lovers (e.g. *Amores* 1.11 and 1.12), a

dynamic that, as Fitzgerald notes, is 'both a convenience and a source of friction'; see Fitzgerald, *Slavery*, p. 51. McCarthy contends that slaves and women are used in love poetry 'as instruments to express the selfhood of the author'; see Kathleen McCarthy, '*Servitium amoris: amor servitii*', in S.R. Joshel and S. Murnaghan (eds), *Women and Slaves in Greco-Roman Culture: Differential Equations* (London and New York, 1998), p. 175.

83 For more on these troubling poems, see Sharon James, 'Slave-rape and female silence in Ovid's love poetry', *Helios*, 24/1 (1997), pp. 60–76. In his *Ars Amatoria*, Ovid outlines at greater length – and with greater brutality and detachment – the role of the maid in a mistress's seduction (351–398), at one point openly deliberating the value of raping the slave (375 ff.). For James, Ovid's brutal treatment of slave women seeks to expose the precariousness of the slave woman's position at Rome; see James, 'Slave-rape', p. 74.

84 John T. Davis, *Dramatic Pairings in the Elegies of Propertius and Ovid*, Noctes Romanae 15 (Bern and Stuttgart, 1977), p. 100.

II. AUTHOR AND *EGO*

1 Allen traces the influence of Catullus' formulation on later Roman writers in Archibald W. Allen, '"Sincerity" and the Roman elegists', *Classical Philology*, 45/3 (1950), pp. 152–153.

2 For a fuller discussion of ancient views of the authorial persona, see Diskin Clay, 'The theory of the literary persona in antiquity', *Materiali e discussioni per l'analisi dei testi classici*, 40 (1998), pp. 9–40.

3 The phrase is taken from Paul Veyne, *Roman Erotic Elegy: Love, Poetry, and the West*, tr. D. Pellauer (Chicago and London, 1988), p. 50.

4 See Victoria Pedrick, 'The abusive address and the audience in Catullan poems', *Helios*, 20/2 (1993), pp. 173–196.

5 David Wray, *Catullus and the Poetics of Roman Manhood* (Cambridge and New York, 2001), p. 65.

6 See the helpful overview of modern scholars' attitudes towards Catullus at Wray, *Catullus and the Poetics*, pp. 9–13. See also Eric Havelock, *The Lyric Genius of Catullus* (New York, repr. 1967) and William Fitzgerald, *Catullan Provocations: Lyric Poetry and the Drama of Position* (Berkeley, Los Angeles and London, 1995).

7 Paul Allen Miller, *Lyric Texts and Lyric Consciousness: The Birth of a Genre from Archaic Greece to Augustan Rome* (London and New York, 1994), p. 52.

8 Ibid., pp. 55–57. See also Daniel L. Selden, '*Caveat lector*: Catullus and the rhetoric of performance', in R. Hexter and D. Selden (eds), *Innovations of Antiquity* (New York and London, 1992), pp. 461–512.

9 Micaela Janan, '*When the Lamp is Shattered*': *Desire and Narrative in Catullus* (Carbondale and Edwardsville, 1994), p. x.

10 Richard F. Thomas, 'Sparrows, hares, and doves: a Catullan metaphor and its tradition', *Helios*, 20/2 (1993), pp. 132–133.

11 Regarding the ongoing debate, see G. Giangrande, 'Catullus' lyrics on the passer',

Museum Philologum Londiniense, 1 (1975), pp. 137–146; H.D. Jocelyn, 'On some unnecessarily indecent interpretations of Catullus 2 and 3', *American Journal of Philology*, 101/4 (1980), pp. 421–441; Richard Hooper, 'In defence of Catullus' dirty sparrow', *Greece and Rome*, 32/2 (October 1985), pp. 162–178; and Thomas, 'Sparrows, hares, and doves', pp. 131–142.

12 Cf. Sappho 105c. See Paul Allen Miller, 'Sappho 31 and Catullus 51: the dialogism of lyric', *Arethusa*, 26/2 (1993), p. 193.

13 Catullus reuses the same image in his own wedding poem, 62.39–47.

14 See Elizabeth Manwell, 'Gender and masculinity', in Marilyn B. Skinner (ed.), *A Companion to Catullus* (Malden, 2007), pp. 116–117.

15 For more on the question, see also M.L. Clarke, 'Latin love poets and the biographical approach', *Greece and Rome*, 23/2 (1976), pp. 132–139.

16 Allen describes the scholarly treatment of Propertius at Archibald W. Allen, '*Sunt qui Propertium malint*', in J.P. Sullivan (ed.), *Critical Essays on Roman Literature: Elegy and Lyric* (Cambridge, MA, 1962), pp. 113–114.

17 Ibid., pp. 115–117.

18 Ibid., p. 117.

19 J.P. Postgate, *Select Elegies of Propertius* (London, 1881), p. lxxxix.

20 Allen, 'Sincerity', p. 147.

21 Ibid., pp. 146–147. See also, R. Heinze, '*Fides*', *Hermes*, 64 (1929), pp. 140–166.

22 Allen, 'Sincerity', p. 153.

23 See, for example, R.O.A.M. Lyne, *The Latin Love Poets from Catullus to Horace* (Oxford, 1980), p. viii.

24 For more background, see Maria Wyke, 'In pursuit of love: the poetic self and a process of reading: Augustan elegy in the 1980s', *Journal of Roman Studies*, 79 (1989), pp. 165–173.

25 See, for example, Duncan F. Kennedy, *The Arts of Love: Five Studies in the Discourse of Roman Love Elegy* (Cambridge, 1993). There have been important critiques of the overall shift; see, for example, Jasper Griffin, *Latin Poets and Roman Life* (Chapel Hill, 1986), p. 49.

26 The work of Maria Wyke is crucial in this area; see, for example, Maria Wyke, 'Mistress and metaphor in Augustan elegy', rev. and repr. in ead., *The Roman Mistress: Ancient and Modern Representations* (Oxford, 2002), pp. 11–45.

27 While the role of women in Rome has been studied in great depth in recent decades, begin with Moses Finley, 'The silent women of Rome', *Horizon*, 7 (1965), pp. 57–64.

28 For female poets in antiquity, see Emily Hemelrijk, *Matrona Docta: Educated Women in the Roman Elite from Cornelia to Julia Domna* (London and New York, 1999), pp. 146–184. Also, more generally, Jane M. Snyder, *The Woman and the Lyre: Women Writers in Classical Greece and Rome* (Carbondale and Edwardsville, 1989).

29 See Cicero, *Brutus* 58.211; Tacitus, *Annals* 4.53.3; Pliny, *Natural History* 7.46.

30 For more on this later Sulpicia, see C.U. Merriam, 'The other Sulpicia', *Classical World*, 84 (1991), pp. 303–305; Holt Parker, 'Other remarks on the other Sulpicia', *Classical World*, 86 (1992), pp. 89–95; and Judith P. Hallett, 'Martial's Sulpicia

and Propertius' Cynthia', in Mary DeForest (ed.), *Woman's Power, Man's Game: Essays on Classical Antiquity in Honor of Joy K. King* (Wauconda, IL, 1993), pp. 322–353.

31 Thomas Hubbard, 'The invention of Sulpicia', *Classical Journal*, 100/2 (2004), p. 188.

32 Notably, a tablet with 'the earliest known example of writing in Latin by a woman' was found in Britain and connected with the birthday celebrations of a Claudia Severa; see Alan K. Bowman and J. David Thomas, 'New texts from Vindolanda', *Britannia*, 18 (1987), p. 138.

33 Hubbard, 'The invention of Sulpicia', p. 177.

34 Cicero intriguingly reports that women spoke Latin differently from men at *On Oratory* 3.45, although his argument has more to do with the use of archaic speech patterns. See Matthew Santirocco, 'Sulpicia reconsidered', *Classical Journal*, 74/3 (1979), p. 236.

35 For a thoughtful and balanced discussion of her distinct style, see N.J. Lowe, 'Sulpicia's syntax', *Classical Quarterly*, 38/1 (1988), pp. 193–205.

36 Kristina Milnor, 'Sulpicia's (corpo)reality: elegy, authorship, and the body in {Tibullus} 3.13', *Classical Antiquity*, 21/2 (2002), p. 262.

37 Barbara Flaschenriem, 'Sulpicia and the rhetoric of disclosure', *Classical Philology*, 94/1 (1999), p. 37.

38 As Laurel Fulkerson observes, in many ways, 'Sulpicia's poetry is a "drag" performance: the positioning of a woman as elegiac poet is a reversal of elegiac norms'; see Laurel Fulkerson, 'The *Heroides*: female elegy', in Peter E. Knox (ed.), *A Companion to Ovid* (Malden and Oxford, 2009), p. 84.

39 One line (3.13.10) acknowledges sexual relations with Cerinthus, which commentators over the years have agonized over. See Mathilde Skoie, 'Sulpicia Americana: a reading of Sulpicia in the commentary by K. F. Smith (1913)', *Arethusa*, 33/2 (2000), pp. 302–304.

40 Hubbard, 'Invention of Sulpicia', p. 179.

41 One suggestion is that a later post-Ovidian poet composed all the poems in Book 3 in an attempt to imitate Tibullus' work; see Niklas Holzberg, 'Four poets and a poetess or a portrait of the poet as a young man? Thoughts on Book 3 of the *Corpus Tibullianum*', *Classical Journal*, 94 (1998–1999), pp. 169–191.

42 The cycle of these Sulpicia poems might be related to Tibullus 2.2, a birthday poem for Cornutus, whom some have identified as Cerinthus. That poem also expands on the attributes of the perfect marriage.

43 Hubbard, 'Invention of Sulpicia', p. 183.

44 Hallett has also emphasized Sulpicia's potential authorship of the 'Petale inscription'; see, for example, Judith P. Hallett, 'Human connections and paternal evocations: two elite Roman women writers and the valuing of others', in Ralph Rosen and Ineke Sluiter (eds), *Valuing Others in Classical Antiquity* (Leiden and Boston, 2010), pp. 367–370.

45 Toril Moi, 'Feminist, female, feminine', in C. Belsey and J. Moore (eds), *The Feminist Reader: Essays in Gender and the Politics of Literary Criticism* (New York, 1989), p. 126.

46 For a critical examination of later scholars' reconstructions of her life and poetic aims, including her same-sex desire, begin with Holt Parker, 'Sappho Schoolmistress', in Ellen Greene (ed.), *Re-reading Sappho: Reception and Transmission* (Berkeley, Los Angeles and London, 1996), pp. 146–183.

47 Havelock, *Lyric Genius*, p. 118; cf. Marilyn B. Skinner, '*Ego mulier*: the construction of male sexuality in Catullus', in J.P. Hallett and Marilyn B. Skinner (eds), *Roman Sexualities* (Princeton, 1997), p. 131.

48 Miller, *Lyric Texts*, p. 99.

49 Miller, 'Sappho 31 and Catullus 51', p. 185.

50 Sappho 31 was preserved only because the later writer Longinus used it as an example of excellence in his treatise *On the Sublime* 10.

51 Miller, 'Sappho 31 and Catullus 51', p. 190.

52 Ellen Greene, 'Re-figuring the feminine voice: Catullus translating Sappho', *Arethusa*, 32/1 (1999), pp. 4–5.

53 Ibid., pp. 7 and 9. On the two poems, see also Dolores O'Higgins, 'Sappho's splintered tongue: silence in Sappho 31 and Catullus 51', in Greene (ed.), *Re-reading Sappho*, pp. 68–78.

54 T.P. Wiseman, *Catullus and His World* (Oxford, 1985), p. 154.

55 Greene, 'Re-figuring', p. 11.

56 Here Ovid suggests that women are more likely to fall short in matters of Latin usage and grammar, a condescending remark that might find echo in modern views of 'ladies' Latin'. For further discussion, see Roy K. Gibson, *Excess and Restraint: Propertius, Horace, and Ovid's* Ars Amatoria (London, 2007), pp. 107–109. On documentary evidence for women's letters, see Raffaella Cribiore, *Gymnastics of the Mind: Greek Education in Hellenistic and Roman Egypt* (Princeton and Oxford, 2001), pp. 88–101.

57 For discussion of Ovid's assertion, see Albert R. Baca, 'Ovid's claim to originality and *Heroides* 1', *Transactions and Proceedings of the American Philological Association*, 100 (1969), pp. 1–10; and Maurice P. Cunningham, 'The novelty of Ovid's *Heroides*', *Classical Philology*, 44/2 (1949), pp. 100–106.

58 On Arethusa's letter, begin with Maria Wyke, 'The elegiac woman at Rome: Propertius' Book 4', in ead., *The Roman Mistress*, pp. 85–93.

59 This change in format that has led some scholars to argue that the pairs are not part of the original work, but were only later added to the corpus. See, for example, Howard Jacobson, *Ovid's* Heroides, (Princeton, 1974), p. ix; Jacobson asserts that they were written by Ovid himself, but at a later period.

60 Important early studies include Jacobson, *Ovid's* Heroides and Florence Verducci, *Ovid's Toyshop of the Heart:* Epistulae Heroidum (Princeton, 1985). See also Joseph Farrell, 'Reading and writing the *Heroides*', *Harvard Studies in Classical Philology*, 98 (1998), pp. 307–338.

61 See, for example, Patricia Rosenmeyer, *Ancient Epistolary Fictions: The Letter in Greek Literature* (Cambridge, 2001) and, more broadly, Linda Kauffman, *Discourses of Desire: Gender, Genre and Epistolary Fictions* (Ithaca, 1986).

62 Duncan F. Kennedy, 'The epistolary mode and the first of Ovid's *Heroides*', *The*

Classical Quarterly, NS 34/2 (1984), p. 415. See also Gareth Williams, 'Ovid's Canace: dramatic irony in *Heroides* 11', *The Classical Quarterly*, NS 42/1 (1992), pp. 201–209.

63 Kennedy, 'The epistolary mode', p. 413.

64 Ibid., p. 416.

65 Ibid., pp. 416–418.

66 Alessandro Barchiesi, 'Future reflexive: two modes of allusion and Ovid's *Heroides*', *Harvard Studies in Classical Philology*, 95 (1993), pp. 333–334. See also Sergio Casali, 'Tragic irony in Ovid, *Heroides* 9 and 11', *The Classical Quarterly*, NS 45/2 (1995), pp. 505–511.

67 Barchiesi, 'Future reflexive', p. 346. Knox considers whether the Medea letter is actually in conversation with Ovid's own lost tragedy in Peter E. Knox, 'Ovid's *Medea* and the authenticity of *Heroides* 12', *Harvard Studies in Classical Philology*, 90 (1986), pp. 207–223.

68 In this way, the writers of the *Heroides* might resemble Sulpicia herself; see Jacqueline Fabre-Serris, 'Sulpicia: an/other female voice in Ovid's *Heroides*: a new reading of *Heroides* 4 and 15', *Helios*, 36/2 (2009), pp. 149–173.

69 Barchiesi, 'Future reflexive', p. 350.

70 Kennedy, 'The epistolary mode', p. 421.

71 Smith similarly argues that the differences between Ariadne in *Heroides* 10 and Catullus 64 allow Ovid to suggest the 'personal growth' of Ariadne's character; see R. Alden Smith, 'Fantasy, myth, and love letters: text and tale in Ovid's *Heroides*', *Arethusa*, 27 (1994), p. 251.

72 See also Gareth Williams, 'Writing in the mother-tongue: Hermione and Helen in *Heroides* 8 (a Tomitan approach)', *Ramus*, 26/2 (1997), pp. 113–137.

73 Pamela Gordon, 'The lover's voice in *Heroides* 15: or, why is Sappho a man?' in Hallett and Skinner (eds), *Roman Sexualities*, p. 280.

74 Efrossini Spentzou, *Readers and Writers in Ovid's* Heroides: *Transgressions of Genre and Gender* (Oxford and New York, 2004), p. 3.

75 Laurel Fulkerson, *The Ovidian Heroine as Author: Reading, Writing, and Community in the* Heroides (Cambridge, 2005). Bloch has suggested that the letters addressed to Jason by Hypsiple and Medea be read in dialogue in David J. Bloch, 'Ovid's *Heroides* 6: preliminary scenes from the life of an intertextual heroine', *Classical Quarterly*, 50/1 (2000), pp. 197–209.

76 See Marilynn Desmond, 'When Dido reads Vergil: gender and intertextuality in Ovid's *Heroides* 7', *Helios*, 20/1 (1993), pp. 56–68.

77 Drinkwater, however, demonstrates some of the forms of writing that certain letter-writers are associated with in their original myths in Megan O. Drinkwater, '*Which* letter? Text and subtext in Ovid's *Heroides*', *American Journal of Philology*, 128 (2007), pp. 367–387.

78 Richard Tarrant, 'The authenticity of the letter of Sappho to Phaon (*Heroides* XV)', *Harvard Studies in Classical Philology*, 85 (1981), pp. 148–149.

79 Pamela Gordon provides a quick overview of the issues concerned at Gordon, 'The lover's voice', pp. 274–275. See also Gianpiero Rosati, 'Sabinus, the *Heroides* and the

poet-nightingale: some observations on the authenticity of the *Epistula Sapphus*', *Classical Quarterly*, 46 (1996), pp. 207–216.

80 Gordon, 'The lover's voice', p. 277.

81 Smith, 'Fantasy, myth, and love letters', pp. 267–268.

82 For more background on Roman attitudes towards female same-sex desire, see Judith P. Hallett, 'Female homoeroticism and the denial of Roman reality in Latin literature', in Hallett and Skinner (eds), *Roman Sexualities*, pp. 255–273.

83 Gordon, 'The lover's voice', p. 275.

84 Ibid., pp. 281–282.

85 Victoria Rimell, *Ovid's Lovers: Desire, Difference and the Poetic Imagination* (Cambridge and New York, 2006), p. 154.

86 Lucille Haley, 'The feminine complex in the *Heroides*', *The Classical Journal*, 20/1 (1924), p. 23.

87 Sara H. Lindheim, *Mail and Female: Epistolary Narrative and Desire in Ovid's Heroides* (Madison, 2003), p. 183.

III. POWER AND PLAY

1 Paul Veyne, *Roman Erotic Elegy: Love, Poetry, and the West*, tr. D. Pellauer (Chicago and London, 1988), p. 90. Veyne, for one, argues that it is essential that the protagonists in elegy not be married at the end. Flaschenriem calls the frequent allusions to death (especially in Propertius) 'a metaphor for the "impossibility" of desire' in elegy: see Barbara Flaschenriem, 'Loss, desire, and writing in Propertius 1.19 and 2.15', *Classical Antiquity*, 16/2 (1997), p. 262.

2 Veyne, *Roman Erotic Elegy*, p. 86; Veyne expands that 'everything is a humorous simulacrum with no trace of irony or harshness, including the vexations of love and evil company.'

3 Skinner focuses especially on the term '*scortillum*' ('little whore') and the phrase '*ut decuit cinaediorem*' (which she translates 'as suits a whoring faggot' on p. 8) at Marilyn B. Skinner, '*Ut decuit cinaediorem*: power, gender, and urbanity in Catullus 10', *Helios*, 16 (1989), p. 16. The latter insult in particular is complex in gender terms, given that the *cinaedus*, although it generally references contexts of prostitution, refers to a male subject 'in all other instances of its occurrence in classical Latin' (p. 17).

4 Ibid., p. 14.

5 Sharon James, 'Slave-rape and female silence in Ovid's love poetry', *Helios*, 24/1 (1997), p. 62. Another significant 'asymmetrical' relationship in love poetry is that of poet and patron. See Parshia Lee-Stecum, *Powerplay in Tibullus: Reading Elegies Book One* (Cambridge and New York, 1998), p. 20.

6 Both are discussed at Lee-Stecum, *Powerplay in Tibullus*, pp. 22–23.

7 J.P. Sullivan, *Propertius: A Critical Introduction* (Cambridge, 1976), p. 83; cf. Georg Luck, *The Latin Love Elegy* (New York, 1959), p. 15.

8 Sullivan, *Propertius*, p. 83. It is this 'demi-monde' that Ovid identifies as the primary audience of his *Ars Amatoria*, as we shall see in Chapter 6.

9   Dixon places the relationship of real women and their textual representations at the heart of her approach in Suzanne Dixon, *Reading Roman Women* (London, 2001); her final chapter 'The allure of "la dolce vita" in Ancient Rome' examines how and why certain ideas about Roman women have persisted across the centuries, pp. 133–156. See also Jane F. Gardner, *Women in Roman Law and Society* (Bloomington and Indianapolis, 1986), especially her final chapter entitled 'The emancipation of Roman women', pp. 257–266.

10   Maria Wyke, 'Mistress and metaphor in Augustan elegy', rev. and repr. in ead., *The Roman Mistress: Ancient and Modern Representations* (Oxford, 2002), pp. 39–40.

11   Edwards also urges greater caution in linking ancient accounts to 'real' women's activities at Catharine Edwards, *The Politics of Immorality in Ancient Rome* (Cambridge and New York, 1993), pp. 35–36.

12   Veyne, *Roman Erotic Elegy*, argues that the *puella* of Latin love poetry is by conscious design 'someone irregular, a woman one did not marry' (p. 2), while Gardner argues that 'the marginality of these women becomes, for the *amator*, the very basis of their allure' at Hunter H. Gardner, 'Ariadne's lament: the semiotic impulse of Catullus 64', *Transactions of the American Philological Association*, 137/1 (2007), p. 175.

13   On the contradictory representations of Tibullus' Delia, see, for example, Veyne, *Roman Erotic Elegy*, p. 50. Such variable social roles open class as well as ethnic distinctions, as some scholars have identified the women in love poetry specifically as Greek freedwomen; cf. R.O.A.M. Lyne, *The Latin Love Poets from Catullus to Horace* (Oxford, 1980), pp. 8–18.

14   Alison R. Sharrock, 'Womanufacture', *The Journal of Roman Studies*, 81 (1991), p. 49.

15   Ingrid E. Holmberg, 'The *Odyssey* and female subjectivity', *Helios*, 22/2 (1995), p. 104. The role of desire has also featured in Lacanian interpretations of Latin love poetry. Janan offers one definition of Lacanian desire as 'that which propels us to recover a blessed state we believe we once enjoyed' in Micaela Janan, '*When the Lamp is Shattered': Desire and Narrative in Catullus* (Carbondale and Edwardsville, 1994), p. 25.

16   Holmberg, 'The *Odyssey* and female subjectivity', p. 107.

17   Ibid., p. 111.

18   Ibid., p. 120.

19   On the various pseudonyms in love poetry, see Sullivan, *Propertius*, pp. 78–79. Fredrick notes that the name of Sulpicia's lover, Cerinthus, 'has associations with bees, wax, and writing' at David Fredrick, 'Reading broken skin: violence in Roman elegy', in Judith P. Hallett and Marilyn B. Skinner (eds), *Roman Sexualities* (Princeton, 1997), p. 187.

20   Ovid deftly recognizes this dynamic when he remarks that the name Corinna continuously inspires the desire to know who she 'really' is (*Ars* 3.538).

21   Veyne, *Roman Erotic Elegy*, pp. 60–61. Wyke has used the phrase 'the elegiac woman' to denote the women of elegy collectively as a type, countering the specificity implied by their individual names; see Maria Wyke, 'Reading female flesh: *Amores*

3.1', in A. Cameron (ed.), *History as Text: The Writing of Ancient History* (Chapel Hill and London, 1989), p. 117.

22 Veyne, *Roman Erotic Elegy*, p. 60.

23 Ibid., p. 64.

24 Corinna is discussed in detail at J.P. Sullivan, 'Two problems in Roman love elegy', *Transactions and Proceedings of the American Philological Association*, 92 (1961), pp. 522–536.

25 Moreover, the *puella*'s elusiveness becomes enmeshed in love poetry's own poetics since one of the central characteristics of elegy is also its 'lightness' (*levitas*). For a lengthier discussion of the *puella*'s 'levity', see Denise E. McCoskey, 'Reading Cynthia and sexual difference in the poems of Propertius', *Ramus*, 28/1 (1999), pp. 22–26.

26 See Barbara K. Gold, '"But Ariadne was never there in the first place": finding the female in Roman poetry', in N.S. Rabinowitz and A. Richlin (eds), *Feminist Theory and the Classics* (New York and London, 1993), p. 89.

27 Flaschenriem similarly equates the textual and sexual dimensions of Cynthia, noting that Cynthia 'becomes a focus of literary as well as erotic unease'; see Flaschenriem, 'Loss, desire, and writing', p. 259.

28 For a broader perspective, see Maria Wyke, 'Woman in the mirror: the rhetoric of adornment in the Roman world', in Léonie J. Archer, Susan Fischler and Maria Wyke (eds), *Women in Ancient Societies: An Illusion of the Night* (New York, 1994), pp. 134–151.

29 See Lawrence Richardson, jr, *Propertius: Elegies I–IV* (Norman, 1977), p. 150. See also Sharrock, 'Womanufacture', pp. 39–40 and Robert J. Gariépy, 'Beauty unadorned: a reading of Propertius I.2', *Classical Bulletin*, 57 (1980), pp. 12–14.

30 Gillian Rose, *Feminism and Geography: The Limits of Geographical Knowledge* (Minneapolis, 1993), p. 32.

31 Mary Hamer, *Signs of Cleopatra: Reading an Icon Historically*, (2nd edn., Exeter, 2008), p. 21; the actual triumph is described in ancient sources at Cassius Dio, *Roman History* 51.21.8 and Plutarch, *Antony* 86.1–3.

32 Wyke, 'Mistress and metaphor', p. 45.

33 This is not to say, however, that illegitimate children were routinely stigmatized in Roman culture; see Edwards, *Politics of Immorality*, pp. 49–51.

34 For a fuller account of ancient abortion, see Konstantinos Kapparis, *Abortion in the Ancient World* (London, 2002). In regard to Ovid's poem, see also W.J. Watts, 'Ovid, the law and Roman society on abortion', *Acta Classica*, 16 (1973), pp. 89–101.

35 For a critique of such tendencies, see Dixon, *Roman Women*, pp. 59–65.

36 Mary-Kay Gamel, '*Non sine caede*: abortion politics and poetics in Ovid's *Amores*', *Helios*, 16/2 (1989), p. 189.

37 Balsdon calls them 'singularly tasteless' at J.P.V.D. Balsdon, *Roman Women* (London, 1962), p. 192.

38 Gamel, '*Non sine caede*', pp. 190–192.

39 Ibid., p. 193.

40 The use of the gaze as a potential way of tracking gendered power was inspired

in large part by Mulvey's groundbreaking work on film; see Laura Mulvey, *Visual and Other Pleasures* (Bloomington, 1989). For the Roman era, begin with David Fredrick (ed.), *The Roman Gaze: Vision, Power, and the Body* (Baltimore, 2002). For a related discussion of art, see John R. Clarke, *Looking at Lovemaking: Constructions of Sexuality in Roman Art, 100 B.C. – A.D. 250* (Berkeley, Los Angeles and London, 1998).

41 See Saara Lilja, *The Roman Elegists' Attitude to Women* (Helsinki, 1978), pp. 119–132.

42 O'Neill, for example, uses a Lacanian perspective to argue that the recipient of the gaze in Propertius' poetry also holds a position of power at Kerill O'Neill, 'The lover's gaze and Cynthia's glance', in Ronnie Ancona and Ellen Greene (eds), *Gendered Dynamics in Latin Love Poetry* (Baltimore, 2005), p. 245. For similar dynamics in Horace, see Elizabeth H. Sutherland, 'How (not) to look at a woman: bodily encounters and the failure of the gaze in Horace's *C.* 1.19', *The American Journal of Philology*, 124/1 (2003), pp. 57–80.

43 Flaschenriem, 'Loss, desire, and writing', p. 270.

44 See, for example, Ellen Greene, *The Erotics of Domination: Male Desire and the Mistress in Latin Love Poetry* (Baltimore and London, 1998), p. 81.

45 Joan Booth, 'The *Amores*: Ovid making love', in Peter E. Knox (ed.), *A Companion to Ovid* (Malden and Oxford, 2009), p. 65.

46 See Walters, 'Invading the Roman body', p. 38.

47 The Roman soldier occupied a paradoxical position in Roman law and social attitudes given his reliance on his body; see ibid., p. 40.

48 See Leslie Cahoon, 'The bed as battlefield: erotic conquest and military metaphor in Ovid's *Amores*', *Transactions of the American Philological Association*, 118 (1988); the author notes that, in many ways, this 'is a perfect reversal' (p. 302) of the completed sexual act of 1.5.

49 Alison R. Sharrock, 'The drooping rose: elegiac failure in *Amores* 3.7', *Ramus*, 24/2 (1995), pp. 156 and 172.

50 Ibid., p. 157.

51 Sharrock notes that the closest parallels in Latin literature come from Horace's *Epodes* (11, 12, 14 and 17). Tibullus makes indirect reference to a similar experience of impotence in 1.5.39–42; see ibid., pp. 156–157.

52 The Catullus translation is taken from Sharrock; see her discussion of both passages at ibid., pp. 169–170.

53 Kirk Ormand, *Controlling Desires: Sexuality in Ancient Greece and Rome* (Westport, 2009), p. 186.

54 Catullus calls it 'a tidy, if not large sum'; see Kenneth Quinn (ed.), *Catullus: The Poems*, (2nd edn., London, 1973), p. 443. The same amount appears in poem 103, where Catullus seems to be asking for a refund from the pimp Silo.

55 See Fredrick, 'Reading broken skin', pp. 176–177. See also Marilyn B. Skinner, 'The dynamics of Catullan obscenity: cc. 37, 58 and 11', *Syllecta Classica*, 3 (1991), pp. 1–11. J.N. Adams' *The Latin Sexual Vocabulary* (Baltimore, 1982) is an essential aid for reading Catullus.

56 See Julie Hemker, 'Rape and the founding of Rome', *Helios*, 12 (1985), pp. 41–47. See also Susan Deacy and Karen F. Pierce (eds), *Rape in Antiquity* (London, 1997).

57 Gardner, *Women in Roman Law*, pp. 118–121.

58 See Leo Curran, 'Rape and rape victims in the *Metamorphoses*', in J. Peradotto and J.P. Sullivan (eds), *Women in the Ancient World: The Arethusa Papers* (Albany, 1984), pp. 263–286; and Amy Richlin, 'Reading Ovid's rapes', in ead. (ed.), *Pornography and Representation in Greece and Rome* (New York and Oxford, 1992), pp. 158–179.

59 For bodily inscriptions in antiquity, see C.P. Jones, '*Stigma*: tattooing and branding in Graeco-Roman antiquity', *Journal of Roman Studies*, 77 (1987), pp. 139–155.

60 Fredrick, 'Reading broken skin', p. 172.

61 Sharon L. James, *Learned Girls and Male Persuasion: Gender and Reading in Roman Love Elegy* (Berkeley, Los Angeles and London, 2003), p. 185.

62 See Julia H. Gaisser, '*Amor, rura*, and *militia* in three elegies of Tibullus: 1.1, 1.5 and 1.10', *Latomus*, 42 (1983), pp. 58–72.

63 In passages like these, love poetry seems to point to some of its origins in epigram; for a detailed discussion of the use of epigrammatic inscriptions in Roman poetry, see Teresa R. Ramsby, *Textual Permanence: Roman Elegists and the Epigraphic Tradition* (London, 2007).

64 Cahoon, 'The bed as battlefield', p. 294.

65 See Sharon L. James, 'Her turn to cry: the politics of weeping in Roman love elegy', *Transactions of the American Philological Association*, 133/1 (2003), pp. 99–122.

66 Lilja, *Roman Elegists' Attitude*, p. 165.

67 Greene maintains that the poem overall forges a potent bond between 'pleasure and male domination' at Ellen Greene, 'Travesties of love: violence and voyeurism in Ovid *Amores* 1.7', *The Classical World*, 92/5 (1999), p. 415.

68 Ibid.

69 Ibid., p. 417.

70 Greene, *Erotics of Domination*, p. xvi.

71 Fredrick, 'Reading broken skin', p. 190.

72 James L. Butrica, 'Propertius 3.8: unity and cohesion', *Transactions of the American Philological Association*, 111 (1981), p. 24.

73 For an overview, see James H. Dee, 'Elegy 4.8: a Propertian comedy', *Transactions of the American Philological Association*, 108 (1978), pp. 41–53.

74 See Dee, 'Elegy 4.8', for example; the author rightly emphasizes the graphic nature of the verbs describing Cynthia's actions, p. 50.

75 Richardson, *Propertius*, p. 462.

76 For the background on each myth, see Francis M. Dunn, 'The lover reflected in the *exemplum*: a study of Propertius 1.3 and 2.6', *Illinois Classical Studies*, 10/2 (1985), pp. 239–250. Significantly, Ovid parodies Propertius' opening in *Amores* 1.10.1–6.

77 See especially Hérica Valladares, 'The lover as a model viewer: gendered dynamics in Propertius 1.3', in Ancona and Greene (eds), *Gendered Dynamics*, pp. 206–242. For a bibliography on the connections of the poem to Roman art, see also Dunn, 'The lover reflected', pp. 242–243.

78 R.O.A.M. Lyne, 'Propertius and Cynthia: Elegy 1.3', *Proceedings of the Cambridge Philological Society*, NS 16 (1970), p. 76.

79 Brian W. Breed, 'Portrait of a lady: Propertius 1.3 and ecphrasis', *The Classical Journal*, 99/1 (2003), p. 51.

80 Cf. Greene, *Erotics of Domination*, p. 58; the author presents a more pessimistic view of Cynthia's speech.

81 See the important article by Judith de Luce, '"O, for a thousand tongues to sing": a footnote on metamorphosis, silence, and power', in Mary DeForest (ed.), *Woman's Power, Man's Game: Essays on Classical Antiquity in Honor of Joy K. King* (Wauconda, IL, 1993), pp. 305–321.

82 Breed, 'Portrait of a lady', p. 42.

83 Judith Hallett, 'Women's voices and Catullus' poetry', *The Classical World*, 95/4 (2002), pp. 421–424.

84 Hallett, 'Women's voices', pp. 422–423; although, Hallett suggests that in fact 2a and 51 can be assigned to Lesbia (pp. 423–424). For an example of Lesbia's potential ability to 'talk back' in poem 36, see David Wray, *Catullus and the Poetics of Roman Manhood* (Cambridge and New York, 2001), p. 180.

85 In providing a detailed description of a work of art (i.e. the embroidered cloth) within a literary text, Catullus takes advantage of a popular form of ancient narrative called ecphrasis; see Andrew Laird, 'Sounding out ecphrasis: art and text in Catullus 64', *Journal of Roman Studies*, 83 (1993), pp. 18–30.

86 Julia H. Gaisser, 'Threads in the labyrinth: competing views and voices in Catullus 64', *The American Journal of Philology*, 116/4 (1995), p. 595.

87 See, for example, Breed, 'Portrait of a lady', p. 35.

88 Gardner, 'Ariadne's lament', pp. 147 and 148.

89 Ibid., pp. 170–175.

90 In relation to other negative speech acts, Propertius accuses Cynthia of saying bad things about him in 2.9.21–22.

91 Maria Wyke, 'The elegiac woman at Rome: Propertius' Book 4', in ead., *The Roman Mistress*, p. 85.

92 See, for example, John Warden, *Fallax Opus: Poet and Reader in the Elegies of Propertius* (Toronto, Buffalo and London, 1980). See also Basil Dufallo, *The Ghosts of the Past: Latin Literature, the Dead, and Rome's Transition to a Principate* (Columbus, 2007), pp. 77–84.

93 Wyke, 'The elegiac woman at Rome', p. 106.

94 William C. Helmbold, 'Propertius IV.7: prolegomena to an interpretation', *University of California Publications in Classical Philology*, 13/9 (1949), p. 342.

95 Dorothy K. Lange, 'Cynthia and Cornelia: two voices from the grave', in C. Deroux (ed.), *Studies in Latin Literature and Roman History I*, Collection Latomus 164 (Brussels, 1979), p. 338.

96 Warden, *Fallax Opus*, p. 70.

97 For the sexual connotations of her phrasing, see Theodore D. Papanghelis, *Propertius: A Hellenistic Poet on Love and Death* (Cambridge and New York, 1987), p. 23.

98   Compare Lesbia's oath in Catullus 36 that she will burn 'the worst poet's most select writings' (6–7).

99   Barbara Flaschenriem, 'Speaking of women: "female voice" in Propertius', *Helios*, 25/1 (1998), p. 61.

100 Lange, 'Cynthia and Cornelia', p. 336.

101 For a critical response to the poem, see Judith Hallett, 'Queens, *princeps* and women of the Augustan elite: Propertius' Cornelia-elegy and the *Res Gestae Divi Augusti*', in R. Winkes (ed.), *The Age of Augustus*, Archaeologia Transatlantica 5 (Belgium, 1985), p. 73.

102 Richardson, *Propertius*, p. 481.

103 See Greene, *Erotics of Domination*, p. xii; the author argues that critics have tended too much to focus on (and identify with) the workings of male desire in elegy.

104 Propertius uses the term *pudor* here to speak of the appropriate behaviour for women; for the related concept of *pudicitia*, see Rebecca Langlands, *Sexual Morality in Ancient Rome* (Cambridge and New York, 2006).

105 See Molly Myerowitz, *Ovid's Games of Love* (Detroit, 1985), pp. 117–120.

106 Aliston Keith, '*Tandem venit amor*: a Roman woman speaks of love', in Hallett and Skinner (eds), *Roman Sexualities*, p. 307.

107 For a brief introduction to the Greek myth of the Amazons, see Elaine Fantham et al., *Women in the Classical World* (New York and Oxford, 1994), pp. 128–135.

108 See John Warden, 'Another would-be Amazon: Propertius 4.4.71–72', *Hermes*, 106 (1978), pp. 177–187. Also Jeri B. DeBrohun, *Roman Propertius and the Reinvention of Elegy* (Ann Arbor, 2003), pp. 194–195.

109 See Livy, *From the Foundation of the City* 1.11.5–9. For other versions of the story, see Jennifer A. Rea, *Legendary Rome: Myth, Monuments, and Memory on the Palatine and Capitoline* (London, 2007), p. 114.

110 A permanent record of it was enshrined in the so-called Tarpeian rock, a site of sheer drop along the Capitoline from which traitors were said to be tossed to their deaths.

111 For the Augustan use of Tarpeia's myth, see Tara S. Welch, *The Elegiac Cityscape: Propertius and the Meaning of Roman Monuments* (Columbus, 2005), pp. 58–62.

112 For these sites as ways of referring to the Capitoline hill, see Richardson, *Propertius*, p. 435.

113 Welch, *Elegiac Cityscape*, p. 57.

114 Ibid.

115 For background on the Vestal Virgins, begin with Mary Beard, 'Re-reading (Vestal) virginity' in R. Hawley and B. Levick (eds), *Women in Antiquity: New Assessments* (London and New York, 1995), pp. 166–177.

116 See Welch, *Elegiac Cityscape*, pp. 74–76.

117 Richardson, *Propertius*, p. 440.

118 Welch, *Elegiac Cityscape*, p. 57.

119 See, for example, Micaela Janan, *The Politics of Desire: Propertius* IV (Berkeley, Los Angeles, and London, 2001), pp. 70–84.

120 Welch, *Elegiac Cityscape*, p. 68.

121 See Monica Silveira Cyrino, 'Heroes in d(u)ress: transvestism and power in the myths of Herakles and Achilles', *Arethusa*, 31/2 (1998), pp. 207–241.

122 DeBrohun, *Roman Propertius*, p. 22.

123 Welch, *Elegiac Cityscape*, pp. 114–115, 124–126.

124 Richardson, *Propertius*, p. 471.

125 In fact, the politician Clodius had caused a public scandal by sneaking into the rites in 62 BCE dressed as a woman; see Welch, *Elegiac Cityscape*, p. 117. Tibullus warns a man whose wife is going to attend the Bona Dea that she may be using the occasion for something else (1.6.21–24); cf. Welch, *Elegiac Cityscape*, p. 123.

126 Ibid., p. 119.

127 DeBrohun, *Roman Propertius*, pp. 121–125. See also, W.S. Anderson, '*Hercules exclusus*: Propertius 4.9', *The American Journal of Philology*, 85 (1964), pp. 1–12. Emblematic of the barriers that persist in love poetry, the '*paraclausithyron*' refers to an impassioned appeal to the inanimate door standing between lovers, e.g. Catullus 67, Tibullus 1.2, Propertius 1.16 and Ovid, *Amores* 1.6. See Christopher Nappa, 'Elegy on the threshold: generic self-consciousness in Propertius 1.16', *Classical World*, 101/1 (2007), pp. 57–73.

128 See Nicole Loraux, 'Herakles: the super-male and the feminine', in D.M. Halperin, J.J. Winkler and F.I. Zeitlin (eds), *Before Sexuality: The Construction of Erotic Experience in the Ancient Greek World* (Princeton, 1990), pp. 21–52.

129 DeBrohun, *Roman Propertius*, pp. 139–140; the author sees the boundary-crossing as one of genre more than gender.

130 For one way to read the effects of the poem's progression, i.e. through its resolution in a 'violent reassertion' of 'rigid gender roles', see Welch, *Elegiac Cityscape*, p. 114.

131 Ibid., p. 131.

132 Janan, *Politics of Desire*, pp. 144–145.

133 See Shane Butler, 'Notes on a *membrum disiectum*', in S.R. Joshel and S. Murnaghan (eds), *Women and Slaves in Greco-Roman Culture: Differential Equations* (London and New York, 1998), pp. 236–255. For the broader context of Cybele's cult, see Jacob Latham, '"Fabulous clap-trap": Roman masculinity, the cult of Magna Mater, and literary constructions of the *galli* at Rome from the Late Republic to Latin antiquity', *Journal of Religion*, 92/1 (2012), pp. 84–122.

134 Marilyn B. Skinner, '*Ego mulier*: the construction of male sexuality in Catullus', in Hallett and Skinner (eds), *Roman Sexualities* (Princeton, 1997), p. 137.

135 Ibid., pp. 141 and 142.

136 Alison Sharrock, 'Constructing characters in Propertius', *Arethusa*, 33/3 (2000), p. 266.

137 Ibid., p. 270.

138 Greene, *Erotics of Domination*, p. 104.

139 Quoted at Greene, 'Re-figuring the feminine', p. 5, n. 10.

140 See, for example, B. Heiden, '*Sic te servato*: an interpretation of Propertius 1.21', *Classical Philology*, 90 (1995), pp. 161–167.

141 Miller reviews the arguments against at Paul Allen Miller, *Subjecting Verses: Latin Love Elegy and the Emergence of the Real* (Princeton, 2004), pp. 80–83. For Janan,

it is precisely the myriad problems generated by the varying images of Gallus that determine his centrality to the Propertian corpus; see Janan, *Politics of Desire*, p. 18.

142 See, for example, Richardson, *Propertius*, p. 207; the author prefers a more open-ended reading, especially when it comes to 1.21.

143 Miller, *Subjecting Verses*, p. 86.

144 Ibid., p. 84.

145 Ibid., p. 85.

146 Recent studies include Craig A. Williams, *Roman Homosexuality: Ideologies of Masculinity in Classical Antiquity* (New York and Oxford, 1999) and Ormand, *Controlling Desires*.

147 See Walters, 'Invading the Roman body', pp. 30–31.

148 Ormand, *Controlling Desires*, p. 198.

149 Holt Parker, 'The teratogenic grid', in Hallett and Skinner (eds), *Roman Sexualities*, p. 47.

150 Walters, 'Invading the Roman body', p. 31.

151 Judith Hallett, '*Perusinae Glandes* and the changing image of Augustus', *American Journal of Ancient History*, 2 (1977), p. 157. One bullet even seems to have turned his name into a feminine form.

152 See Edwards, *Politics of Immorality*, p. 91.

153 Wray, *Catullus and the Poetics*, p. 120.

154 For further discussion of this category, see Parker, 'The teratogenic grid', pp. 60–62. See also Amy Richlin, 'Not before homosexuality: the materiality of the *cinaedus* and the Roman law against love between men', *Journal of the History of Sexuality*, 3/4 (1993), pp. 523–573.

155 See Wray, *Catullus and the Poetics*, pp. 156–160 and Ormand, *Controlling Desires*, pp. 194–198.

156 Ormand, *Controlling Desires*, pp. 192–193.

157 Frederick, 'Reading broken skin', p. 176.

158 Ormand, *Controlling Desires*, p. 194.

159 James, *Learned Girls*, pp. 9–10. Virgil has often also been labelled 'homosexual' in modern times, although, as we have seen, the term can be misleading when applied to Roman culture; see Parker, 'The teratogenic grid', p. 56.

160 Lee-Stecum, *Powerplay in Tibullus*, p. 287; Lilja suggests that 'Tibullus reacts to the infidelity of Marathus far more passionately than to the infidelity of Delia and Nemesis' at Lilja, *Roman Elegists' Attitude*, p. 221.

161 Lee-Stecum: *Powerplay in Tibullus*, p. 288.

162 See Brenda H. Fineberg, 'Repetition and the poetics of desire in Tibullus 1.4', *The Classical World*, 92/5 (1999), pp. 426–427.

163 Fredrick, 'Reading broken skin', pp. 174–175. See also, Konstantinos P. Nikoloutsos, 'Beyond sex: the poetics and politics of pederasty in Tibullus 1.4', *Phoenix*, 61 (2007), pp. 55–82.

164 James, *Learned Girls*, p. 12.

165 See Edwards, *Politics of Immorality*, pp. 71–72.

166 Toril Moi, 'Feminist, female, feminine', in C. Belsey and J. Moore (eds), *The Feminist*

Reader: Essays in Gender and the Politics of Literary Criticism (New York, 1989), pp. 117–118.

167 See, for example, the special issue of *Helios*, 17 (1990), which initiated important discussions of Ovid and feminism.

168 Paul Allen Miller and Chuck Platter, 'Introduction', *The Classical World*, 92/5 (1999), p. 405. See also the account of contemporary feminist criticism at James, *Learned Girls*, pp. 28–30, and Maria Wyke, 'Taking the woman's part: gender and scholarship on love elegy', in ead., *The Roman Mistress*, pp. 155–191.

169 Janan, *Politics of Desire*, p. 165.

170 Gold describes Augustan elegy as emerging from an 'unsettled political climate, the concomitant shakeup of societal values, and the search for an individual response to the failure of the patriarchal state in Rome at that time' at Gold, 'But Ariadne was never there', p. 77.

171 Paul Allen Miller, 'Why Propertius is a woman: French feminism and Augustan elegy', *Classical Philology*, 96/2 (2001), p. 132.

172 Ibid., p. 127.

173 Judith P. Hallett, 'The role of women in Roman elegy: counter-cultural feminism', *Arethusa*, 6 (1973), p. 108.

174 Aya Betensky, 'Forum', *Arethusa*, 6 (1973), p. 267. Hallett and Betensky replied to one another in *Arethusa*, 7 (1974).

175 Wyke, 'Mistress and metaphor', p. 13.

176 Ibid., pp. 42–43.

177 Gardner, 'Ariadne's lament', p. 176.

178 James, *Learned Girls*, p. 210.

179 Gold, 'But Ariadne was never there', p. 92.

180 Gold expands that 'Propertius's figure of the female defies any identification and, at least by that act of defying identification, manages to elude the traditional categories that have been used to describe the female in Western literature' at ibid., p. 93.

181 Ibid., p. 83.

182 Ormand, *Controlling Desires*, p. 198.

183 Greene, *Erotics of Domination*, p. xiii.

184 Miller, 'Why Propertius is a woman', p. 143.

185 Ibid., p. 144.

186 Paul Allen Miller and Chuck Platter, 'Crux as symptom: Augustan elegy and beyond', *The Classical World*, 92/5 (1999), p. 446.

187 Sharrock, 'Constructing characters', p. 267.

188 Vicki Kirby, '"Feminisms, reading, postmodernisms": rethinking complicity', in S. Gunew and A. Yeatman (eds), *Feminism and the Politics of Difference* (Boulder and San Francisco, 1993), p. 32.

189 Kathryn J. Gutzwiller and Ann N. Michelini,'Women and other strangers: feminist perspectives in classical literature', in J.E. Hartman and E. Messer-Davidow (eds), *(En)Gendering Knowledge: Feminists in Academe* (Knoxville, 1991), pp. 77 and 78. See also Mary-Kay Gamel, 'Reading as a man: performance and gender in Roman elegy', *Helios*, 25/1 (1998), pp. 79–95.

IV. READERS AND WRITERS

1   Calvus also appears in 53 and 96. Horace insults Catullus and Calvus in *Satires* 1.10. For Catullus' attitudes towards other authors, see also 22, 36 and 95.

2   See Catullus' poems 74, 80, 88, 89, 90, and 91.

3   Lawrence Richardson, jr, *Propertius: Elegies I–IV* (Norman, 1977), p. 315.

4   For a detailed analysis of Ovid's literary lists, see Richard Tarrant, 'Ovid and ancient literary history', in P. Hardie (ed.), *The Cambridge Companion to Ovid* (Cambridge, 2002), pp. 13–33; and Barbara Weiden Boyd, *Ovid's Literary Loves: Influence and Innovation in the* Amores (Ann Arbor, 1997), pp. 19–48.

5   Alessandro Barchiesi, *The Poet and the Prince* (Berkeley, 1997), p. 26.

6   Peter E. Knox, 'A Poet's life', in id. (ed.), *A Companion to Ovid* (Malden and Oxford, 2009), p. 4.

7   Sharon L. James, *Learned Girls and Male Persuasion: Gender and Reading in Roman Love Elegy* (Berkeley, Los Angeles and London, 2003), pp. 219–220. On the *puella* as reader, see Sharon James, 'Slave-rape and female silence in Ovid's love poetry', *Helios*, 24/1 (1997), pp. 61–62. For a number of occasions where Ovid points to a specifically female readership, see Mary-Kay Gamel, '*Non sine caede*: abortion politics and poetics in Ovid's *Amores*', *Helios*, 16/2 (1989), p. 186.

8   For Cynthia's problematic reading of Helen in the *Iliad*, see Denise E. McCoskey, 'Reading Cynthia and sexual difference in the poems of Propertius', *Ramus*, 28/1 (1999), p. 16. Ovid cagily attempts to circumvent the importance of the *puella*'s literary verdict when he professes himself susceptible to all sorts of women, including those who consider Callimachus' poetry 'rustic' compared to his and those who find fault with his own verse (*Amores* 2.4.19–22).

9   James, *Learned Girls*, pp. 106–107.

10 The most common metre in Catullus' poetry was hendecasyllabic, a metre that featured in some forty of his poems and became strongly associated with him in later centuries. See Julia H. Gaisser, *Catullus and His Renaissance Readers* (Oxford, 1993), p. 195.

11 See Robert J. Baker, '*Duplices tabellae*: Propertius 3.23 and Ovid, *Amores* 1.12', *Classical Philology*, 68/2 (1973), pp. 109–113. See also Elizabeth Meyer, 'Wooden wit: *tabellae* in Latin poetry', in E. Tylawsky and C. Weiss (eds), *Essays in Honor of Gordon Williams: Twenty-Five Years at Yale* (New Haven, 2001), pp. 201–212.

12 On Ovid 1.10, see Leo Curran, 'Ovid, *Amores* 1.10', *Phoenix*, 18/4 (1964), pp. 314–319.

13 Nisbet, for example, reassures his readers that 'a Cynthia would not expect payment cash down: like the poets themselves in relation to their patrons, mistresses did better when their recompense was undefined' in R.G.M. Nisbet, 'Pyrrha among roses: real life and poetic imagination in Augustan Rome', *Journal of Roman Studies*, 77 (1987), p. 187.

14 Sharon L. James, 'The economics of Roman elegy: voluntary poverty, the *recusatio*, and the greedy girl', *The American Journal of Philology*, 122/2 (2001), p. 225. See also Suzanne Dixon, 'Exemplary housewife or luxurious slut?: Cultural representations

of women in the Roman economy', in F. McHardy and E. Marshall (eds), *Women's Influence on Classical Civilization* (London and New York, 2004), pp. 56–74.

15   James, 'The economics', p. 227; see also ead., *Learned Girls*, p. 213.

16   James, 'The economics', p. 239.

17   As Myers notes, there is a distinct cultural hostility expressed against older women in classical literature; see K. Sara Myers, 'The poet and the procuress: the *lena* in Latin love elegy', *Journal of Roman Studies*, 86 (1996), p. 6. Also, on Ovid's 'advice' to ageing women, see Victoria Rimell, 'Facing facts: Ovid's *Medicamina* through the looking glass', in Ronnie Ancona and Ellen Greene (eds), *Gendered Dynamics in Latin Love Poetry* (Baltimore, 2005), p. 178.

18   In fact, she functions as a kind of scapegoat in Tibullus, allowing Tibullus to claim at one point that 'the *lena* is the one who injures me, the girl herself is good' (2.6.44).

19   Myers, 'The poet and the procuress', p. 7.

20   See Kathryn J. Gutzwiller, 'The lover and the *lena*: Propertius 4.5', *Ramus*, 14/2 (1985), pp. 108–112; cf. Myers, 'The poet and the procuress', pp. 19–20.

21   Compare the famous designation of poetry as a 'monument' in Horace, *Ode* 3.30.1.

22   Richardson, *Propertius*, p. 8.

23   For the significance of this description, see Maria Wyke, 'Reading female flesh: *Amores* 3.1', in A. Cameron (ed.), *History as Text: The Writing of Ancient History* (Chapel Hill and London, 1989), pp. 148–151.

24   Some scholars have posited that 2.10 is actually the first poem of the next book, and that the current Book 2 of Propertius contains the remains of two separate books; see Margaret Hubbard, *Propertius* (New York, 1975), p. 41 and Chapter 1.

25   Maria Wyke, 'Written women: Propertius' *scripta puella* (2.10–13)', in ead., *The Roman Mistress: Ancient and Modern Representations* (Oxford, 2002), p. 52.

26   Richardson, *Propertius*, p. 242.

27   On the highly literary nature of this poem, see Parshia Lee-Stecum, 'Poet/reader, authority deferred: re-reading Tibullan elegy', *Arethusa*, 33/2 (2000), pp. 200–211.

28   For the correlation of women with '*materia*' in *Ars Amatoria*, see Molly Myerowitz, *Ovid's Games of Love* (Detroit, 1985), pp. 111–116.

29   See Trevor Fear, 'The poet as pimp: elegiac seduction in the time of Augustus', *Arethusa*, 33 (2000), pp. 217–240. See also Ellen Greene, *The Erotics of Domination: Male Desire and the Mistress in Latin Love Poetry* (Baltimore and London, 1998), pp. 108–113.

30   A.M. Keith, '*Corpus eroticum*: elegiac poetics and elegiac *puellae* in Ovid's *Amores*', *The Classical World*, 88/1 (1994), p. 31.

31   Kathleen McNamee, 'Propertius, poetry, and love', in Mary DeForest (ed.), *Woman's Power, Man's Game: Essays on Classical Antiquity in Honor of Joy K. King* (Wauconda, IL, 1993), p. 224.

32   Ibid., p. 215.

33   Wyke, 'Written women', p. 51.

34   Wyke, 'Reading female flesh', pp. 118–124.

35   See, for example, Paul Allen Miller, *Subjecting Verses: Latin Love Elegy and the Emergence of the Real* (Princeton, 2004), pp. 66–67.

36   For Tibullus' possible influence on Propertius, see Hubbard, *Propertius*, pp. 55–64.

37   Sharon James explains that 'in the *recusatio* the lover-poet gives up the financial rewards of both military service and public poetry (epic, tragedy, scientific didaxis), in favor of serving his mistress' at James, 'The economics', p. 227.

38   On the device of *recusatio* in Augustan poetry in relation to Callimachus, see Alan Cameron, *Callimachus and His Critics* (Princeton, 1995), pp. 454–483.

39   Indicative of his rich use of landscape in the poem, the final two lines allude to a passage from Virgil's sixth *Eclogue* featuring Gallus; see Jeffrey W. Tatum, 'Aspirations and divagations: the poetics of place in Propertius 2.10', *Transactions of the American Philological Association*, 130 (2000), pp. 395–396.

40   J.P. Sullivan, *Propertius: A Critical Introduction* (Cambridge, 1976), pp. 122–126.

41   Ibid., p. 71.

42   Hubbard, *Propertius*, p. 100.

43   Gregson Davis, *Polyhymnia: The Rhetoric of Horatian Lyric Discourse* (Berkeley, 1991), p. 11.

44   Hubbard, *Propertius*, pp. 70–71.

45   For a discussion of the historical episodes Propertius credits to Ennius' verse, see Francis Cairns, 'Propertius the historian (3.3.1–12)?', in D.S. Levene and D.P. Nelis (eds), *Clio and the Poets: Augustan Poetry and the Traditions of Ancient Historiography* (Leiden, Boston and Köln, 2002), pp. 25–44.

46   On the relationship between Horace and Propertius, see Sullivan, *Propertius*, pp. 12–31. Nethercut argues that Propertius' humour in responding to Horace has often been underestimated; see William R. Nethercut, 'The ironic priest', *American Journal of Philology*, 91/4 (1970), pp. 385–407.

47   Katharina Volk, *Ovid* (Malden and Oxford, 2010), p. 50.

48   Archibald W. Allen, '"Sincerity" and the Roman elegists', *Classical Philology*, 45/3 (1950), p. 157.

49   Patricia Watson, 'Mythological *exempla* in Ovid's *Ars Amatoria*', *Classical Philology*, 78/2 (April, 1983), p. 118.

50   Fritz Graf, 'Myth in Ovid', in Hardie (ed.), *Cambridge Companion*, p. 113.

51   Watson, 'Mythological *exempla*', p. 119.

52   Richardson, *Propertius*, p. 147.

53   For further discussion of the passage, including its influence on Ovid's use of the myth, see Francis Cairns, 'Some observations on Propertius 1.1', *Classical Quarterly*, 24 (1974), pp. 94–99.

54   Graf, 'Myth in Ovid', pp. 114–115. See also Mary H.T. Davisson, '"*Quid moror exemplis?*": mythological *exempla* in Ovid's pre-exilic poems and the elegies from exile', *Phoenix*, 47/3 (1993), pp. 213–237.

55   Boyd, *Ovid's Literary Loves*, p. 10.

56   See James, *Learned Girls*; the author proposes more particularly that certain poems of the *Amores* are 'designed to showcase particular issues and problems in elegy' (p. 156).

57   Boyd, *Ovid's Literary Loves*, p. 18; cf. James, *Learned Girls*, p. 155.

58   The identity of Macer has been debated. In his *Epistulae ex Ponto* Ovid tags him as 'Ilian'

Macer (*Ex Ponto* 4.16.6) referring probably to the latter's preoccupation with an epic about the events before and after the *Iliad*. This is most likely the same Aemilius Macer whom Ovid also mentions in the legacy list in the *Tristia* (4.10.41–54), the author of didactic poetry. See Peter Green, *Ovid: Erotic Poems* (London, 1982), pp. 26–28.

59   The reason for Ovid's address to Macer in 2.18 can be explained as an attempt to bring Macer, a devotee of serious genres, to Ovid's camp of love poets by showing him that love elegy is also suited for a genre as serious as tragedy and thus is not to be taken lightly.

60   Paul Zanker, *The Power of Images in the Age of Augustus*, tr. A. Shapiro (Ann Arbor, 1990), p. 195.

61   Green, *Ovid: Erotic Poems*, p. 269.

62   For a more detailed discussion of Propertius' and Tibullus' influences on Ovid, see S.J. Heyworth, 'Propertius and Ovid', in Knox (ed.), *Companion to Ovid*, pp. 265–278; and Robert Maltby, 'Tibullus and Ovid', in Knox (ed.), *Companion to Ovid*, pp. 279–293.

63   Paul Allen Miller (ed.), *Latin Erotic Elegy* (London and New York, 2002), p. 247.

64   Green, *Ovid: Erotic Poems*, p. 325.

65   Ibid.

66   Ibid.

67   Joan Booth, 'The *Amores*: Ovid making love', in Knox (ed.), *Companion to Ovid*, pp. 66–67.

68   The dichotomy of *poeta* and *vates* was initiated by Virgil in his *Eclogues* (*c.*39 BCE); it acquired special poignancy in love elegy as the poets sought to establish the significance of their work. The most detailed discussion of the concept during this period can be found in J.K. Newman, *The Concept of Vates in Augustan Poetry* (Brussels, 1967). See also Molly Pasco-Pranger, '"*Vates operosus*": vatic poetics and antiquarianism in Ovid's *Fasti*', *The Classical World*, 93/3 (2000), pp. 275–291.

69   See Caroline A. Perkins, 'Ovid's erotic *vates*', *Helios*, 27/1 (2000), pp. 53–62.

70   Boyd, *Ovid's Literary Loves*, p. 5.

71   Steven Green, 'Lessons in love: fifty years of scholarship on the *Ars Amatoria* and *Remedia Amoris*', in Roy Gibson, Steven Green and Alison Sharrock (eds), *The Art of Love: Bimillennial Essays on Ovid's* Ars Amatoria *and* Remedia Amoris (Oxford, 2006), p. 5.

72   Ibid., p. 7.

73   J.M. Fyler, '*Omnia vincit amor*: incongruity and the limitations of structure in Ovid's elegiac poetry', *Classical Journal*, 66 (1971), pp. 196–203.

74   S. Harrison, 'Ovid and genre: evolutions of an elegist', in Hardie (ed.), *Cambridge Companion*, p. 84.

75   Green, 'Lessons in love', pp. 14–15.

76   Christopher Brunelle, 'Form vs. function in Ovid's *Remedia Amoris*', *The Classical Journal*, 96/2 (December 2000 – January 2001), p. 123.

77   Gian Biagio Conte, 'Love without elegy: the *Remedia Amoris* and the logic of a genre', tr. G. Most, repr. in *Genres and Readers: Lucretius, Love Elegy, Pliny's Encyclopedia* (Baltimore, 1994), pp. 465–467.

78 Conte proposes that 'the use Ovid makes of the aetiological scheme proves to be considerably more playful than had been thought' at Gian Biagio Conte, *Latin Literature: A History*, tr. J.B. Solodow, rev. Don Fowler and Glen W. Most (Baltimore and London, 1994), p. 356; on the *Fasti*'s politics, see also A.J. Boyle, 'Postscripts from the edge: exilic *fasti* and imperialised Rome', *Ramus*, 26/1 (1997), pp. 7–28.

79 Harrison, *Ovid and Genre*, p. 85.

V. COUNTRY AND CITY

1 Catharine Edwards, *Writing Rome: Textual Approaches to the City* (Cambridge, 1996), p. 42.

2 Jennifer A. Rea, *Legendary Rome: Myth, Monuments, and Memory on the Palatine and Capitoline* (London, 2007), p. 7.

3 As Claude Nicolet has argued, representations of space and geography were employed in unprecedented ways during the Augustan period; see Claude Nicolet, *Space, Geography, and Politics in the Early Roman Empire* (Ann Arbor, 1991). The love poets' recourse to spatial ideas also reflects their intense engagement with earlier literary traditions. See, for example, Ann Vasaly's interpretation of Cicero's use of space in Ann Vasaly, *Representations: Images of the World in Ciceronian Oratory* (Berkeley, Los Angeles and Oxford, 1993).

4 See, for example, Vasaly, *Representations*, pp. 156–190.

5 In the same poem he jokes that those who do not want to hurt his feelings refer to his farm as 'near Tivoli' rather than the less fashionable 'Sabine' (1–3).

6 In the opening poem of the *Eclogues*, Tityrus, a country dweller, tells Meliboeus, an exiled shepherd deprived of his land by a war veteran, about his journey to Rome, revealing his amazement at the grandeur of the city, which, in Tityrus' imagination, completely dwarfs his own humble rustic surroundings (19–25).

7 Rea, *Legendary Rome*, p. 13.

8 Harold G. Gotoff, 'Tibullus: *nunc levis est tractanda Venus*', *Harvard Studies in Classical Philology*, 78 (1974), p. 232.

9 David O. Ross, 'Tibullus and the country', *Atti del Convegno internazionale di studi su Albio Tibullo* (Roma, 1986), p. 251. For a different approach to Tibullus' use of landscape, see P. Lowell Bowditch, 'Tibullus and Egypt: a postcolonial reading of elegy 1.7', *Arethusa*, 44/1 (2011), pp. 89–122.

10 Gotoff, 'Tibullus', p. 232.

11 On the programmatic nature of Tibullus' first elegy, see Barbara Weiden Boyd, '*Parva seges satis est*: the landscape of Tibullan elegy in 1.1 and 1.10', *Transactions of American Philogical Association*, 114 (1984), pp. 273–280.

12 Michael Putnam, *Tibullus: A Commentary* (Oklahoma, 1973), p. 49.

13 Gotoff, 'Tibullus', p. 238.

14 Julia H. Gaisser, 'Tibullus 2.3 and Vergil's tenth *Eclogue*', *Transactions of American Philogical Association*, 107 (1977), p. 135.

15 Francis Cairns, *Tibullus: A Hellenistic Poet at Rome* (Cambridge, 1979), p. 14.

16 Allen Miller, *Subjecting Verses: Latin Love Elegy and the Emergence of the Real* (Princeton, 2004), p. 119.

17 See Gaisser, 'Tibullus 2.3', p. 141; and Guy Lee, '*Otium cum dignitate*: Tibullus 1.1', in T. Woodman and D. West (eds), *Quality and Pleasure in Latin Poetry* (Cambridge, 1974), p. 103.

18 Eleanor W. Leach, 'Poetics and poetic design in Tibullus' first elegiac book', *Arethusa*, 13 (1980), p. 86.

19 Miller observes that Messalla becomes 'the fly in the ointment with regards to Tibullus' dream of Arcadia' at Miller, *Subjecting Verses*, p. 119.

20 White observes that towards the end of the 20s BCE, 'Vergil, Tibullus, and Propertius each produced vignettes depicting the site of Rome as it looked before a city has risen there' at Peter White, *Promised Verse: Poets in the Society of Augustan Rome* (Cambridge and London, 1993), p. 182. See also Philip Hardie, 'Augustan poets and the mutability of Rome', in Powell (ed.), *Roman Poetry and Propaganda in the Age of Augustus* (London, 1992), pp. 59–82; Rhiannon Evans, 'Searching for paradise: landscape, utopia, and Rome', *Arethusa*, 36/3 (2003), pp. 285–307; and R. Maltby, 'Tibullus 2.5 and the early history of Rome: a comparison of Tibullus 2.5, Virgil's *Aeneid* and Propertius 3.9 and 4.1', *Kleos*, 7 (2002), pp. 291–304.

21 On Evander, see Sophia Papaioannou, 'Founder, civilizer, and leader: Vergil's Evander and his role in the origins of Rome', *Mnemosyne*, 56/6 (2003), pp. 680–702; cf. Elaine Fantham, 'The role of Evander in Ovid's *Fasti*', *Arethusa*, 25/1 (1992), pp. 155–171.

22 Rea, *Legendary Rome*, pp. 89–95.

23 Evidencing even greater intricacy, we can discern in such accounts the mobilization of two distinct past eras: what Rea calls 'proto-Rome, or Rome-prior-to-Romulus, and archaic Rome, or the Rome-of-Romulus', each of which holds its own set of connotations; see ibid., p. 5.

24 Ibid., p. 15.

25 Putnam, *Tibullus*, pp. 182–183.

26 Rea, *Legendary Rome*, p. 4.

27 Significantly, Tibullus transfers Rome's earliest human habitation from the Palatine to the Capitoline, underlining the prominence of Jupiter throughout the poem; see ibid., pp. 96 and 135.

28 Rea argues that Tibullus' poem invites a reading of the myth that emphasizes not fratricide, but a more positive act – a 'human sacrifice protecting the city's boundaries'; see ibid., p. 98.

29 Edwards, *Writing Rome*, p. 87.

30 The connection of women to nature was treated by Sherry Ortner in her famous essay 'Is female to male as nature is to culture?'; this work is reprinted, along with a later essay rethinking the question, in Sherry B. Ortner, *Making Gender: The Politics and Erotics of Culture* (Boston, 1996).

31 Propertius also addresses Tullus in 1.1, in effect dedicating the work to him. Tullus was presumably a nephew of Lucius Volcacius Tullus, the proconsul of Asia in 30–29 BCE; see Richardson, *Propertius*, p. 147. Tullus is also addressed in 1.14, 1.22 and 3.22.

32   In epigram 1.62, Martial professes of one woman that she arrived at Baiae a Penelope and left a Helen; cf. *Ars Amatoria* 1.255–258.

33   Solmsen lists a number of potential Hellenistic and Roman models for this type of poem at Friedrich Solmsen, 'Three elegies of Propertius' first book', *Classical Philology*, 57 (1962), pp. 73–74. Hubbard points specifically to Acontius in Callimachus' *Aetia* as a model at Margaret Hubbard, *Propertius* (New York, 1975), p. 11.

34   Richardson, *Propertius*, p. 403.

35   Richardson notes that the district 'was created by Augustus' extension of the pomoerium' and '[b]eing a new district and far from the Forum it was probably not fashionable' at Richardson, *Propertius*, p. 409.

36   On the Campus Martius, see Horace, *Ode* 1.8 and the interpretation of its use of space by Mary Jaeger, 'Reconstructing Rome: the Campus Martius and Horace, *Ode* 1.8', *Arethusa*, 28 (1995), pp. 177–191.

37   Edwards, *Writing Rome*, p. 23. For discussion of the theatre of Pompey and its adjoining portico, see Diane Favro, *The Urban Image of Augustan Rome* (Cambridge and New York, 1996), pp. 59–60; see also Jane D. Evans, 'Prostitutes in the portico of Pompey?: a reconsideration', *Transactions of the American Philological Association*, 139 (2009), pp. 123–145.

38   Equally suggestive, Propertius begins the very next poem with the word 'peace': 'Love is the god of peace, and lovers worship peace' (3.5.1). See Donald N. Levin, 'War and peace in early Roman elegy', in Hildegard Temporini and Wolfgang Haase (eds), *Aufstieg und Niedergang der römischen Welt: Geschichte und Kultur Roms im Spiegel der neueren Forschung*, 2.30.1 (1982), pp. 418–538.

39   For an excellent study on the subject, see Mary Beard, *The Roman Triumph* (Cambridge, MA, 2007).

40   There is now a consensus that this stanza refers to Julius Caesar and his future Parthian triumph, not to Octavian's triumph over Cleopatra. See R.J. Anderson, P.J. Parsons and R.G.M. Nisbet, 'Elegiacs by Gallus from Qaṣr Ibrîm', *Journal of Roman Studies*, 69 (1979), p. 141, which also contains the *editio princeps* (first publication) of Gallus' new fragment. This clarification is important in dating the fragment since it means that it could have been written only before March 44 BCE.

41   Anderson, Parsons and Nisbet, 'Elegiacs by Gallus', p. 140.

42   Peter Green, *Ovid: The Poems of Exile: Tristia and the Black Sea Letters* (Berkeley, Los Angeles and London, 2005), p. 256.

43   See Michèle Lowrie, 'Ovid's triumphs in exile: representation and power', in ead., *Writing, Performance, and Authority in Augustan Rome* (Oxford, 2009), pp. 259–275.

44   Horace also penned a poem about the temple's opening: *Ode* 1.31.

45   On the significance of the Danaid portico, see Ellen O'Gorman, 'Love and the family: Augustus and Ovidian elegy', *Arethusa*, 39 (1977), pp. 103–123. On the role of gender in the temple's decoration, especially in relation to the Danaid portico, see Barbara Kellum, 'Concealing/revealing: gender and the play of meaning in the monuments of Augustan Rome', in T. Habinek and A. Schiesaro (eds), *The*

Roman Cultural Revolution (Cambridge and New York, 1997), pp. 158–161; and Kristina Milnor, *Gender, Domesticity, and the Age of Augustus: Inventing Private Life* (Oxford, 2005), pp. 50–53. Corinna is shown at the portico in *Amores* 2.2.

46   For a more extensive interpretation of the poem, begin with Lowell Bowditch, 'Palatine Apollo and the imperial gaze: Propertius 2.31 and 2.32,' *American Journal of Philology*, 130/3 (2009), pp. 401–438.

47   William R. Nethercut, 'Propertius 2.15.41–48: Antony at Actium', *Rivista di Studi Classici*, 19 (1971), p. 301.

48   See Danijel Dzino, 'The *praetor* of Propertius 1.8 and 2.16 and the origins of the province of Illyricum', *Classical Quarterly*, 58/2 (2008), pp. 699–703.

49   See Lowell Bowditch, 'Propertius and the gendered rhetoric of luxury and empire: a reading of 2.16', *Comparative Literature Studies*, 43/3 (2006), pp. 306–325.

50   Two different huts associated with Romulus existed during the Augustan period: one on the Palatine and one on the Capitoline. See Edwards, *Writing Rome*, pp. 32–37; and Rea, *Legendary Rome*, pp. 35–38.

51   The worship of Isis was evidently quite popular in Rome; see R.E. Witt, *Isis in the Graeco-Roman World* (London, 1971); Sharon K. Heyob, *The Cult of Isis among Women in the Graeco-Roman World* (Leiden, 1975); and Friedrich Solmsen, *Isis among the Greeks and Romans* (Cambridge, MA and London, 1979). For discussion of the elegists' representation of Isis' rites, see Heyob, *Cult of Isis*, pp. 58–60; and Solmsen, *Isis among the Greeks*, pp. 68–72.

52   See John F. Miller, 'Propertius' tirade against Isis (2.33a)', *Classical Journal*, 77/2 (1981–1982), pp. 104–111.

53   Maria Wyke, 'Augustan Cleopatras: female power and poetic authority', in Powell (ed.), *Roman Poetry and Propaganda*, p. 107. For a fuller account of such practices, see Eric M. Orlin, 'Octavian and Egyptian cults: redrawing the boundaries of Romanness', *American Journal of Philology*, 129 (2008), pp. 231–253.

54   On general Augustan representations of Cleopatra, see Wyke, 'Augustan Cleopatras'; also Gottfried Mader, 'Heroism and hallucination: Cleopatra in Horace C. 1.37 and Propertius 3.11', *Grazer Beiträge*, 16 (1989), pp. 183–201.

55   For Cleopatra's actual visit to the city, see Erich Gruen, 'Cleopatra in Rome: facts and fantasies', in D. Braund and C. Gill (eds), *Myth, History and Culture in Republican Rome: Studies in Honor of T.P. Wiseman* (Exeter, 2003), pp. 257–274.

56   See Cassius Dio, *Roman History* 51.21.8 and Plutarch, *Antony* 86.1–3.

57   The exact order and meaning of these lines is disputed, see William R. Nethercut, 'Propertius 3.11', *Transactions of the American Philological Association*, 102 (1971), pp. 429–436.

58   On Propertius and Antony, see Jasper Griffin, *Latin Poets and Roman Life* (Chapel Hill, 1986), pp. 32–47.

59   On the ordering of poems here, see William R. Nethercut, 'Propertius 3.12–14', *Classical Philology*, 65/2 (1970), pp. 99–102. On the import of luxury goods, start with Grant Parker, '*Ex oriente luxuria*: Indian commodities and the Roman experience', *Journal of the Economic and Social History of the Orient*, 45/1 (2002), pp. 40–95.

60   Jeri B. DeBrohun, *Roman Propertius and the Reinvention of Elegy* (Ann Arbor, 2003), p. 8.
61   Ibid., p. 22. The concurrence of *amor* and *Roma* runs throughout Roman thought, including a proposition recorded in some ancient sources that 'the secret name of Rome, key to the possession and preservation of the city, was Amor' at Kellum, 'Concealing/revealing', p. 177.
62   DeBrohun, *Roman Propertius*, p. 96.
63   Ibid., p. 172.
64   Tara S. Welch, *The Elegiac Cityscape: Propertius and the Meaning of Roman Monuments* (Columbus, 2005), p. 3.
65   Ibid., p. 12.
66   On the use of Remus' hut here, see Rea, *Legendary Rome*, p. 109.
67   See, for example, Elaine Fantham, 'Images of the city: Propertius' new-old Rome', in Habinek and Schiesaro (eds), *Roman Cultural Revolution*, pp. 122–135. See also K.S. Rothwell, 'Propertius on the site of Rome', *Latomus*, 55/4 (1996), pp. 829–854.
68   Hans-Peter Stahl, *Propertius: 'Love' and 'War': Individual and State under Augustus* (Berkeley, 1985), pp. 256–257.
69   Welch, *Elegiac Cityscape*, p. 22.
70   Ibid., p. 24.
71   DeBrohun, *Roman Propertius*, p. 16.
72   On Vertumnus, see Welch, *Elegiac Cityscape*, pp. 35–42.
73   Ibid, p. 133.
74   Ibid, pp. 135–137.
75   Richardson, *Propertius*, p. 477.
76   Welch, *Elegiac Cityscape*, pp. 137–138.
77   Ibid., p. 145.
78   Ibid., p. 134.
79   Ibid., p. 162; cf. DeBrohun, *Roman Propertius*, p. 198.
80   DeBrohun, *Roman Propertius*, p. 89.
81   Welch, *Elegiac Cityscape*, p. 79. For one interpretation, see Francis Cairns, 'Propertius and the Battle of Actium (4.6)', in Anthony Woodman and David West (eds), *Poetry and Politics in the Age of Augustus* (Cambridge, 1984), pp. 129–168.
82   DeBrohun, *Roman Propertius*, pp. 210–214.
83   Welch, *Elegiac Cityscape*, pp. 102–103.
84   On Apollo's intersecting political and poetic roles in this era, see John F. Miller, *Apollo, Augustus, and the Poets* (Cambridge and New York, 2009).
85   DeBrohun, *Roman Propertius*, p. 68; Wickkiser similarly argues that Ovid appropriates architectural language in the *Metamorphoses* to describe his poetic contributions at Bronwen Wickkiser, 'Famous last words: putting Ovid's *sphragis* back into the *Metamorphoses*', *Materiali e discussioni per l'analisi dei testi classici*, 42 (1999), p. 129.
86   Welch, *Elegiac Cityscape*, p. 2.
87   Green, *Ovid: Erotic Poems* (London, 1982), pp. 322–323.
88   Ibid., p. 323.

89   These sentiments are resonant of the moralizing at the end of Catullus 64.

90   This view can also be found in Tibullus (e.g. 2.3.39).

91   James E.G. Zetzel, 'Poetic baldness and its cure', *Materiali e discussioni per l'analisi dei testi classici*, 36 (1996), p. 91.

92   On the passage's reliance on Propertius, see DeBrohun, *Roman Propertius*, pp. 113–115.

93   Thomas Habinek, 'Ovid and empire', in P. Hardie (ed.), *The Cambridge Companion to Ovid* (Cambridge, 2002), p. 50.

94   Green, *Ovid: Erotic Poems*, p. 385.

95   Teresa R. Ramsby and Beth Severy-Hoven, 'Gender, sex, and the domestication of the empire in art of the Augustan Age', *Arethusa*, 40 (2007), pp. 63–64. See also Habinek, 'Ovid and empire', p. 50.

96   As, for example, in *Amores* 3.4.37: 'that man is overly unrefined who gets offended if his wife is adulterous'.

97   E.K. Rand, *Ovid and His Influence* (Boston, 1925), p. 77.

98   R.O.A.M. Lyne, *The Latin Love Poets from Catullus to Horace* (Oxford, 1980), p. 259.

99   A.J. Boyle, *Ovid and the Monuments* (Bendigo, 2003), p. 4.

100 P.J. Davis, '*Praeceptor Amoris*: Ovid's *Ars Amatoria* and the Augustan idea of Rome', *Ramus*, 24 (1995), p. 187.

101 Ibid. On the porticoes of Octavia and Livia, see also Milnor, *Gender, Domesticity*, pp. 56–64.

102 Green, *Ovid: The Erotic Poems*, p. 340.

103 See Davis, '*Praeceptor Amoris*', p. 187.

104 Mario Labate, 'Erotic aetiology: Romulus, Augustus, and the rape of the Sabine women', in Roy Gibson, Steven Green and Alison Sharrock (eds), *The Art of Love: Bimillennial Essays on Ovid's* Ars Amatoria *and* Remedia Amoris (Oxford, 2006), p. 195. See also Eva Stehle, 'Venus, Cybele, and the Sabine women: the Roman construction of female sexuality', *Helios*, 16/2 (1989), pp. 143–164; and Gary B. Miles, 'The first Roman marriage and the theft of the Sabine women', in R. Hexter and D. Selden (eds), *Innovations of Antiquity* (New York and London, 1992), pp. 161–196.

105 Richard Brilliant, *Visual Narratives: Storytelling in Etruscan and Roman Art* (Ithaca and London, 1984), pp. 28–29.

106 Labate, 'Erotic aetiology', p. 199.

107 Ibid., p. 212.

VI. LOVE AND EXILE

1   Jo-Marie Claassen, '*Tristia*', in Peter E. Knox (ed.), *A Companion to Ovid* (Malden and Oxford, 2009), p. 170.

2   Allen Miller, *Subjecting Verses: Latin Love Elegy and the Emergence of the Real* (Princeton, 2004), p. 212.

3   The theory that Ovid was never in fact relegated to Tomi at all but was merely

adopting the persona of an exile seems implausible. See Peter Green, *Ovid: The Poems of Exile:* Tristia *and the* Black Sea Letters (Berkeley, Los Angeles and London, 2005), pp. x, xxiii. For more detailed refutation of that theory, see D. Little, 'Ovid's last poems: cry of pain from exile or literary frolic in Rome?', *Prudentia*, 22 (1990), pp. 23–39.

4   Miller, *Subjecting Verses*, p. 212; see also Gareth Williams, *Banished Voices: Readings in Ovid's Exile Poetry* (Cambridge, 1994), p. 7.

5   Jo-Marie Claassen, 'Ovid's poetic Pontus', in F. Cairns (ed.), *Papers of Leeds International Latin Seminar*, 6 (1990), pp. 72–73. See also J. Richmond, 'The latter days of a love poet: Ovid in exile', *Classics Ireland*, 2 (1995), pp. 97–120. The poet even admits that his repeated attacks on Tomi and its inhabitants have caused much resentment against him among the locals who gave him a place of honour and valued his presence (*Ex Ponto* 4.14.17–19).

6   Thibault suggests that Ovid's indiscretion may have been in aiding and abetting Julia's affair or that she was encouraged in her improper behaviour by merely reading the *Art of Love*; see John C. Thibault, *The Mystery of Ovid's Exile* (Berkeley and Los Angeles, 1964), p. 55.

7   See ibid., pp. 68–74: the work offers a survey of these suggestions, ranging from Ovid's accidental intrusion upon a scene of some delicacy involving Augustus' daughter's adultery to the *princeps'* practice of pederasty and Livia's preparation of poison for Agrippa Postumus, Augustus' grandson.

8   For the political theory, see Aldo Luisi and Nicoletta F. Berrino, Culpa Silenda: *Le Elegie dell'error Ovidiano* (Bari, 2002).

9   Gian Biagio Conte, *Latin Literature: A History*, tr. J.B. Solodow, rev. Don Fowler and Glen W. Most (Baltimore and London, 1994), p. 340. For more on the theories of sexual intrigue, see R. Verdière, *Le Secret du voltigeur d'amour, ou, Le Mystère de la relégation d'Ovide* (Brussels, 1992).

10   For a detailed account, see Thibault, *Mystery*, pp. 4–19.

11   This enmity, moreover, did not die with the *princeps*; even after Augustus' death, both Tiberius (Augustus' adopted son and successor) and Livia (Augustus' wife and Tiberius' mother) refused to allow Ovid to return to Rome despite his many tearful appeals (see *Epistulae ex Ponto* 2.8.37, 2.8.43, 3.1.97).

12   Matthew McGowan, *Ovid in Exile: Power and Poetic Redress in the* Tristia *and* Epistulae ex Ponto (Leiden and Boston, 2009), p. 2. McGowan's book focuses on Ovid's relationship with Augustus in light of his exilic poetry.

13   For more on the notion of 'political opposition' to Augustus, see K.A. Raaflaub and L.J. Samons, 'Opposition to Augustus', in K.A. Raaflaub and M. Toher (eds), *Between Republic and Empire: Interpretations of Augustus and His Principate* (Berkeley, Los Angeles and London, 1990), pp. 417–454. They argue against any notion of organized opposition (p. 454).

14   Although Ovid blames the *Ars Amatoria* alone for his banishment, some scholars single out the *Metamorphoses* as another possibility because it was irreverent towards traditional religion. See Maurice W. Avery, 'Ovid's *apologia*', *Classical Journal*, 32 (1936), p. 101.

15 Thibault, *Mystery*, p. 35.
16 Ibid., p. 36.
17 Green, *Poems of Exile*, p. xxiv.
18 Ronald Syme, *History in Ovid* (Oxford 1978), p. 222.
19 On Julia's plight, see Richard A. Bauman, *Women and Politics in Ancient Rome* (London and New York, 1992), pp. 108–119.
20 Syme, *History in Ovid*, p. 190.
21 Alessandro Barchiesi, *The Poet and the Prince* (Berkeley, 1997), p. 272. See also Alessandro Barchiesi, 'Voices and narrative: instances in the *Metamorphoses*', in id., *Speaking Volumes: Narrative and Intertext in Ovid and Other Latin Poets* (London, 2001), p. 76.
22 Paul Allen Miller, 'Introduction', in id. (ed.), *Latin Erotic Elegy* (London and New York, 2002), p. 32.
23 Thomas Habinek, 'Ovid and empire', in P. Hardie (ed.), *The Cambridge Companion to Ovid* (Cambridge, 2002), p. 46.
24 Adultery among the upper class was a prominent theme in Roman public discourse beginning in the late Republic; we should use some caution, however, in taking these texts as evidence of actual sexual practices. See Chapter 3 and Catharine Edwards, *The Politics of Immorality in Ancient Rome* (Cambridge and New York, 1993), pp. 35–36, 42–62.
25 See Cassius Dio, *Roman History* 54.19.
26 Edwards, *Politics of Immorality*, p. 27.
27 As this suggests, despite Augustus' continual claims that he was merely restoring the earlier Republic, the Augustan period increasingly featured a 'realignment of authority in many areas of Roman culture around the figure of Augustus'; see Parshia Lee-Stecum, 'Poet/reader, authority deferred: re-reading Tibullan elegy', *Arethusa*, 33/2 (2000), p. 179.
28 P.J. Davis, *Ovid and Augustus: A Political Reading of Ovid's Erotic Poems* (London, 2006), pp. 85–86.
29 As Little observes, 'it elaborates, codifies, and clarifies, but the underlying assumptions and attitudes are unchanged' at Douglas Little, 'Politics in Augustan poetry', in Hildegard Temporini and Wolfgang Haase (eds), *Aufstieg und Niedergang der römischen Welt: Geschichte und Kultur Roms im Spiegel der neueren Forschung*, 2.30.1 (1982), p. 254.
30 Sergio Casali, 'The art of making oneself hated: rethinking (anti-)Augustanism in Ovid's *Ars Amatoria*', in Roy Gibson, Steven Green and Alison Sharrock (eds), *The Art of Love: Bimillennial Essays on Ovid's* Ars Amatoria *and* Remedia Amoris (Oxford, 2006), p. 219.
31 Green, *Poems of Exile*, p. xi.
32 For a survey of the different opinions on the relationship between the poem and the mistake, see Thibault, *The Mystery*, p. 32.
33 Miller, 'Introduction', p. 32. As Bowditch phrases it, in the *Ars Amatoria*, 'the various conventions and topoi of elegy are revealed as a semiotic (often behavioural) system, one whose principles become [...] objective material to be taught and manipulated

for the purposes of seduction', at Phebe Lowell Bowditch, 'Hermeneutic uncertainty and the feminine in Ovid's *Ars Amatoria*: the Procris and Cephalus digression', in Ronnie Ancona and Ellen Greene (eds), *Gendered Dynamics in Latin Love Poetry* (Baltimore, 2005), p. 272.

34   Bowditch, 'Hermeneutic uncertainty', p. 272. Earlier in Book 1, when advising that the best time to approach a girl is when she is happy, Ovid equates the *puella* to the city of Troy: 'then, when she was sad, Troy was defended by arms: when happy she welcomed the horse heavy with the soldiers' (*Ars* 1.363–364).

35   Molly Myerowitz, *Ovid's Games of Love* (Detroit, 1985), pp. 57–72.

36   Davis, *Ovid and Augustus*, p. 88.

37   See Little, 'Politics in Augustan poetry', p. 319. Little argues that freedwomen would also have been regarded at the time as free citizens and thus should have been off limits as far as the *lex Iulia* is concerned.

38   R.K. Gibson, '*Meretrix* or *matrona*? Stereotypes in Ovid, *Ars Amatoria* 3', *Papers of the Leeds International Latin Seminar*, 10 (1998), pp. 295–312. See also Steven Green, 'Lessons in love: fifty years of scholarship on the *Ars Amatoria* and *Remedia Amoris*', in Gibson, Green and Sharrock (eds), *Art of Love*, p. 14.

39   Susan Treggiari, *Roman Marriage: Iusti Coniuges from the Time of Cicero to the Time of Ulpian* (Oxford, 1991), pp. 279 ff. See also Thomas A. McGinn, *Prostitution, Sexuality, and the Law in Ancient Rome* (Oxford, 1998), p. 155. Davis points out that Ovid's didactic strategy in the *Ars Amatoria* was 'based on a false premise' at Davis, *Ovid and Augustus*, p. 89.

40   For more on the opposition of *cultus* and *rusticitas* in the *Ars*, see Myerowitz, *Ovid's Games of Love*, pp. 41–72.

41   Alexander Dalzell, *The Criticism of Didactic Poetry: Essays on Lucretius, Virgil, and Ovid* (Toronto, 1996), pp. 138–139.

42   Green, 'Lessons in love', p. 13.

43   Eric Downing, 'Anti-Pygmalion: the praeceptor in *Ars Amatoria*, Book 3', *Helios*, 17 (1990), p. 238.

44   John F. Miller, 'Apostrophe, aside and the didactic addressee: poetic strategies in *Ars Amatoria* III', in A. Schiesaro, P. Mitsis and J. Clay (eds), 'Mega Nepios: il destinario nell'epos didascalisco', *Materiali e discussioni per l'analisi dei testi classici*, 31 (1993), pp. 231–241.

45   For a summary of the leading opinion of earlier scholarship, see Christopher Brunelle, 'Ovid's satirical remedies', in Ancona and Greene (eds), *Gendered Dynamics*, p. 141.

46   Ibid.

47   Miller, *Subjecting Verses*, p. 211.

48   Richard Tarrant, 'Ovid and ancient literary history', in Hardie (ed.), *Cambridge Companion*, p. 29.

49   Claassen, '*Tristia*', p. 174.

50   Green, *Poems of Exile*, p. xxxviii.

51   For more details on the pattern of addressees in the *Epistulae ex Ponto*, see A.L. Wheeler, Tristia, Ex Ponto (London, 1924), 2nd edn., rev. G.P. Goold (London and Cambridge, 1988).

52 Gareth Williams, 'Ovid's exile poetry: *Tristia, Epistulae ex Ponto* and *Ibis*', in Hardie (ed.), *Cambridge Companion*, p. 234.

53 Efrossini Spenzou, 'Silenced subjects: Ovid and the heroines in exile', in Ancona and Greene (eds), *Gendered Dynamics*, p. 319.

54 Green, *Poems of Exile*, p. xxxviii.

55 Patricia Rosenmeyer, 'Ovid's *Heroides* and *Tristia*: voices from exile', *Ramus*, 26/1 (1997), p. 29.

56 Rosenmeyer observes: 'the desperation, the longings, the self-deception, and the resistance to fate found in the *Tristia* are all prefigured in the *Heroides*' at ibid., p. 32.

57 Jo-Marie Claassen, *Displaced Persons: The Literature of Exile from Cicero to Boethius* (Madison, 1999), p. 12.

58 Spentzou, 'Silenced subjects', p. 319.

59 Raphael Lyne, 'Love and exile after Ovid', in Hardie (ed.), *Cambridge Companion*, p. 290.

60 A.J. Boyle, *Ovid and the Monuments* (Bendigo, 2003), p. 19.

61 Ibid., p. 18.

62 According to Ovid, Getic and Sarmatian were the languages most often heard at Tomi; the Greek spoken there was a bowdlerized version of the language, full of local words (see *Tristia* 5.7.52, 5.10.34–36). Latin, Ovid kept insisting, was a language utterly unfamiliar to the locals (see *Tristia* 5.10.37, 5.7.53–54).

63 Tarrant, *Ovid and Ancient Literary History*, p. 30.

64 Davis, *Ovid and Augustus*, p. 8.

65 Barchiesi, *Poet and the Prince*, p. 27.

66 Williams, 'Ovid's exile poetry', p. 238.

67 Ibid., p. 239.

68 Green, *Poems of Exile*, p. liv.

69 Robert Graves, 'The Virgil cult', *The Virginia Quarterly Review*, 38 (1962), p. 13.

70 Theodore Ziolkowski, 'Ovid in the twentieth century', in Knox (ed.), *Companion to Ovid*, p. 455.

VII. DEATH AND AFTERLIFE

1 The elegiac couplet, however, retained its popularity in antiquity and even appeared in later prose novels such as Petronius' *Satyricon* (*c.*66 CE) and Apuleius' *The Golden Ass* (*c.*160 CE). For a survey of elegy across the centuries and into the modern period, see Karen Weisman (ed.), *The Oxford Handbook of the Elegy* (Oxford and New York, 2010).

2 For more on the classical tradition, begin with Craig W. Kallendorf (ed.), *A Companion to the Classical Tradition* (Oxford, 2007).

3 The term *Rezeptionsästhetik* (sometimes translated as 'the poetics of reception') was coined in 1967 by the German academic Hans Robert Jauss and has subsequently been applied to discussions of the European reception of antiquity. See Lorna Hardwick and Christopher Stray (eds), *A Companion to Classical Receptions* (Oxford,

2008); and Charles Martindale and Richard Thomas (eds), *Classics and the Uses of Reception* (Cambridge, 2006), pp. 1–13.

4   See, for example, Rosalind Thomas, *Literacy and Orality in Ancient Greece* (Cambridge and New York, 1992), pp. 117–127.

5   This period saw the marked rise of textual criticism itself, including close study and preservation of earlier Greek literature.

6   Kenneth Quinn, 'The poet and his audience in the Augustan Age', in Hildegard Temporini and Wolfgang Haase (eds), *Aufstieg und Niedergang der römischen Welt: Geschichte und Kultur Roms im Spiegel der neueren Forschung*, 2.30.1 (1982), pp. 83–87.

7   See ibid., pp. 88–93; see also Holt Parker, 'Books and reading Latin poetry', in W.A. Johnson and H.N. Parker (eds), *Ancient Literacies: The Culture of Reading in Greece and Rome* (Oxford and New York, 2009), pp. 186–229.

8   See Raymond J. Starr, 'The circulation of literary texts in the Roman world', *The Classical Quarterly*, NS 37/1 (1987), pp. 213–223. Significantly, Catullus refers to 'book stalls' in his work (14) suggesting the presence of a public trade in books. See also Peter White, 'Bookshops in the literary culture of Rome', in Johnson and Parker (eds), *Ancient Literacies*, pp. 268–287.

9   The most extensive discussion of ancient literacy can be found in William V. Harris, *Ancient Literacy* (Cambridge, 1989). Harris makes the critical point that Latin was not the first language for many residents of the Empire during that period, including those in Italy (pp. 175 ff). On the different ways in which literacy might be defined, see also Greg Woolf, 'Literacy or literacies in Rome?', in Johnson and Parker (eds), *Ancient Literacies*, pp. 46–68.

10 On Martial's interest in Ovid, see also Craig Williams, 'Ovid, Martial, and poetic immortality: traces of *Amores* 1.15 in the *Epigrams*', *Arethusa*, 35/3 (2002), pp. 417–433.

11 Sven Lorenz, 'Catullus and Martial', in Marilyn B. Skinner (ed.), *A Companion to Catullus* (Malden, 2007), pp. 424–426.

12 Propertius' work alone can be identified in three different instances; see James Butrica, 'The transmission of the text of Propertius', in H.-C. Günther (ed.), *Brill's Companion to Propertius* (Leiden and Boston, 2006), p. 31. Virgil is the most prominent intertext in graffiti, however; see Kristina Milnor, 'Literary literacy in Roman Pompeii: the case of Vergil's *Aeneid*', in Johnson and Parker (eds), *Ancient Literacies*, pp. 288–319.

13 For more information and bibliography for these poets, see Gian Biagio Conte, *Latin Literature: A History*, tr. J.B. Solodow, rev. Don Fowler and Glen W. Most (Baltimore and London, 1994), pp. 655–661.

14 See L.D. Reynolds, 'Introduction', in id. (ed.), *Texts and Transmission: A Survey of the Latin Classics* (Oxford, 1983), p. xiv.

15 For an excellent survey of the textual transmission of most Roman writers, see Reynolds (ed.), *Text and Transmission*.

16 Reynolds, 'Introduction', p. xvii.

17 See Roberto Weiss, *The Renaissance Discovery of Classical Antiquity* (New York, 1969).

18 For an excellent account of how Latin texts are edited, see Richard Tarrant, 'Classical Latin literature', in D.C. Greetham (ed.), *Scholarly Editing: A Guide to Research* (New York, 1995), pp. 95–147.

19 Julia H. Gaisser, 'Catullus in the Renaissance', in Skinner (ed.), *Companion to Catullus*, p. 439. See also Julia H. Gaisser, *Catullus and His Renaissance Readers* (Oxford, 1993), p. 15.

20 As Gaisser argues, Martial reinforced the sense of Catullus as a 'light and racy epigrammatist, witty and often obscene, without emotional complexity, political animus, or Alexandrian intricacy' at Gaisser, 'Catullus in the Renaissance', p. 441.

21 James Butrica, 'History and transmission of the text', in Skinner (ed.), *Companion to Catullus*, pp. 26–28.

22 See Aulus Gellius, *Attic Nights* 6.20.6; see also Butrica, 'History and transmission', p. 15.

23 As Butrica writes, 'among ancient Latin poets, perhaps only the text of Propertius was corrupted to a comparable degree' at Butrica, 'History and transmission', p. 30.

24 Gaisser, 'Catullus in the Renaissance', p. 445.

25 Butrica, 'History and transmission', p. 32. See also John M. Trappes-Lomax, *Catullus: A Textual Reappraisal* (Swansea, 2007).

26 Francis Newton, 'Tibullus in two grammatical florilegia of the Middle Ages', *Transactions of American Philological Association*, 93 (1962), p. 254.

27 Ibid., p. 258.

28 Butrica, 'The transmission of the text', pp. 36–37.

29 Although relationships between the various manuscripts and their descendants continue to be contested, critics generally identify two distinct families deriving from A and N. Butrica identifies a third branch beginning with X, a now-lost manuscript dated to around 1425; see ibid., pp. 39–42. Tarrant treats this copy as part of N's family; see Richard Tarrant, 'Propertius', in Reynolds (ed.), *Texts and Transmission*, pp. 325–326. For a fuller account, see James Butrica, *The Manuscripts of Propertius* (Toronto, Buffalo and London, 1984).

30 Butrica, 'The transmission of the text', p. 41. See also Tarrant, 'Propertius', pp. 324–325.

31 Paolo Fedeli, 'The history of Propertian scholarship', in Günther (ed.), *Brill's Companion to Propertius*, pp. 3–4.

32 See D. Thomas Benediktson, *Propertius: Modernist Poet of Antiquity* (Carbondale and Edwardsville, 1989).

33 Butrica helpfully identifies five specific types of error that entered Propertius' text over the centuries at Butrica, 'The transmission of the text', pp. 31–36.

34 For an excellent survey, see Fedeli, 'The history of Propertian scholarship', pp. 1–21.

35 Paul Allen Miller, 'What is a Propertian poem?', *Arethusa*, 44 (2011), pp. 331–333.

36 See the thoughtful discussion of this issue at ibid., pp. 329–352.

37 Richard Tarrant, 'Propertian textual criticism and editing', in Günther (ed.), *Brill's Companion to Propertius*, pp. 47–48, 65.

38 On Heyworth's use of Housman, see G. Luck, 'Lessons learned from a master', in D.J. Butterfield and C.A. Stray (eds), *A. E. Housman: Classical Scholar* (London, 2009), pp. 249–250.

39 See S.J. Heyworth, 'Housman and Propertius', in Butterfield and Stray (eds), *A. E. Housman: Classical Scholar*, pp. 11–28.

40 Ibid., pp. 23–25.

41 Tom Stoppard, *The Invention of Love* (New York, 1997), p. 69. See also Kenneth Reckford, 'Stoppard's Housman', *Arion*, 9/2 (2001), pp. 108–149.

42 Stoppard, *Invention of Love*, p. 56.

43 John Richmond, 'Manuscript traditions and the transmission of Ovid's works', in B.W. Boyd (ed.), *Brill's Companion to Ovid* (Leiden and Boston, 2002), p. 443. As Possanza observes, 'we can glimpse from the indirect tradition what is happening to the text, and what we see is not encouraging' at Mark Possanza, 'Editing Ovid: immortal works and material texts', in Peter E. Knox (ed.), *A Companion to Ovid* (Malden and Oxford, 2009), p. 316.

44 Possanza, 'Editing Ovid', p. 316. There is only one fragment dated to the second half of the fifth century CE, which contains twenty-four lines of Ovid's exilic poetry.

45 Our account of Ovid's manuscript tradition closely follows the survey provided at Richmond, 'Manuscript traditions', pp. 450–451.

46 A few words should also be said about an unexpected and curious resource for restoring Ovid's elegiac texts: the Byzantine monk Maximus Planudes (*c*.1255–*c*.1305), who translated the *Amores* and the *Heroides*, along with the epic *Metamorphoses*, into Greek. His translation was so literal that it has allowed scholars to reconstruct some of the readings and the proper spelling of Greek names in the lost Latin manuscripts that he was relying on. See ibid., p. 456; and Possanza, 'Editing Ovid', p. 317.

47 For more on editing and the amended editions, see Richmond, 'Manuscript traditions', pp. 457–459; and Possanza, 'Editing Ovid', pp. 318–323.

48 Conte, *Latin Literature*, p. 329.

49 Gaisser, *Catullus and His Renaissance Readers*, p. 193; see also pp. 220–229.

50 Ibid., p. 233.

51 Simona Gavinelli, 'The reception of Propertius in Latin antiquity and Neolatin and Renaissance literature', in Günther (ed.), *Brill's Companion to Propertius*, p. 404. The changing status of the Latin love poets in schools continued to shape their reception over the centuries. See, for example, Ronnie Ancona and Judith P. Hallett, 'Catullus in the secondary school curriculum', in Skinner (ed.), *Companion to Catullus*, pp. 481–502. On the other hand, knowledge of ancient poetry for many people was limited over the centuries to what was recorded in 'commonplace books'; see Julia H. Gaisser, 'Introduction', in ead. (ed.), *Catullus in English* (London and New York, 2001), p. xxxi.

52 Gordon Braden, 'Classical love elegy in the Renaissance (and after)', in Weisman (ed.), *Oxford Handbook of the Elegy*, p. 158.

53 Braden, 'Classical love elegy', p. 158 ff.

54 Conte, *Latin Literature*, p. 329.

55 See Jeremy Dimmick, 'Ovid in the Middle Ages: authority and poetry', in P. Hardie (ed.), *The Cambridge Companion to Ovid* (Cambridge, 2002), pp. 264–287.

56 Michael L. Stapleton, *Harmful Eloquence: Ovid's* Amores *from Antiquity to Shakespeare* (Ann Arbor, 1996), p. 65.

57 John M. Fyler, 'The medieval Ovid', in Knox (ed.), *Companion to Ovid*, p. 413.

58 Ibid., p. 416.

59 G. Martelotti (ed.), *Francesco Petrarca: Prose* (Milan, 1955), p. 532.

60 Conte, *Latin Literature*, p. 362.

61 Raphael Lyne, 'Love and exile after Ovid', in Hardie (ed.), *Cambridge Companion*, p. 291.

62 Yvonne LeBlanc, 'Queen Anne in the lonely, tear-soaked bed of Penelope: rewriting the *Heroides* in sixteenth-century France', in Carol Poster and Richard Utz (eds), *The Late Medieval Epistle* (Evanston, 1996), p. 71.

63 Ibid., p. 72.

64 Ibid., p. 81.

65 For both Andrelini and Cretin, Ovid's work provided an opportunity to open a 'space of exchange' with classical antiquity. See Paul White, *Renaissance Postscripts* (Columbus, 2009), p. 187.

66 See Bernhard Zimmermann, 'The reception of Propertius in the Modern Age: Johann Wolfgang von Goethe's *Römische Elegien* and Ezra Pound's *Homage to Sextus Propertius*', tr. J. Grethlein, in Günther (ed.), *Brill's Companion to Propertius*, pp. 420–424.

67 Ibid., p. 424. Goethe seems especially influenced by Propertius in the work (see p. 424), and he even offers a seeming parallel for the sleeping Cynthia of Propertius 1.3 in his poem 13 (p. 422).

68 Ibid., pp. 424.

69 Heather James, 'Ovid in Renaissance English literature', in Knox (ed.), *Companion to Ovid*, p. 432.

70 Braden, 'Classical love elegy', pp. 164–165.

71 James, 'Ovid in Renaissance', pp. 436–437.

72 Notably, Skelton also wrote a dead sparrow poem: see Jacob Blevins, *Catullan Consciousness and the Early Modern Lyric in England: From Wyatt to Donne* (Aldershot and Burlington, 2004), pp. 19–22.

73 John B. Emperor, 'The Catullan influence in English lyric poetry, circa 1600–1650', *The University of Missouri Studies*, 3/3 (1928), pp. 21–28, 100–112.

74 Gaisser, 'Introduction', p. xxviii. By that point, however, English writers had also become familiar with Catullus' earlier receptions in Europe, making Catullus' direct link to English poetry often difficult to pinpoint (see pp. xxix f.).

75 Eleanor Shipley Duckett, *Catullus in English Poetry* (Northampton, MA, 1925) organizes poetic responses to Catullus by poem number; for responses to the sparrow poems, see pp. 10–25, and for Catullus 5 and 7, about Lesbia, see pp. 30–45. See also Gaisser (ed.), *Catullus in English*.

76 See Duckett, *Catullus in English Poetry*, p. 39.

77 Gaisser, 'Introduction', pp. xxxv.

78 Ibid., pp. xxxv f.

79 See Brian Arkins, 'The modern reception of Catullus', in Skinner (ed.), *Companion to Catullus*, p. 464.

80 Ibid., p. 465. See also Thomas J. Brennan, 'Creating from nothing: Swinburne and

Baudelaire in "Ave Atque Vale", *Victorian Poetry*, 44/3 (2006), pp. 251–271. For broader background on the Victorian period, see Vance Norman, *The Victorians and Ancient Rome* (Oxford and Cambridge, MA, 1997). For visual material from the same period, including discussion of Lawrence Alma-Tadema's 1865 work *Catullus at Lesbia's* (p. 36 and fig. 3), see George P. Landow, 'Victorianized Romans: images of Rome in Victorian painting', *Browning Institute Studies*, 12 (1984), pp. 29–51.

81 Sara Teasdale, 'On the death of Swinburne', in *Helen of Troy and Other Poems* (New York and London, 1911), p. 93.

82 Edna St. Vincent Millay, 'Passer mortuus est', repr. in Gaisser (ed.), *Catullus in English*, p. 288.

83 Dorothy Parker, 'From a letter from Lesbia', repr. in Gaisser (ed.), *Catullus in English*, p. 289.

84 Gaisser, 'Catullus in the Renaissance', p. 457.

85 Arkins, 'Modern reception', pp. 463–464.

86 Gaisser, 'Introduction', p. xxxix.

87 Arkins, 'Modern reception', p. 473.

88 Sidney Keyes, 'A translation of *Carmen* XI by Catullus', in M. Meyer (ed.), *The Collected Poems of Sidney Keyes*, (London and New York, 1988), p. 129. The translation is taken from a letter, and Keyes deflected some of its intensity by writing, 'I enclose also my own inept effort to translate Catullus. You may wonder Why Catullus? and I can only say that there is a volume of him in the local library with crib opposite' (p. 129).

89 On Keyes's short life and poetry, see Linda M. Shires, *British Poetry of the Second World War* (New York, 1985), pp. 99–112; and John Guenther, *Sidney Keyes: A Biographical Inquiry* (London, 1967).

90 Ira B. Nadel, *The Cambridge Introduction to Ezra Pound* (Cambridge and New York, 2007), p. 8.

91 Quoted in Arkins, 'Modern reception', p. 466.

92 Ibid., pp. 466–470. See also Ron Thomas, *The Latin Masks of Ezra Pound* (Ann Arbor, 1983), pp. 21–37.

93 On his hostility to Virgil, see Thomas, *Latin Masks*, pp. 9–20; for use of Ovid in the *Cantos*, see pp. 59–116.

94 The *Homage to Sextus Propertius* was not Pound's first involvement with Propertius: on Propertius' presence in Pound's earlier work, see Thomas, *Latin Masks*, pp. 39–46; for a comparison of Pound's two different treatments of the same poem, see Brian Arkins, 'Pound's Propertius: what kind of homage?', *Paideuma*, 17/1 (1988), p. 39.

95 For an account of its publishing, see J.P. Sullivan, *Ezra Pound and Sextus Propertius: A Study in Creative Translation* (Austin, 1964), pp. 4–6.

96 Ibid., p. 3. Sullivan provides a short survey of translations of Propertius beginning with John Nott in 1782 and culminating with more open-ended efforts by Yeats (responding to 2.2.5–10) and Robert Lowell, who composed a response to 4.7 (see pp. 173–183).

97 Arkins, 'Pound's Propertius', p. 30.

98 Quoted in Sullivan, *Ezra Pound and Sextus Propertius*, p. 4.

99 Quoted in ibid., p. 6.

100 Quoted in ibid., p. 9.

101 Ibid., p. 27.

102 Quoted in Thomas, *Latin Masks*, p. 49.

103 Thomas, *Latin Masks*, pp. 44–45. Notably, Pound pointed to the poem he called 'Ride to Lanuvium' (i.e. 4.8) as a clear example of Propertian humour; for more on Pound's sense of this poem, see Sullivan, *Ezra Pound and Sextus Propertius*, pp. 71–72.

104 Sullivan, *Ezra Pound and Sextus Propertius*, p. 65.

105 Arkins, 'Pound's Propertius', p. 33. As Arkin notes, Pound relied on a text from 1892 that is somewhat different from the text of Propertius today, making some of Pound's attempts to follow full poems seem choppy (see p. 34). See also Sullivan, *Ezra Pound and Sextus Propertius*, pp. 112–113.

106 Ezra Pound, 'XI', from the *Homage to Sextus Propertius*, repr. in *Personae: The collected poems of Ezra Pound* (New York, 1926), p. 226.

107 Sullivan, *Ezra Pound and Sextus Propertius*, p. 28.

108 To this day, the best study on Ovid's overall reception in the twentieth century is Theodore Ziolkowski, *Ovid and the Moderns* (Ithaca and London, 2005). See also Duncan F. Kennedy, 'Recent receptions of Ovid', in Hardie (ed.), *Cambridge Companion*, pp. 320–335.

109 Ziolkowski, *Ovid and the Moderns*, p. 104.

110 Jo-Marie Claassen, *Displaced Persons: The Literature of Exile from Cicero to Boethius* (Madison, 1999), p. 1.

111 This phrase belongs to Hartmut Froesch and is cited at Ziolkowski, *Ovid and the Moderns*, p. 243.

112 Ibid., p. 105.

113 Lyne, 'Love and exile', p. 289.

114 Ziolkowski, *Ovid and the Moderns*, p. 113. Ziolkowski also offers a chronological survey of Ovidian revival in Romania; see pp. 112–121.

115 We are grateful to Carmen Fenechiu and Dana LaCourse Munteanu for allowing us to use their forthcoming essay 'Reinventing Ovid's exile: *Ex Ponto* ... Romanian style', which addresses in detail all the Romanian authors discussed on these pages.

116 This essay can be found in A. Codrescu, *The Disappearance of the Outside: A Manifesto for Escape* (Boston, 1990).

117 This phrase is taken from Richard Thomas, *Vergil and the Augustan Reception* (Cambridge, 2001), p. 222.

118 Svetlana Boym, *The Future of Nostalgia* (New York: Basic Books, 2001), p. xix.

119 For a detailed discussion of Pushkin's and Mandelshtam's reception of Ovid, see Zara M. Torlone, *Russia and the Classics: Poetry's Foreign Muse* (London, 2009), pp. 36–54 and 132–152 respectively.

120 Iosif Brodskii [Joseph Brodsky], *Sochineniia Iosifa Brodskogo* [Works of Joseph Brodsky], 7 vols. (St Petersburg, 2001), ii. p. 100. Unless otherwise noted all translations from the Russian are Zara Torlone's.

121 Ibid., p. 124.

122 Ibid., iii. p. 11.

RECOMMENDED READING

GENERAL STUDIES

Ancona, Ronnie and Ellen Greene (eds), *Gendered Dynamics in Latin Love Poetry* (Baltimore, 2005)

Conte, Gian Biagio, *Latin Literature: A History*, tr. Joseph B. Solodow, rev. Don Fowler and Glen W. Most (Baltimore, 1994)

Day, Archibald, *The Origins of Latin Love Elegy* (repr., Oxford, 1972)

Greene, Ellen, *The Erotics of Domination: Male Desire and the Mistress in Latin Love Poetry* (Baltimore, 1998)

James, Sharon, *Learned Girls and Male Persuasion: Gender and Reading in Roman Love Elegy* (Berkeley, 2003)

Kennedy, Duncan, *The Arts of Love: Five Studies in the Discourse of Roman Love Elegy* (Cambridge and New York, 1993)

Luck, Georg, *The Latin Love Elegy* (New York, 1959)

Lyne, R.O.A.M., *The Latin Love Poets from Catullus to Horace* (Oxford and New York, 1980)

Miller, Paul A., *Subjecting Verses: Latin Love Elegy and the Emergence of the Real* (Princeton, 2004)

Ross, David O., *Backgrounds to Augustan Poetry: Gallus, Elegy, and Rome* (Cambridge and New York, 1975)

Veyne, Paul, *Roman Erotic Elegy: Love, Poetry, and the West*, tr. D. Pellauer (Chicago, 1988)

POETRY IN THE AUGUSTAN CONTEXT

Barchiesi, Alessandro, *The Poet and the Prince: Ovid and Augustan Discourse* (Berkeley, 1997)
Galinsky, Karl, *Augustan Culture: An Interpretive Introduction* (Princeton, 1996)
Griffin, Jasper, *Latin Poets and Roman Life* (Chapel Hill, 1986)
Lowrie, Michèle, *Writing, Performance, and Authority in Augustan Rome* (Oxford and New York, 2009)
Powell, Anton (ed.), *Roman Poetry and Propaganda in the Age of Augustus* (London, 1992)
White, Peter, *Promised Verse: Poets in the Society of Augustan Rome* (Cambridge, 1993)
Woodman, Tony J. and David West (eds), *Poetry and Politics in the Age of Augustus* (Cambridge and New York, 1984)

CATULLUS

Fitzgerald, William, *Catullan Provocations: Lyric Poetry and the Drama of Position* (Berkeley, 1995)
Havelock, Eric A., *The Lyric Genius of Catullus* (repr., New York, 1967)
Janan, Micaela, *"When the Lamp Is Shattered": Desire and Narrative in Catullus* (Carbondale, 1994)
Quinn, Kenneth, *Catullus: An Interpretation* (London, 1972)
Skinner, Marilyn B., *Catullus in Verona: A Reading of the Elegiac Libellus, Poems 65–116* (Columbus, 2003)
Wiseman, T.P., *Catullus and His World: A Reappraisal* (Cambridge and New York, 1985)
Wray, David, *Catullus and the Poetics of Roman Manhood* (Cambridge and New York, 2001)

TIBULLUS

Cairns, Francis, *Tibullus: A Hellenistic Poet at Rome* (Cambridge and New York, 1979)
Lee-Stecum, Parshia, *Powerplay in Tibullus: Reading Elegies Book One* (Cambridge and New York, 1998)

PROPERTIUS

Benediktson, D. Thomas, *Propertius: Modernist Poet of Antiquity* (Carbondale, 1989)
DeBrohun, Jeri Blair, *Roman Propertius and the Reinvention of Elegy* (Ann Arbor, 2003)
Hubbard, Margaret, *Propertius* (New York, 1975)
Janan, Micaela, *The Politics of Desire: Propertius IV* (Berkeley, 2001)
Johnson, Walter R., *A Latin Lover in Ancient Rome: Readings in Propertius and His Genre* (Columbus, 2009)
Keith, Alison, *Propertius: Poet of Love and Leisure* (London, 2008)
Papanghelis, Theodore D., *Propertius: A Hellenistic Poet on Love and Death* (Cambridge and New York, 1987)

Stahl, Hans-Peter, *Propertius: "Love" and "War": Individual and State under Augustus* (Berkeley, 1985)

Sullivan, John P., *Propertius: A Critical Introduction* (Cambridge and New York, 1976)

Welch, Tara S., *The Elegiac Cityscape: Propertius and the Meaning of Roman Monuments* (Columbus, 2005)

OVID

Boyd, Barbara Weiden, *Ovid's Literary Loves: Influence and Innovation in the* Amores (Ann Arbor, 1997)

Fulkerson, Laurel, *The Ovidian Heroine as Author: Reading, Writing, and Community in the* Heroides (Cambridge and New York, 2005)

Gibson, Roy, Steven Green and Alison Sharrock (eds), *The Art of Love: Bimillennial Essays on Ovid's* Ars Amatoria *and* Remedia Amoris (Oxford, 2006)

Holzberg, Niklas, *Ovid: The Poet and His Work* (Ithaca, 2002)

Jacobson, Howard, *Ovid's* Heroides (Princeton, 1974)

Knox, Peter, *A Companion to Ovid* (Malden and Oxford, 2009)

Lindheim, Sara H., *Mail and Female: Epistolary Narrative and Desire in Ovid's* Heroides (Madison, 2003)

Myerowitz, Molly, *Ovid's Games of Love* (Detroit, 1985)

Rimell, Victoria, *Ovid's Lovers: Desire, Difference and the Poetic Imagination* (Cambridge and New York, 2006)

Spentzou, Efrossini, *Readers and Writers in Ovid's* Heroides: *Transgressions of Genre and Gender* (Oxford and New York, 2003)

Thibault, John C., *The Mystery of Ovid's Exile* (Berkeley, 1964)

Verducci, Florence, *Ovid's Toyshop of the Heart:* Epistulae Heroidum (Princeton, 1985)

Ziolkowski, Theodore, *Ovid and the Moderns* (Ithaca, 2005)

INDEX